R. Paul Caudill

FIRST CORINTHIANS
A Translation with Notes

BROADMAN PRESS
Nashville, Tennessee

To my grandfather,
the Reverend John Jackson Caudill,
and to my grandmother,
Nancy Emaline Rash Caudill,
whose exemplary lives
remain fragrant memory

Dewey Decimal Classification: 227.2
Library of Congress Catalog Card Number: 82-71220

Printed in the United States of America

CONTENTS

CONTENTS

PREFACE

This book, as the title suggests, is a translation of the First Epistle to the Corinthians with notes. The notes are not to be regarded as a critical commentary on the extant texts of the epistle, for that is not their purpose. The purpose of this work is to help the average pastor, teacher, and Bible student obtain a clearer and fuller understanding of the literal meaning of the Greek text of the first epistle to the Corinthians. While no attempt has been made to deal critically with the various readings in the epistle as presented in the diverse extant manuscripts, a critical study has been made of the words and syntax of the texts relied upon in making this translation; the third edition of *The Greek New Testament* (United Bible Societies, 1975) edited by Aland, Black, Martini, Metzger, and Wikgren has been used as the basis of the translation, together with the texts of Brooke Foss Westcott and Fenton John Anthony Hort (The Macmillan Company, New York, 1929), and Professor Eberhard Nestle (British and Foreign Bible Society, London, 1934).

The copious footnotes and brief outline that accompany each page of the translation, and the explanatory notes that follow, have been prepared for the convenience of the Bible student who wishes to pursue a careful study of the epistle, observing the various usages of the given words, without the use of numerous lexicons and commentaries. In the preparation of the translation and notes, I have relied chiefly on etymology and grammatical syntax. I have endeavored, however, to present fruitful gleanings from many commentaries on the epistle but have sought to avoid excessive editorializing and paraphrasing, in order to allow the original text to speak for itself, as literally as possible. To this end, and in an effort to let the Greek text speak for itself in contemporary language, I consulted no other translations (apart from the study of particular words, phrases, and clauses in the lexicons and commentaries).

I am deeply indebted to those who have shared in the effort to make this book possible. My special thanks go to my wife, Fern, for her excellent proofreading; to my capable secretary, Mrs. Eugenia Price, for her splendid typing and proofreading; to Miss Alice Faye Easterling for her English critique; and to Dr. Frank Stagg, Dr. James A. Brooks, and Dr. John B. Polhill for their careful reading of the manuscript and for their scholarly suggestions, many of which have been incorporated in the book.

R. PAUL CAUDILL
October 1, 1982

INTRODUCTION
The Text

Fortunately, the Chester Beatty papyrus 46 which contains the entire 1 Corinthians letter has been preserved. Parts of 1 Corinthians have also been preserved in seven other papyri. This is significant in that it brings scholars a step closer to the original text.[1] How the epistles were collected and edited, no one knows. Some think that the Muratorian Canon which placed 1 and 2 Corinthians at the head of the Pauline Epistles "took shape in Corinth" and that the location of Romans in the forefront was a later development.

Chronology and Occasion of the Epistle

Paul was in Ephesus at the time of the writing (16:8), and the occasion of the letter was a letter Paul had received from Corinth (7:1). A copy of the letter has not been preserved, and for this reason we can only infer, partially, its contents from Paul's first letter to Corinth.

The chronology of Paul's First Epistle to the Corinthians may be dated by the proconsulship of Gallio (Acts 18:12) and by Luke's mention of Aquila and Prisc(ill)a.

Aquila and Prisca came to Corinth directly from Rome, after having been expelled by the edict of Claudius against the Jews (Rom. 16:3; Acts 18:2,18,26). The exact date of the epistle probably falls around the year AD 55, and few would question its authenticity.

The language of the epistle reflects the full mainstream of the Koine and likewise displays "the well-known characteristics of the language of Paul."[2] The language is varied with elements of colloquial speech standing alongside elements of "the higher Koine (and the classical language)."[3]

The student of Greek grammar finds delightful "figures of rhetoric" which fall together like precious stones into the perfect whole. Antithesis, catch words, antistrophe, asyndeton, all abound together with the "customary metaphors of the diatribe."[4]

Paul observed some "formalities of the epistolary style," but at the same time wrote as an apostle. The epistle reflects a minimum of homiletic schema. Paul dealt plainly with matters raised by the Corinthians in their letter to him, matters which affected the day-to-day life-style of the Corinthians in their interpersonal relationships and in their relationship to God. At the heart of Paul's words is his discussion of the saving work of Christ "and actualizes itself in the gospel, the 'word of the cross.'"[5] This theological character further reflects itself in the freedom of those who are "in Christ." Those who make up the body of Christ have their marked social, cultural, and psychological differences, and yet the body is one.[6] The ground around the cross is level where the Lord's slave and the Lord's freeman stand side by side.

The Pauline Letters in General

The letters of Paul, for the most part, were addressed to specific situations which demanded his immediate attention. Sometimes a problem had a "threatening" mood, and Paul wrote to deal with that need. Usually the character of the need was of more than passing interest. That is why his epistles throb with meaning for the contemporary Christian. After all, the critical problems of human beings, in the realm of the spirit and of morality, are common to every generation and to every race of people. Human situations change, but the modus operandi of life goes on much the same. Thus Corinthians throws a brilliant spotlight on the Corinthian church and upon the character of the disciples of Christ, the saints who are truly in Christ *(en Christōi)*. Paul's style, says Robertson, "is unhellenic in arrangement but in Ro. 8 and 1 Cor. 13 he reaches the elevation and dignity of Plato."[7]

The City of Corinth

Corinth (Greek *Korinthos*) is "both an ancient and a modern city of the Peloponnessus in Greece."[8] According to ancient history, Corinthian settlers founded Corinth, "the best port site on the east coast," around 733 BC. Originally the location was an island site that later was linked to the mainland by a causeway. Apparently most of the settlers were from the Achaean cities and were quick to seize the opportunities the strategic location afforded them both in agriculture and in merchandising.

The history of Corinth is marked by both greatness and tragedy. "Thucydides, the Greek historian, claims that it was in Corinth that the first triremes, the Greek battleships, were built. Legend has it that it was in Corinth that the Argo was built, the ship in which Jason sailed the seas, searching for the golden fleece."[9]

But in 146 BC, the great city of Corinth met with disaster at the hands of the Roman general Lucius Mummius who captured the city and sacked it completely, leaving all of her architectural and commercial grandeur in a heap of ruins. The fierce devastation was in retaliation for the opposition of Greece to the conquering hordes of Rome. One hundred years later (46 BC) Julius Caesar rebuilt Corinth and made her a Roman colony and the capital city of the Roman province of Achaea. The population in those days was a heterogeneous mixture of Roman veterans, Jews, Venetians, Phrygians, people from the East, and people from the West. "Farrar speaks of 'this mongrel and heterogeneous population of Greek adventurers and Roman bourgeois, with a tainting infusion of Phoenicians; this mass of Jews, ex-soldiers, philosophers, merchants, sailors, freedmen, slaves, trades-people, hucksters and agents of every form of vice.' He characterizes her as a colony 'without aristocracy, without traditions and without well-established citizens.'"[10]

Corinth was a great and powerful city. The city was located on the isthmus, without which all southern Greece would have been an island. The city became a great trading center, a place of commerce that served the ancient world. Practically all traffic from East to West and North to South passed through Corinth. This was also true of Mediterranean traffic, for the southern tip of Greece then known as Cape Malea (now Cape Matapan) knew dangers, such as later seamen knew of Cape Horn. Barclay tells us that the Greeks had "two sayings" which reflect the seaman's fear of the cape: "Let him who sails round Malea forget his home," and "Let him who sails round Malea first make his will."[11]

In order to avoid the cape, seamen with small boats would often drag their boats across the isthmus on rollers. If the boats were too large for this, they unloaded them and used porters to transmit the cargo to where they could reembark by ship on the other side of the isthmus. The little four-mile journey saved the sailors more than two hundred miles by way of the dangerous cape.

Corinth was not only a wealthy, populous city but it was also a city of wickedness and shame. "The very name Corinth was synonymous with debauchery."[12] Moreover, standing high on the hill near the acropolis was the temple of Aphrodite, goddess of love. "To that temple there were attached one thousand priestesses who were sacred prostitutes, and at evening time they descended upon the Acropolis and plied their trade upon the streets of Corinth, until it became a Greek proverb, 'It is not every man who can afford a journey to Corinth.'"[13] Conzelmann calls this "often-peddled statement that Corinth was a seat of sacred prostitution (in the service of Aphrodite)" a fable.[14] Some say this was not true of the new Corinth. But right or wrong, tradition has its own story of the wickedness of Corinth. And the word *korinthiazesthai,* "to live like a Corinthian," came to have a meaning that denigrates morality and is associated with all kinds of debauchery whether immoral or drunken.

The religious syncretism resulting from the conquest of Alexander the Great left the people hungering for true guidance. There were the devotees of astrology whose basic conviction held that "the heavenly bodies were deities that in a direct way control life and events on earth."[15] And there were likewise those who turned to philosophy for a solution to the riddle of the universe and life in general. Socrates, whose life and works took place in the fifth century BC, led in the search for the "good" life. In the third century BC, Zeno founded Stoicism, a doctrine which held that "all reality was material but was animated by a rational principle that was at the same time both the law of the universe and of the human soul."[16] In addition to these, there were the mystery religions and Cynicism, "a philosophy that maintained a cosmic view of life with a method of dealing with crisis by reducing man's needs to a minimum."[17]

It was into the heart of this cosmopolitan center with its diverse religious views and disturbing life-styles that Paul came with the Christian message which proclaimed Jesus Christ as Lord and Savior of the world.

Paul's Stay in Corinth

Paul remained in Corinth some eighteen months. This was longer than he spent in any other city with the exception of Ephesus. Apart from Luke's words in Acts 18:1-17, we know little of what took place in Paul's life during his stay there. Upon his arrival, he stayed with Aquila and Prisca, and he was well-received when he preached in the synagogue there. But the Jews were hostile to his presence, and he left the synagogue and went to live with Titus Justus (Acts 18:7).

When Gallio came to Corinth in AD 51, as the new governor, the Jews rallied in their effort to stop Paul's teaching in Corinth. But Gallio took no action in the case, and Paul had freedom to complete his work before he went on to Syria.

It is too bad that we do not have a copy of Paul's letter to the Corinthians which antedated the first Corinthian letter (1 Cor. 5:9). Some scholars believe that part of the previous letter is incorporated in 2 Corinthians (6:14 to 7:1), for the passage does hark back to what Paul wrote about in 1 Corinthians. One thing we do know is that one of the sources of the news which Paul had about the problems in Corinth came from those of the household of Chloe (1 Cor. 1:11). Then there was the news that came by way of Stephanas, Fortunatus, and Achaicus, when they visited Ephesus during Paul's stay (1 Cor. 16:17). Paul would have had an excellent opportunity to get a firsthand story from them of conditions in Corinth. Then there was the letter that came from the Corinthians themselves (1 Cor. 7:1) in which they obviously sought Paul's guidance in matters that affected the church there. The influence of the cult of Orphism may have made an impact on the Corinthian Christians, as reflected in their disposition toward ecstasy and escapism. Like the ancient Greeks (that is, Plato and others), the Corinthians held to the idea that the soul is immortal, but there is no resurrection of the body and spirit. This belief led to a dualistic concept in which the body was not regarded as the real self. This paved the way for unbridled carnal indulgence. At any rate, Paul's concern for the Corinthian church was so great that he dispatched Timothy with a letter bearing the message with which we are concerned in this translation.

The Hope of Resurrection

In chapter 15, Paul summarized the meaning of the resurrection of Christ and pointed out how that, apart from the resurrection of the Christ, Christ's followers have utterly no grounds for hope.

It is a happy thing that the position of the chapter is near the end of the epistle, for the divine meditation in that chapter "brings to consciousness what was contained from the start in the hope of resurrection."[18] Nowhere else in the New Testament does one find presented so clearly the lines of hope concerning life after death. Theologically, the glorious fact of the resurrection of Jesus from among the dead ones is the foundation stone upon which all feet must rest in the agelong grasp of the human spirit for the eschatological hopes of the soul. Conzelmann sums up the matter beautifully: "The concept of the 'cross' predominates in 1 Corinthians over that of justification, which was the prevailing concept in Galatians and Romans, but has in substance no other intention than the latter, namely, to present the ideas of *sola gratia—sola fide,* of the destruction of human . . . 'boasting,' and of the transportation into the freedom of faith."[19]

It is as though Paul were saying, "Hear me, ye who profess to be followers of Jesus Christ, hear me: he is arisen, he is alive, and by his resurrection he has nullified death. Now you need only to think on him, the Exalted One, for in him you have forgiveness of sin; you have the basis for your faith; you can go on with your preaching of the good news; for you too will rise from the dead at the last day, just as he arose; for he has destroyed the last enemy which is death!"

The letter closes with a very personal note from Paul who wanted the Corinthians to know that he placed his own signature at the end. They needed to have no doubt that the letter came from him.

Notes

1. Hans Conzelmann, James W. Leitch, trans., *A Commentary on the First Epistle to the Corinthians, Hermeneia* series (Philadelphia: Fortress Press, 1975), p. 1.

2. Ibid., p. 5.

3. Ibid.

4. Ibid.
5. Ibid., p. 9.
6. Ibid.
7. A. T. Robertson, *A Grammar of the Greek New Testament in the Light of Historical Research,* fifth ed. (New York: Richard R. Smith, Inc., Hodder and Stoughton, [n.d.]), p. 129.
8. "Corinth," *Encyclopaedia Britannica, Micropaedia,* Vol. III (Chicago: Encyclopaedia Britannica, Inc., 1979), p. 150.
9. William Barclay, *The Letters to the Corinthians* (Philadelphia: The Westminster Press, 1956), p. 3.
10. Ibid., p. 4.
11. Ibid., p. 1.
12. Ibid., p. 3.
13. Ibid.
14. Conzelmann, p. 12.
15. "Biblical Literature," *Encyclopaedia Britannica, Macropaedia,* Vol. 2 (Chicago: Encyclopaedia Britannica, Inc., 1979), p. 947.
16. Ibid.
17. Ibid.
18. Conzelmann, p. 11.
19. Ibid.

Sources Mentioned in Notes on Translation

Bauer—*A Greek-English Lexicon of the New Testament* (Chicago: University of Chicago Press, 1979).

Bruce—"I and II Corinthians," *New Century Bible* (London: Oliphants, 1971).

Caudill—*Ephesians: A Translation with Notes* (Nashville, Tennessee: Broadman Press, 1979).

Caudill—*Philippians: A Translation with Notes* (Boone, North Carolina: Blue Ridge Press of Boone, Inc., 1980).

Conzelmann—*A Commentary on the First Epistle to the Corinthians,* translated by James W. Leitch (Philadelphia: Fortress Press, 1975).

Findlay—"St. Paul's First Epistle to the Corinthians," *The Expositor's Greek Testament,* Vol. 3 (Grand Rapids, Michigan: William B. Eerdmans Publishing Co., [n.d.]).

Gould—"Commentary on the Epistles to the Corinthians," *An American Commentary on the New Testament,* Vol. 5 (Philadelphia: American Baptist Publication Society, 1887).

Polhill—Personal correspondence with Dr. John B. Polhill.

Robertson—*A New Short Grammar of the Greek Testament,* Parts I, III, and IV (New York: Richard R. Smith, Inc., 1931).

Robertson—*Word Pictures in the New Testament* (Nashville, Tennessee: Sunday School Board of the SBC, 1931).

Robertson & Plummer—"A Critical and Exegetical Commentary on the First Epistle of St. Paul to the Corinthians," *International Critical Commentary* (New York: Charles Scribner's Sons, 1911).

Souter—*A Pocket Lexicon to the Greek New Testament* (Oxford University Press, 1943).

Thayer—*Greek-English Lexicon of the New Testament* (Grand Rapids, Michigan: Baker Book House, 1977).

Vincent—"The Epistles of Paul," *Word Studies in the New Testament,* Vol. 3 (Grand Rapids, Michigan: William B. Eerdmans Publishing Co., 1946).

ANALYSIS OF THE EPISTLE

Salutation (1:1-3)
Thanksgiving and Praise (1:4-9)
 I. Divisions in the Corinthian Church and the Gospel (1:10 to 4:21)
    A. A Plea for Unity (1:10)
    B. Party Strife (1:11-17)
    C. The Talk About the Cross (1:18-25)
    D. The Matter of Boasting (1:26-31)
    E. Paul and His Preaching (2:1-5)
    F. The Wisdom of God (2:6-9)
    G. The Things of the Spirit (2:10 to 3:2)
    H. God's Fellow Workers (3:3-9)
    I. The Foundation and the Building (3:10-17)
    J. The Christian and the World (3:18-23)
    K. The Judgment of God (4:1-5)
    L. A Lesson in Humility (4:6-13)
    M. Some Fatherly Counsel (4:14-21)
 II. Social and Moral Problems (5—7)
    A. The Matter of Incest (5:1-8)
    B. Evil Associations (5:9-13)
    C. Christians and Law Courts (6:1-8)
    D. The Kingdom Inheritance (6:9-11)
    E. The Christian and His Body (6:12-20)
    F. Celibacy and Marriage (7:1-9)
    G. The Problem of Divorce (7:10-16)
    H. The Believer's Life-Style (7:17-24)
    I. Concerning Virgins (7:25-38)
    J. Concerning Remarriage (7:39-40)
III. Idolatry and Spiritual Freedom (8:1 to 11:1)

FIRST CORINTHIANS

CHAPTER 1

Salutation (1:1-3)

1   Paul,[1] a called apostle[2] of Jesus Christ through the will of God,[3] and Sosthenes our brother,

2   to the church[4] of God that is in Corinth,[5] they that are sanctified[6] in Christ Jesus, called saints, with all that call upon the name of our Lord Jesus Christ (theirs and ours) in every place;

---

1. *Paulos*—Paul, the Roman surname of the apostle whose Jewish name was Saul. The name Paul is Graeco-Roman.

2. *apostolos*—"One commissioned and sent forth by another to represent him in some way—an envoy, a delegate, messenger, missionary" (Caudill, *Ephesians*).

3. *dia thelēmatos Theou*—Paul's apostleship did not spring from self or men but from God.

4. *tē ekklēsia*—The church that belongs to God rather than to "any individual or faction, as this genitive case shows" (Robertson, *Word Pictures*).

5. *Korinthōi*—Mummius destroyed the city in 146 BC, but Julius Caesar restored it in 44 BC. A hundred years later the city became "very rich and very corrupt."

6. *hēgiasmenois*—Perfect, "Holy, sacred, consecrated; worthy of veneration; used of sacrifices and offerings prepared for God with solemn rites; in a moral sense, pure, sinless, upright; in the New Testament used of those whose lives are set apart for or unto God, to be exclusively his; hence saints" (Caudill, *Ephesians*).

3   grace[7] to you and peace[8] from God our Father and Lord Jesus
       Christ.

Thanksgiving and Praise (1:4-9)

4   I give[9] thanks[10] to my God at all times concerning you for the grace
       of God given to you in Christ Jesus,
5   that in everything[11] you were enriched in him, in every utterance
       and all knowledge,
6   even as the testimony concerning Christ[12] was confirmed[13] in you,
7   so that you are not lacking in any gift, as you eagerly await the
       revelation[14] of our Lord Jesus Christ
8   who also will confirm you unto the end[15] blameless in the day of our
       Lord Jesus Christ.

---

7. *charis*—"A lovely, unmerited, God-given experience of his favoring
   presence felt in the life of man. One can have peace only after he has
   received grace" (Caudill, *Ephesians*).
8. *eirēnē*—"Related to *shalom* and so used by the ancient Hebrew scholars."
   The word means "well being under God's sovereign rule." That tranquil state
   of mind and heart that is independent of circumstance and that results from
   being in Christ and in doing God's will in all things. Note: One must first
   receive grace before he can obtain peace" (Caudill, *Ephesians*).
9. *dotheisē*—First aorist passive participle of *didōmi*, I give, bestow, grant,
   impart—as something to someone.
10. *eucharistō*—From *eucharisteō*, to thank, be thankful, feel obligated, give
    thanks, to return or render thanks.
11. *en panti*—Every good and every perfect gift is from above, coming down
    from the Father (Jas. 1:17).
12. *marturion tou Christou*—Objective genitive. Hence, Paul's preaching
    amounted to a testimony "to or concerning Christ."
13. *ebebaiōthē*—From *bebaioō*, from *bebaios*, from *bainō*, "to make to
    stand, to make stable" (Robertson, *Word Pictures*).
14. *apokalupsin*—From *apokalupsis*—disclosure, revelation, used of the
    revelation of truth and of "revelations of a particular kind, through visions,
    etc." (Bauer).
15. *heōs telous*—"End of the age until Jesus comes, final preservation of the
    saints" (Robertson, *Word Pictures*).

9   Faithful is God through whom[16] you were called into a fellowship of
his Son, Jesus Christ our Lord.

I. Divisions in the Corinthian Church and the Gospel (1:10 to 4:21)
A. A Plea for Unity (1:10)

10   I beseech[17] you brothers, through the name of our Lord Jesus
Christ, that you all keep on speaking the same thing,[18] and that
there be no divisions[19] among you, but that you be made
complete[20] with the same mind and with the same purpose.

B. Party Strife (1:11-17)

11   For it was revealed to me concerning you, my brothers, by the
family of Chloe,[21] that there are contentions[22] among you.

---

16. *di'hou*—Through whom. God is both "the agent" and the "ground" for the
call of the Corinthians into their fellowship with the Lord.

17. *parakalō*—From *parakaleō*, to summons, call to one side, call for help,
urge, encourage, appeal to, exhort, implore, request, entreat. Also to
cheer up, comfort, encourage. Used in the New Testament more than 100
times.

18. *to auto*—Divisions usually come over things spoken, hence the need for
unity in speaking.

19. *schismata*—From *schizō*, to rend or to split and so to cause a rent (Matt.
9:16; Mark 2:21), hence divisions. Used in the papyri for "a splinter of wood
and for plowing" (Robertson, *Word Pictures*).

20. *katērtismenoi*—Paraphrastic perfect passive subjunctive, from *katartizō*,
to restore, put in order, complete, put in proper condition, prepare, make,
make something complete (Bauer).

21. *hupo tōn Chloēs*—By them of Chloe, "Whether the children, the
kinspeople, or the servants of Chloe we do not know" (Robertson, *Word
Pictures*). We also do not know where Chloe lived—whether in Ephesus or in
Corinth.

22. *erides*—From Greek *eris*, discord, contention, quarrel.

12   Now this I mean, that each of you says that I myself am indeed of
      Paul, but I am of Apollos,[23] but I am of Cephas,[24] but I am of
      Christ.

13   Is Christ divided;[25] was Paul crucified in behalf of you, or were you
      baptized[26] in the name of Paul?

14   I am thankful that I baptized none of you save Crispus[27] and Gaius

15   lest anyone should say that you were baptized in my name.[28]

16   But I did also baptize the household of Stephanas;[29] beyond that I
      do not recall that I baptized any other.

17   For Christ did not send me to be a baptizer but to evangelize,[30] not
      in wisdom of speech, lest the cross of Christ be made ineffective.[31]

C. The Talk About the Cross (1:18-25)

18   For the talk about the cross[32] is indeed foolishness to those who are

---

23. **Apollō**—Little is known of Apollos apart from Paul's references to him in his
    epistles and from the passages in Acts (18:24). He was "a learned exegete"
    from Alexandria (Conzelmann).

24. **Kēpha**—Greek Cēphas, the name (Aramaic) which Jesus gave to Simon
    (John 1:42), (Petros, Greek).

25. **memeristai**—Perfect passive indicative of merizō, separate, divide—as
    into component parts.

26. **ebaptisthēte**—From baptizō, to immerse, dip (dip oneself), baptize.

27. **Krispon**—Prior to his conversion (Acts 18:8), ruler of the synagogue in
    Corinth.

28. **eis to emon**—Paul wanted no special significance attached to any baptism
    he might perform. The importance of baptism was not to be regarded as
    enhanced by the person performing the baptism.

29. **Stephana**—Stephanas was "a firstfruit of Achaia" (1 Cor. 16:15).

30. **euaggelizesthai**—From euaggelizō, announce or bring good news. Used
    often in the New Testament "of the divine message of salvation, the
    Messianic proclamation, the gospel" (Bauer).

31. **kenōthē**—From kenoō (first aorist passive subjunctive, effective aorist),
    from kenos "to make empty."

32. **logos**—The word of the cross. Paul's reference to his preaching and
    conversation concerning the cross.

perishing, but to us who are being saved it is the power of God.[33]

19 For it is written[34]

I will destroy[35] the wisdom of the wise,[36]
and the understanding of the intelligent ones
I will reject.

20 Where *is* the wise? Where *is* the scribe?[37] Where *is* the debater[38] of this age? Did not God make foolish the wisdom of the world?

21 For since in the wisdom of God[39] the world through its own wisdom[40] did not come to know God, God was pleased through the foolishness of the preaching[41] to save those who believe.

22 Since, indeed, the Jews asked for signs[42] and the Greeks seek wisdom,

---

33. *dunamis theou*—From *dunamis* we get our word *dynamite*. "God's power is shown in the preaching of the Cross of Christ through all the ages, now as always" (Robertson).

34. *gegraptai*—A quotation from Isaiah 29:14 (LXX) follows.

35. *athetēsō*—From *atheteō*, nullify, declare invalid, set aside, reject, thwart, confound.

36. *sophōn*—An old word meaning skillful, clever, experienced, learned, wise "of human intelligence and education above the average" (Bauer).

37. *grammateus*—Literally, clerk, secretary; in the New Testament era an expert; among the Jews, "in the law" a scholar who was "versed in the law."

38. *suzētētēs*—This word occurs nowhere else in the New Testament but in the papyri examples are found for "disputing (questioning together)" (Robertson). Hence, debater, disputant.

39. *en tēi sophiai tou theou*—God's wisdom "has reduced the self-wise world to ignorance" (Findlay).

40. *tēs sophias*—See footnote 36 above. Paul here may have in mind the Greek philosopher.

41. *kērugmatos*—The act of proclamation, preaching, but more—here the emphasis may be on the apostolic, prophetic character of the message proclaimed.

42. *sēmeia*—From *sēmeion* "the sign or distinguishing mark by which something is known, token, indication" (Bauer). The sign can serve as a warning or may consist of "a wonder or miracle, an event that is contrary to the usual course of nature" (Ibid.).

23   we on the other hand preach Christ crucified, to the Jews, indeed, an occasion of stumbling,[43] and to the Gentiles foolishness,

24   but to ourselves the called,[44] both the Jews and the Greeks, Christ the power of God and wisdom of God.

25   For the foolishness[45] of God is wiser than *the wisdom* of men, and the weakness of God[46] is stronger than *the strength* of men.

D. The Matter of Boasting (1:26-31)

26   For behold your calling,[47] brothers, how that not many were wise according to the flesh, not many were prominent,[48] not many were of illustrious birth;[49]

27   but God chose for himself the foolish things of the world that he might put to shame[50] the wise ones, and God chose for himself the

---

43. *skandalon*—A trap, enticement as to apostasy, a temptation to sin, or "that which gives offense or causes revulsion, that which arouses opposition, an object of anger or disapproval" (Bauer).

44. *klētois*—From *klētos*, called, invited as to a meal. See Romans 1:7 for Greek *hagiois* (saints) "who are called by God." Hence, "those who are called," as here.

45. *to mōron*—Abstract neuter singular of the adjective *mōros*, stupid, foolish. A "'foolish thing on God's part' (such as a crucified Messiah), or, better, 'the foolishness of God' (AV.), in a somewhat rhetorical sense, not to be pressed" (Robertson and Plummer).

46. *to asthenes tou Theou*—From *asthenēs*, powerless, weak, sick, feeble, miserable, without influence.

47. *tēn klēsin humōn*—Here "the act of calling rather than the state of being called" (Conzelmann). Maybe there is an implied reference here to the vocational relationship of all Christians. All believers are called to lives of faith and works.

48. *dunatoi*—From old adjective *dunatos*, able, powerful, mighty, strong. Used by the ancients of prominent, powerful people.

49. *eugeneis*—From *eugenēs*, highborn, wellborn, noble minded, high-minded.

50. *kataischunē*—From *kataischunō*, disfigure, dishonor, disgrace, put to shame; in the passive voice, be humiliated, be put to shame, be ashamed.

weak things of the world that he might put to shame the strong things.

28 And God chose for himself the insignificant things[51] of the world and the scorned,[52] the things that are not,[53] that he might put to shame the things that are,

29 that no person[54] should be boastful before God.

30 But of him you are in Christ Jesus,[55] who became wisdom to us from God, both righteousness and holiness and redemption,

31 so that as it stands written,

> The one boasting,
> Let him boast in the Lord.

---

51. **ta agenē**—From *agenēs*, an adjective meaning "not of noble birth," but usually base, insignificant, low (Bauer).

52. **ta exouthenēmena**—From *exoutheneō*, to treat with contempt, reject with contempt, despise, disdain someone (Bauer), scorn.

53. **ta mē onta**—The things that are not.

54. **pasa sarx**—All flesh. That is, every person, used with *mē kauchēsētai*, hence here "no flesh."

55. **en Christōi Iēsou**—That is, you who have been born again . . . who have a viable relationship with Christ as Savior and Lord.

CHAPTER 2

E. Paul and His Preaching (2:1-5)

1 But I myself, in coming to you, brothers, came not as a superior person[1] of speech or of wisdom proclaiming to you the mystery of God.[2]

2 For I decided[3] not to know anything among you save Jesus Christ and him crucified.

3 And I in weakness[4] and in fear and in much trembling came to you,

4 and my speech and my preaching were not in persuasive[5] words of wisdom, but in the demonstration[6] of the Spirit and of power,

5 that your faith should not be in the wisdom of men[7] but in the power of God.

---

1. **kath' huperochēn**—From *huperochē*, prominence, superiority (Bauer).

2. **mustērion**—The secret message revealed as the crucified Christ to save humanity. (Some manuscripts use *marturion*, meaning testimony, rather than *mustērion*. The testimony is still the word of salvation in the cross.)

3. **ekrina**—From *krinō*, distinguish, separate, defer, consider, think, judge—as in legal matters, decide, reach a decision, intend, propose.

4. **astheneiai**—Weakness, as of the body in disease or sickness but here figuratively, timidity (with *phobos*, fear) and *tromos* (trembling) (Bauer).

5. **peithois**—Persuasive. This word is found nowhere else. Dr. A. T. Robertson held that the word "seems to be formed directly from *peithō*, to persuade, as *pheidos (phidos)* is from *pheidomai*, to spare" (Robertson, *Word Pictures*).

6. **apodeixei**—From *apodeiknumi*, to point out, show forth, exhibit, expose to view, literally to point away from oneself.

7. **sophiai anthrōpōn**—See footnote 36, chapter 1.

F. The Wisdom of God (2:6-9)

6 But we speak wisdom among the mature persons,[8] but wisdom not of this age nor of the rulers of this age who are passing away;

7 but we speak God's wisdom in the form of a mystery, the mystery that has been hidden,[9] which God foreordained[10] before time began unto our glory;[11]

8 which none of the rulers of this age has come to know;[12] for if they had known *it,* they would not have crucified the Lord of glory;

9 but it has happened as it is written,

Things which eye has not seen and ear has not heard
And upon the heart of man has not ascended
Whatsoever things God prepared[13] for those who love him.

G. The Things of the Spirit (2:10 to 3:2)

10 But unto us God revealed[14] *them* through the Spirit;[15] for the Spirit searches[16] all things, even the deep things of God.

---

8. *tois teleiois*—From *teleios*, perfect, complete, "having reached the goal," in a moral sense, fully developed, perfect, expert, mature.

9. *apokekrummenēn*—Articular perfect passive participle. From *apokruptō*, I conceal, hide, keep a secret.

10. *proōrisen*—"Constative aorist of God's elective purpose as shown in Christ crucified (1 Cor. 1:18-24)" (Robertson, *Word Pictures*).

11. *eis doxan hēmōn*—"The glory of inward enlightenment as well as of outward exaltation" (Lightfoot, quoted by Robertson in *Word Pictures*).

12. *egnōken*—Perfect indicative active of *ginōskō*, I know, I come to know, understand, comprehend, perceive, realize.

13. *hētoimasen*—First aorist active indicative of *hetoimazō*, to prepare, put or keep in readiness.

14. *apekalupsen*—From *apokaluptō*, to uncover, reveal, disclose, bring to light especially "of divine revelation of certain supernatural secrets" (Bauer).

15. *pneūma*—An old Greek word with variant meanings as movement of air, breath, breath of life, vital spirit by which the body is animated, the Holy Spirit, God's Spirit, as here.

16. *ereunāi*—From *eraunaō*, "The word occurs . . . for a professional searcher's report and *eraunētai*, searchers for customs officials" (Robertson, *Word Pictures*).

11   For who of men has known[17] the things of man save the spirit of man that is in him? Thus also the things of God no one has come to know[18] save the Spirit of God.

12   For we received not the spirit of the world but the Spirit which is of God, that we might know[19] the things graciously given[20] to us by God;

13   which things also we speak not in imparted words of human wisdom, but in *words* taught by the Spirit,[21] combining[22] spiritual matters with spiritual terms.

14   Now a natural[23] man receives not the things of the Spirit from God, for they are foolishness to him, and he is not able to understand,[24] because they are spiritually discerned.

15   The spiritual man, on the other hand, discerns[25] all things, and he himself is judged by no one.

---

17.   **oiden**—Second perfect of root *id* (*eidō*) (Robertson, *Word Pictures*). "The tenses coming from *eidō* and retained by usage form two families, of which one signifies *to see*, the other *to know*" (Thayer).

18.   **egnōken**—First perfect of *ginōskō*, "to know by personal experience." Hence, "has come to know and still knows" (Robertson, *Word Pictures*).

19.   **eidōmen**—Second perfect subjunctive "with *hina* to express purpose" (Robertson, *Word Pictures*). See footnote 17, verse 11.

20.   **charisthenta**—First aorist passive neuter plural participle (with article) of old verb *charizomai*, "to bestow" (Robertson, *Word Pictures*).

21.   **en didaktois pneumatos**—The word *didaktos* simply means taught. When used of persons, instructed, taught. Hence, words taught by the Spirit.

22.   **sugkrinontes**—From *sugkrinō*, combine, bring together, hence, "combining spiritual ideas . . . with spiritual words" (Robertson, *Word Pictures*).

23.   **psuchikos**—"Of or belonging to the *psuchē*" (Thayer), from *psuchē*, breath, or the breath of life, the vital force, life itself. The man possessed of a mere natural life as opposed to regenerate life (*pneumatikos*).

24.   **gnōnai**—From *ginōskō*. See footnote 12.

25.   **anakrinei**—Present active indicative of *anakrinō*, examine, question, call to account, judge, discern.

16   For who has known the mind of the Lord, that he should instruct[26]
him? But we have the mind of Christ.

---

26.   *sumbibasei*—From *sumbibazō*, unite, bring together, knit together, advise, teach, instruct.

CHAPTER 3

1   And I, brothers, was unable to speak to you as unto spiritual persons[1] but as unto the fleshly,[2] as unto babes[3] in Christ.

2   I gave you milk to drink, not solid food,[4] for you were not able,[5] yea, moreover, you are still not able,

3   for you are yet carnal.[6]

H. God's Fellow Workers (3:3-9)

For where there is among you jealousy and strife, are you not fleshly and conduct yourselves[7] like ordinary men?

---

1. *pneumatikois*—Persons who are filled with the Spirit of God and who seek to be governed by him (Thayer).

2. *sarkinois*—Literally, fleshly, "in the manner of the flesh," "belonging to the realm of the flesh" (Bauer).

3. *nēpiois*—Infants or very young children who still have childish ways.

4. *brōma*—Not meat (flesh) in contrast to bread "but all solid food as in 'meats and drinks'" (Robertson, *Word Pictures*). See Hebrews 9:10.

5. *edunasthe*—Literally, to be disabled or powerless. In this case, the powerlessness is due to the dullness of hearing that is brought on by sin on the part of the Corinthians.

6. *sarkikoi*—Fleshly, not altogether in the literal sense here though the unbeliever is still in the grip of the flesh, under the influence of the flesh as to bodily pleasures and appetites. (See Gal. 5:19 ff. for some of the "works of the flesh.") "To have one's total view on earthly realities" (Polhill).

7. *peripateite*—Literally, to walk around, go about. Here the idea is that of life-style, or the walk of life (Bauer).

4   For when one says I indeed am of Paul,[8] and another, I am of
         Apollos,[9] are ye not ordinary men?[10]

5   What then is Apollos? And what is Paul? Ministering servants[11]
         through whom you came to believe, and to each as the Lord gave
         to him.

6   I planted,[12] Apollos[13] watered, but God, all the while, caused the
         growth;[14]

7   so that neither is the one who is planting anything,[15] nor the one
         who is watering, but God who is causing the increase.

8   Both the one who plants and the one who waters are one, and
         each will receive his own reward[16] according to his own labor.

---

8. *Paulou*—Of Paul, meaning that the person was on Paul's side. We have
    here a predicate genitive which could be translated "I belong to Paul."

9. The word *Apollō*, though in form harks back to the Attic second declension,
    carries the same meaning, "I belong to Apollos."

10. *anthrōpoi*—An old word meaning man, or human being in contrast to
    animals.

11. *diakonoi*—An old word used for minister, servant, attendant, deacon—a
    person who carries out the commands of another in a servant role. The same
    word from which we get our word *deacon* (Thayer).

12. *ephuteusa*—From *phuteuō*, to plant something, as a field or vineyard.

13. *Apollōs*—A fellow Christian and fellow worker of Paul who was born and
    educated in Alexandria and witnessed both in Ephesus and Corinth (Acts
    18:24-28).

14. *ēuxanen*—From *auxanō* (and *auxō*) and means, in the transitive use, to
    grow, increase, cause to grow.

15. *ti*—Indefinite pronoun, enclitic, meaning someone, something, anything,
    anyone.

16. *misthon*—Wages, pay, as for work done by someone. Used figuratively of
    "the recompense given (mostly by God) for the moral quality of an action"
    (Bauer).

9   For we are God's fellow workers;[17] you are God's field,[18] God's building.[19]

I. The Foundation and the Building (3:10-17)

10   According to the grace[20] of God given to me, as a wise master builder[21] I laid a foundation, and another builds on it. Each one is to take care[22] how he builds thereon;

11   for another foundation can no one lay beyond[23] the one laid, which is Jesus Christ.

12   Now if anyone is building upon the foundation gold,[24] silver, precious stones, wood, grass, stubble (straw),

13   the work of each will be clearly seen,[25] for the day will reveal it; for it is brought to light with fire,[26] and what sort the work of each is,

---

17. *sunergoi*—Helping, working together with, as here fellow worker.

18. *geōrgion*—A field, or cultivated land.

19. *oikodomē*—An old word used of building "as a process" or construction (Bauer). Used also of an edifice or building which is the result of construction (Ibid.).

20. *charin*—"A word that in early Greek literature had variant meanings of gracefulness, gratitude, a favor. Here the idea seems to be that of a lovely, unmerited, God-given experience of the favoring presence felt in the life of man" (Caudill, *Philippians*).

21. *architektōn*—Our word *architect*, the one who designs buildings and superintends their erection.

22. *blepetō*—From *blepō*, see, look (at). Present imperative, third person singular.

23. *para*—An old preposition meaning beside, alongside, beyond (in comparisons) (Bauer). It is seen in our words: *parable, parallel, paradox.*

24. *chrusion*, etc.—Notice the character of the materials mentioned—both the durable and the perishable.

25. *phaneron*—As an adjective, clear, visible, plainly to be seen, evident, known; as a substantive—that which is open or subject to public notice.

26. *en puri*—With fire, if the preposition *en* is regarded as the so-called instrumental use of *en* as in *en machairēi* (Luke 22:49), or in fire.

the fire itself will test.[27]

14   If the work of anyone which he has built shall abide,[28] he will receive a reward;

15   if the work of any shall be burned, it will be lost, but he himself will be saved,[29] but only as it were through fire.

16   Do you not know that you are a temple[30] of God and that the spirit of God dwells[31] in you?

17   If anyone destroys[32] the temple of God, God will destroy him; for the temple of God is holy,[33] which temple you are.

J. The Christian and the World (3:18-23)

18   No one is to deceive[34] himself; if anyone thinks that he is wise among you in this world, let him become foolish,[35] that he may become wise.

---

27. *dokimasei*—Future third person singular of *dokimazō*, to examine carefully, to put to the test, prove by testing as gold is tested in the laboratory.

28. *menei*—From *menō*, used here in the intransitive sense of something that remains where it is—stays, remains, continues.

29. *sōthēsetai*—From *sōzō*, to rescue, preserve, keep from harm, save. The person is saved, but he loses his reward. The person's works are burned down *(katakaēsetai)* because of a misspent life.

30. *naos*—Literally, temple. Used of the Temple at Jerusalem. "But only of the sacred edifice (or sanctuary) itself, consisting of the Holy place and the Holy of Holies" (Thayer).

31. *oikei*—Intransitive, dwell, have one's habitation, live in someone or something.

32. *phtheirei*—A word which in classical Greek almost invariably meant destroy. Used by Plutarch of "*mixing* pure colors" (Vincent).

33. *hagios*—"Holy, sacred, consecrated: worthy of veneration; used of sacrifices and offerings prepared for God with solemn rites; in a moral sense, pure, sinless, upright; in the New Testament used of those whose lives are set apart for or unto God, to be exclusively his; hence, saints" (Caudill, *Ephesians*).

34. *exapatatō*—To cheat or deceive someone. See 2 Corinthians 11:3.

35. *mōros*—Stupid. Simonides of Ceos 4, 6f., used the word in referring to his opponent, Cleobulus (Bauer).

19 For the wisdom of this world is foolishness with God; for it is written;

> The one who catches[36] the wise in their craftiness;

20 and again,

>> The Lord knows the thoughts of the wise
>> for they are vain.[37]

21 And so, no one is to glory[38] among men; for all are yours.

22 Whether Paul, whether Apollos, whether Cephas, whether the world, whether life, whether death, whether things present, whether things to come, all are yours;[39]

23 but you are Christ's,[40] and Christ is God's.

---

36. ***ho drassomenos***—From *drassomai*, from Homer onward to seize or catch someone, "to grasp with the hand" (Robertson, *Word Pictures*). Used nowhere else in the New Testament. In the papyri (Ibid.).

37. ***mataioi***—An old word for idle, fruitless, empty, useless, powerless, lacking truth (Bauer).

38. ***kauchasthō***—Boast, pride oneself concerning something or someone.

39. ***humōn***—A predicate genitive meaning "all things belong to you."

40. ***Christou***—Another predicate genitive. All believers who have committed their lives to Christ belong to him—totally.

CHAPTER 4

K. The Judgment of God (4:1-5)

1   So, a man is to look upon us as servants[1] of Christ and stewards[2] of the mysteries[3] of God.

2   In this matter, moreover, it is required[4] among the stewards that a person be found faithful.[5]

3   But for myself it is a very small thing[6] that I should be judged by you or by any human tribunal;[7] rather I do not even judge[8] myself.

---

1. *hupēretas*—From *hupo* (under) and *eretēs* from *eressō*, to row. Hence, an under rower or subordinate rower. One who aids another or is an assistant, servant.
2. *oikonomous*—Literally (house) steward, manager, carried the keys and was the one in charge of the house. Servants were under him. So used of the treasurer of the ancient Greek city.
3. *mustēriōn*—Secret teaching, secret rite, secret. A word commonly used in relation to the mystery religions. The mysteries of the kingdom were already open to Christ's disciples (Matt. 13:11).
4. *zēteitai*—Third singular passive from *zēteō*. From Homer on, to seek. Here in the sense of request, demand, or ask for something.
5. *pistos*—Dependable, faithful, trustworthy, one who inspires faith or trust.
6. *eis elachiston estin*—Predicate use of *eis* as in the Hebrew and in the papyri. *Elachiston* is a superlative elative meaning "it counts for very little with me" (Robertson, *Word Pictures*).
7. *anthrōpinēs hēmeras*—Human day as over against Lord's Day. Paul's case, as he sees it, is not for human instruments of examination and judgment.
8. *anakrinō*—An old word meaning to examine, question, judge, call to account, used with reference to judicial hearings.

4   For I know nothing against myself, yet I am not hereby justified;[9] rather it is the Lord who judges me.

5   So quit judging anything before the proper time until the Lord comes[10] who will bring to light the hidden things of the darkness and will reveal the motives[11] of the hearts; and then the praise will come to each from God.

L. A Lesson in Humility (4:6-13)

6   Now these things, brothers, I have applied to myself, and to Apollos for your sakes, so that in us you may learn not *to go* beyond the things[12] that are written,[13] that you be not puffed up— one in behalf of the one against the other.

7   For who makes you to differ?[14] And what do you have that you did not receive? But if indeed you did receive, why do you boast as not receiving?

8   Already you are satisfied;[15] already you are become rich; without us[16] you have become kings; indeed I would that you did reign as kings that we also might reign together with you.

---

9.   *dedikaiōmai*—From *dikaioō*, show or do justice to someone, vindicate, or treat as just. Also make pure or free.

10. *heōs an elthēi ho kurios*—The "Second Coming of the Lord Jesus as Judge" (Robertson, *Word Pictures*).

11. *boulas*—Motives of the heart (Bauer). Decisions, resolutions of men.

12. *meteschēmatisa*—From *meta-schēmatizō*, found in Aristotle and Plato for "changing the form of a thing." Here the figure is rhetorical with "a veiled allusion to Apollos and Paul." "These things" Paul applied to himself and to Apollos for the sake of the Corinthians.

13. *gegraptai*—Some think that Paul may have had in mind Old Testament passages that are quoted in 1 Corinthians 1:19,31; 3:19,20.

14. *diakrinei*—From *diakrinō*, I distinguish, I separate, discern one thing from another. In the middle voice, I doubt, waver, hesitate.

15. *kekoresmenoi*—From *korennumi*, I feel full, glut, fill, sate; hence, satisfied.

16. *chōris hēmōn*—Biting sarcasm. Without our help, our assistance, our company!

9 For I suppose God has exhibited[17] us, the apostles, last as men condemned to die,[18] that we might become a public show to the world—both to angels and to men.

10 We are fools because of Christ, but you are men of prudence[19] in Christ; we are weak, but you are strong; you are honored but we are without honor.

11 Up to the present hour we both hunger and thirst, and we are poorly clothed and roughly treated,[20] and homeless.

12 And we toil,[21] working with our own hands; being abused insultingly, we bless; being persecuted, we put up with[22] it;

13 being slandered, we are conciliatory.[23] We have become as the offscourings[24] of the world—the offscrapings of all things until now.

M. Some Fatherly Counsel (4:14-21)

14 Not to make you ashamed do I write these things, but as instructing[25] my beloved children;

---

17. *apedeixen*—An old word used only twice by Paul from *apodeiknumi*, to appoint, render, proclaim, make, used in the sense of display, show forth, exhibit, as in a procession for spectators.

18. *hōs epithanatious*—From *epithanatios* (*epi*, upon or at, and *thanatos*, death); hence, as used here, condemned to death.

19. *phronimoi*—From *phroneō*, to be wise, have understanding, to think, judge.

20. *kolaphizometha*—From *kolaphizō*, I strike with a fist; hence, I treat roughly, or maltreat violently.

21. *kopiōmen*—From *kopiaō*, I toil, grow weary, work with effort (whether of mental labor or bodily labor).

22. *anechometha*—From *anecho*, used in the New Testament only in the middle voice: to bear with, sustain, hold oneself firm and erect, hold up, endure.

23. *parakaloumen*—From *parakaleō*, to call to one side, summons, entreat, beg, appeal to, request, console, be conciliatory.

24. *perikatharmata*—From *perikathairō*, "cleanse all around" or "on all sides"; that which is removed as a result of a thorough cleansing, that is, refuse, dirt, offscouring (Bauer).

25. *nouthetōn*—To warn, exhort, admonish, instruct (with the accusative of the person) (Bauer).

15   for though you should have many thousands of tutors[26] in Christ,
         yet not many fathers, for in Christ Jesus, through the gospel, I
         became your *spiritual* father.
16   I therefore appeal to you, keep on becoming imitators[27] of me.
17   For this reason I sent you Timothy, who is my beloved[28] child and
         faithful one in the Lord, who will remind you of my life-style in
         Christ (Jesus), as I teach everywhere in every church.
18   Certain people put on airs[29] as though I were not coming to you;
19   but I shall come to you quickly, if the Lord should will, and I will
         acknowledge[30] not the word of the conceited ones but the power;[31]
20   for not in word[32] *is* the kingdom of God but in power.
21   What do you want? With a rod shall I come to you, or with love[33]
         and a spirit of meekness?

---

26. *paidagōgous*—Old word for boy *(pais)* and leader *(agōgos)*; used for the
    attendant who accompanied the child to school (Gal. 3:24) and who served
    as "a sort of tutor who had a care for the child when not in school"
    (Robertson, *Word Pictures*).
27. *mimētai*—*Mimētēs* from *mimeomai*, to emulate, follow, imitate, use as a
    model.
28. *agapēton*—A verbal adjective of *agapaō*; dear, esteemed, favorite,
    beloved.
29. *ephusiōthēsan*—Passive indicative (effective) of *phusioō*; blow up, puff up,
    manifest an arrogant or proud manner—in the passive, to put on airs, be
    conceited or puffed up.
30. *gnōsomai*—From *ginōskō*, know or come to know.
31. *dunamin*—The word *power*, as used here, "certainly does not mean that of
    working miracles (Chrys.); but rather that of winning men over to a Christian
    life" (Robertson and Plummer).
32. *en logōi*—Literally, in a word. The kind of word the puffed up, conceited
    Corinthians had been speaking (v. 19).
33. *en agapēi*—The kind of love that is of the character of God's love for man,
    man's love for God, and man's love for his fellow man as inspired by God's
    love for him.

CHAPTER 5

II. Social and Moral Problems (5—7)
A. The Matter of Incest (5:1-8)

1   Actually fornication[1] is heard of among you, and such immorality
     as is not even among the Gentiles, so as for someone to go on
     having his father's wife.[2]

2   And you are puffed up,[3] and rather you did not even mourn[4] that
     the one who did this deed should be removed from your midst;

3   for I verily, being absent *from you* in body but present *with you* in
     spirit, have already decided,[5] as though being present, with
     regard to the one who did this,

4   in the name of our Lord Jesus, you being assembled and of my
     spirit together with the power[6] of our Lord Jesus,

---

1. *porneia*—Earliest usage for prostitution or sale of sex. Later for sexual
    permission in general. Here habitual immorality, the practice of consorting
    with a male or female prostitute . . . sex outside of marriage.

2. *gunaika*—"It was probably a permanent union (concubine or mistress) of
    some kind without formal marriage" (Robertson, *Word Pictures*). See John
    4:18.

3. *pephusiōmenoi*—See footnote 29, verse 18, chapter 4.

4. *epenthēsate*—To grieve, be sad, mourn, as for the dead.

5. *kekrika*—Perfect of *krinō*, to distinguish, separate, judge, consider, think,
    prefer, reach a decision, decide.

6. *dunamei*—From *dunamis*, power, strength, might, capability, ability,
    resources.

5   to deliver such a one to Satan for the destruction[7] of his flesh, so that his spirit may be saved[8] in the day of the Lord.

6   Not good[9] *is* your boasting. Do you not know that a little leaven ferments the whole lump of dough?

7   Clean out[10] the old yeast so that you may be a fresh batch of dough, just as you are unleavened bread. For our passover,[11] Christ, also has been sacrificed;

8   therefore, let us keep on celebrating[12] the feast, not with the old leaven, and not with the leaven of wickedness and sinfulness, but with the unleavened bread of purity[13] and truth.

B. Evil Associations (5:9-13)

9   I wrote you in my epistle[14] not to be intimate with[15] those who practice sexual immorality,

10   not at all with the immoral persons of this world, or with the covetous or extortioners[16] or idolaters, since in that case you ought to come out from the world.

---

7.   **olethron**—From *olethros*, ruin, destruction, death.
8.   **sōthēi**—From *sōzō*, to keep from harm, rescue, preserve, save. "The final salvation of the man in the day of Christ" (Robertson, *Word Pictures*). A man may be saved though many of his works perish.
9.   **kalon**—From *kalos*, beautiful in outward appearance, of quality, useful, free from defects, noble, praiseworthy, morally good.
10.   **ekkatharate**—From *ekkathairō*, I cleanse, I clean out.
11.   **pascha**—The Passover, a Jewish festival whose observance began on the fourteenth of the month Nisan and continued until the early hours of the fifteenth.
12.   **heortazōmen**—From *heortazō*, to celebrate the festival of the Jewish Passover, used here "as a figure of the Christian life" (Bauer).
13.   **eilikrineias**—Unmixed, sincere, judged by sunlight, pure "in moral sense."
14.   **epistolēi**—Obviously a reference to an earlier epistle to the Corinthians, one that is not preserved for us.
15.   **sunanamignusthai**—From *sunanamignumi*, mix up together, associate or mingle with (with the dative of the person), associate intimately with.
16.   **harpaxin**—From *harpax*, ravenous, as of wolves, rapacious, robber, swindler.

11 But now I write unto you not to associate with *such*. If anyone who is called a brother be a fornicator, or a covetous person,[17] or an idolater or a reviler or a drunkard or a swindler, do not even eat in company with such a one.

12 For what business of mine is it to judge those outside?[18] Is it not those within whom you judge?

13 Those outside *the church* God judges. Remove[19] the evil one from yourselves.

---

17. *pleonektēs*—A person who is greedy for gain notwithstanding the effect of his gain upon others.

18. *tous exō*—Those outside the church. Paul's prime concern was for those within the church for he had no authority over those outside the church.

19. *exarate*—From *exairō*, I remove, I drive away, drive out.

CHAPTER 6

C. Christians and Law Courts (6:1-8)

1   Does any one of you having a lawsuit[1] against another dare to go to law before the unjust,[2] and not before the saints?[3]

2   Or do you not know that the saints will judge the world? And if the world is judged by you, are you incompetent[4] for the smallest lawsuits?

3   Do you not know that we will judge angels, let alone ordinary matters?[5]

4   If you have a law case therefore pertaining to ordinary matters, do

---

1. *pragma*—Something done, an event, thing, deed, matter, affair, also used for dispute, lawsuit, as here.

2. *adikōn*—Used of a person "doing contrary to what is right" (Bauer).

3. *hagiōn*—"Basically used of one who is holy, sacred, consecrated, and *dedicated to God*, i.e., set apart completely unto God and for his service. The word is used of one who is consecrated and worthy of veneration; used of sacrifices and offerings prepared for God with solemn rite; in a moral sense, *pure, sinless, upright*; used in the New Testament of those whose lives are set apart for or unto God, to be exclusively his; hence, *saints*" (Caudill, *Philippians*).

4. *anaxioi*—"Are you not good enough or not competent to settle trivial cases?" (Bauer).

5. *biōtika*—Matters in general that have to do with (daily) life, ordinary matters that embrace even "in daily life" (Bauer).

you appoint *as judges* those that are of no account[6] in the church?

5   For shame to you I speak. So *under these circumstances* is there no wise person among you who will be able to render a decision[7] between brother *and brother*?

6   But brother with brother is judged, and that before[8] unbelievers;

7   indeed it is then already a total defeat[9] for you since you have lawsuits with your own selves? Why not rather be wronged?[10] Why not rather allow yourselves to be robbed?[11]

8   On the contrary, you are doing the wronging[12] and the defrauding, and that your brethren.

D. The Kingdom Inheritance (6:9-11)

9   Or do you not know that the unrighteous will not inherit God's kingdom? Do not be led astray; neither fornicators,[13] nor idolaters, nor adulterers,[14] nor sodomites,[15] nor homosexuals,[16]

---

6. **exouthenēmenous**—From *exoutheneō*, I despise, I ignore, I set at nought. The reference here is for those who have no standing in the church because of the character of their life-style.

7. **diakrinai**—An old compound word, *dia* (through, an interval between) with the resultant idea of between, and *krinai* (first aorist inf. of *krinō*), to decide or judge.

8. **epi**—The meaning of the preposition *epi* is upon and means resting upon "rather than over or above like *huper*" (Robertson, *New Short Grammar*).

9. **hēttēma**—From *hēttaō*, to make inferior, less, to overcome, and hence defeat.

10. **adikeisthe**—Present (permissive) middle indicative of *adikeō*, to act wickedly, unjustly, or to do some wrong or wrong someone.

11. **apostereisthe**—To steal, rob, or defraud.

12. **adikeite**—Present active of *adikeō*. See footnote 10, verse 7.

13. **pornoi**—A male prostitute, a man who practices "unlawful sexual intercourse."

14. **moichoi**—Voluntary sexual intercourse between a married man and a woman who is not his wife, or a married woman with a man who is not her husband.

15. **malakoi**—Men and boys "who allow themselves to be misused homosexually" *(Catamites)*. Used also of persons effeminate, soft (Bauer).

16. **arsenokoitai**—A male homosexual, sodomite, pederast.

10   nor thieves, nor covetous persons,[17] nor drunkards, nor users of abusive language,[18] nor robbers shall inherit the kingdom of God.

11   And these things certain ones of you were; but you had yourselves washed,[19] at least you were consecrated;[20] rather you were justified[21] in the name of the Lord Jesus Christ and in the Spirit of our God.

E. The Christian and His Body (6:12-20)

12   All things for me are lawful,[22] but not all things are expedient;[23] all things for me are permissible, but I myself will not be dominated[24] by anything.

13   The foods *are* for the stomach,[25] and the stomach for the foods, but God will do away with[26] both it and them. But the body is not for the fornication[27] but for the Lord, and the Lord for the body.

---

17. *pleonektai*—From *pleonektēs*, a person who is greedy for gain without regard for other persons.

18. *loidoroi*—A reviler or abusive person. See 1 Corinthians 5:11.

19. *apelousasthe*—First aorist middle of *apolouō*. Their own voluntary act which was an outward expression of God's inner cleansing.

20. *hēgiasthēte*—To make *hagion* (holy), declare sacred or holy or consecrate. "To render or acknowledge to be venerable, to hallow" (Thayer).

21. *edikai ōthēte*—You were set right with God. "These twin conceptions of the Christian state in its beginning appear commonly in the reverse order" (Findlay).

22. *exestin*—An impersonal verb used in the third singular in the sense of "it is permitted, it is proper, it is possible."

23. *sumpherei*—To bring together, to help, benefit, or be advantageous or profitable (Bauer).

24. *exousiasthēsomai*—"Perhaps a conscious play on the verb *exestin* for exousiazō is from *exousia* [capability, might] and that from *exestin*" (Robertson, *Word Pictures*).

25. *koiliai*—Belly, body cavity, of the human stomach.

26. *katargēsei*—Make powerless, ineffective, abolish, wipe out, set aside, bring to an end.

27. *porneiai*—See footnote 13 above.

14   But God both raised up the Lord and will raise up[28] us through his power.

15   Do you not know that your bodies are members[29] of Christ? Having taken[30] therefore the members of Christ, should I make them members of a harlot? May it never come to pass.[31]

16   Or do you not know that he who is joined[32] to the harlot is one body? For they shall be, he says,[33] the two unto one flesh.

17   He who is joined[34] to the Lord is one spirit.

18   Shun every kind of sexual immorality; every sin that a man commits is outside[35] the body, but he who practices sexual immorality sins against his own body.

19   Or do you not know that your body is a temple[36] of the Holy Spirit

---

28.   **exegerei**—Future active indicative of exegeirō, to awaken, as from sleep, raise (awaken) from the dead, raise up.

29.   **melē**—Limb, part, member, as parts of the human body. Here the reference is to the Christian community, the body of Christ, of which Christ is the head. "The individual Christians are members of Christ, and together they form his body" (Bauer).

30.   **aras**—First aorist active participle of airō, "to snatch, carry off like Latin rapio (our rape)" (Robertson, *Word Pictures*).

31.   **mē genoito**—An idiom common in Epictetus, but seldom used in the Septuagint (LXX). Paul used the expression thirteen times, and Luke once (Luke 20:16). The verb is "optative second aorist in a negative wish for the future" (Robertson, *Word Pictures*).

32.   **kollōmenos**—From an old word kollaō, to glue together, glue to, cement, fasten together, cleave to.

33.   **phēsin**—Literally, "he (it) says." "The implied subject may be God or scripture, and either would be equally in line with Paul's thinking" (Bruce). (See Gen. 2:24; Matt. 19:5).

34.   **kollōmenos**—Present passive participle of kollaō. Cf. 32 above.

35.   **ektos tou sōmatos**—The assault on the body comes from outside sources (from without).

36.   **naos**—Basically, temple. Used of the Temple of Jerusalem, of temples in general, and of the heavenly sanctuary.

within you which you have from God, and you do not belong[37] to yourselves?

20 You were bought[38] for a price; therefore glorify[39] God in your body.

---

37. *ouk este heautōn*—Predicate genitive. You are not your own, that is, you do not belong to yourselves.

38. *ēgorasthēte*—From *agorazō*, I purchase, I buy. A marketplace term used only here by Paul with reference to Christian redemption (Bruce).

39. *doxasate*—See Romans 12:1 where Paul entreats the Romans to "present your bodies as a living sacrifice."

CHAPTER 7

F. Celibacy and Marriage (7:1-9)

1   Now concerning the things of which you wrote,[1] it is fitting[2] for a man not to touch a woman;

2   but because of the fornications[3] each man is to have his own wife, and each *woman* is to have her own husband;

3   The man is to fulfill[4] his duty to his wife, and likewise the wife to her husband.

4   The wife does not have dominion[5] over her own body but her husband; and likewise also the husband does not have dominion over his own body, but his wife.

5   Do not deprive each other, except it be by consent for a time that you may devote yourselves to prayer and again be upon the

---

1. *egrapsate*—A letter from the Corinthian church to Paul concerning problems about marriage.
2. *kalon*—Beautiful, fitting, fine, useful, good, free from defects, as in precious stone. Not a condemnation of marriage but a word in favor of celibacy "in certain limitations" (Robertson, *Word Pictures*).
3. *porneias*—Fornication, habitual immorality, consorting with male or female prostitutes, sex outside of marriage.
4. *tēn opheilēn apodidotō*—A bond of mutual obligation exists between both husband and wife. "This dictum defends marital intercourse against rigorists, as that of ver. 1 commends celibacy against sensualists" (Findlay).
5. *exousiazei*—To have power, to be in authority, to have power or right for something or over someone, or the right or the power to act in a given situation, dominion.

same,[6] so that Satan may not tempt you because of your lack of self-control.[7]

6 And this I say as a concession,[8] not as a commandment.

7 Now I would like for all men to be even as I[9] myself; but each has his own gift from God, the one in this manner and the other in that.

8 But I say to the unmarried men and to the widows, it is fine[10] for them if they continue to abide even as I;

9 if then they do not exercise self-control,[11] they are to marry, for it is better to marry than to burn[12] with sexual desire.

G. The Problem of Divorce (7:10-16)

10 But to the married I give orders,[13] not I but the Lord, the wife is not to be separated[14] from her husband.

11 But even if she be separated, let her remain unmarried or else be reconciled[15] to her husband—and the husband is not to leave his wife.

---

6. *epi to auto ēte*—The resumption of the normal sex life between the husband and wife.

7. *akrasian*—Self-indulgence, lack of self-control.

8. *suggnōmēn*—Indulgence, pardon, concession. Papyri for pardon.

9. *hōs kai emauton*—These words suggest that Paul was not then living in a married state. (See v. 8.)

10. *kalon*—See footnote 2 above.

11. *egkrateuontai*—Middle deponent, abstain from something, control oneself, as from evil deeds, and of athletes (1 Cor. 9:25).

12. *purousthai*—Present middle infinitive of *puroō*, I set on fire, I burn up, cause to glow, make red hot, burn, be inflamed, to burn with sexual desire.

13. *paraggellō*—I instruct, I command, I give orders, I direct. Used with reference to "all kinds of persons in authority, worldly rulers, Jesus, the apostles" (Bauer).

14. *chōristhēnai*—From Greek *chōrizō*, to separate or divide something, or in the passive, to be separated by divorce. Frequently used in marriage contracts.

15. *katallagētō*—Second aorist (ingressive) imperative (passive) of *katalassō*. "Old compound verb to exchange coins as of equal value, to reconcile" (Robertson, *Word Pictures*). Used of reconciliation of person's relation to God and to relation to other people.

12   But to the rest, I say, not the Lord:[16] if any brother has an unbelieving wife, and she is willing to go on living with him, he is not to leave her;

13   And if a woman has an unbelieving[17] husband and he agrees to go on living with her, she is not to leave the husband.

14   For the unbelieving husband is treated as sanctified[18] in his wife, and the unbelieving wife is treated as sanctified in her *brother*; else your children are unclean,[19] but now they are holy.

15   But if the unbelieving one is separated, he is to continue to be separated; the brother or the sister is not under bondage[20] in these matters; but God has called you in peace.[21]

16   For how do you know, woman, whether[22] you will save your husband? Or how do you know, man, whether you will save your wife?

---

16.   *ouch ho Kurios*—Paul claimed no divine revelation for his words here, but he in no way disclaims inspiration. He merely said that he had "no word about marriage from Jesus beyond the problem of divorce" (Robertson, *Word Pictures*).

17.   *apiston*—Incredible, unbelievable, but with religious connotation, unbelieving, faithless.

18.   *hēgiastai*—Perfect passive indicative of verb *hagiazō*, to set things aside or "make them suitable for ritual purposes" (Bauer). When used of persons, it carries the idea dedicate, consecrate, sanctify. A person is sanctified when his or her life is set apart and fully committed to God in life-style.

19.   *akatharta*—Used in Acts 10:14 (anything common or unclean). Among the cults of Paul's day the word was used of that which could not be brought into contact with the divinity. The rendering here indicates an ellipse of the condition with *epei*. Robertson has "since, accordingly, if it is otherwise, your children are illegitimate *(akatharta)*" (Robertson, *Word Pictures*).

20.   *dedoulōtai*—Perfect passive indicative of *douloō*, to make a person a *doulos* (a slave), subject, enslave.

21.   *eirēnē*—The meaning is a bit obscure, as Conzelmann notes. Apparently the idea is that of harmony.

22.   *ei*—A widely disputed passage, but apparently the context favors "whether" rather than "whether you will not."

H. The Believer's Life-Style (7:17-24)

17   Only to each as the Lord apportioned,[23] each as God called,[24] so
is one to walk; and likewise in all the churches I give this order.

18   Of the circumcised who is called: he is not to become uncircum-
cised.[25] Who is called in uncircumcision? He is not to be circumcised.

19   Circumcision is nothing, and uncircumcision is nothing, but the
keeping of God's commandments.

20   Each in the calling in which he was called in that *calling* he is to
remain.[26]

21   Were you, a slave,[27] called? It is not to be a bother to you; but if
you are also able to become free, rather use your opportunity.

22   For the one in the Lord called as a slave is a freedman[28] of the
Lord; likewise the one called as a freeman is a slave of Christ.

23   You were bought[29] for a price; stop becoming slaves of men.

24   Each one in that state in which[30] he was called, brothers, in that
state he is to remain with God.[31]

---

23.   **emerisen**—Aorist active indicative of *merizō*, to separate, divide, distrib-
ute, deal out, apportion, assign, as something to someone.

24.   **keklēken**—Perfect passive of *kaleō*. Literally, I call, as a person by name.
Here the idea is that of the divine summons of God to discipleship and the
Christian service.

25.   **mē epispasthō**—Present middle imperative of *epispaō*, to draw on. The
Jew is to remain a Jew, and the Gentile, a Gentile. The Christian church is
free from the rite of circumcision.

26.   **menetō**—From *menō* (intr.), stay, remain, live, lodge, dwell.

27.   **doulos**—A (male) slave, enslaved, subject.

28.   **apeleutheros**—Freedman, used of Christians, as "a freedman of the
Lord." The Christian comes into a new estate in which he possesses a
freedom that is not dependent upon earthly circumstance, for his Master is
the Lord.

29.   **ēgorasthēte**—From *agorazō*, I buy.

30.   **en hōi**—In whatever state.

31.   **para theōi**—"This may mean 'in the presence of God,' or 'in God's
household,' or 'on God's side.' The last agrees well with *menetō*, and makes
a good antithesis to *anthrōpōn*" (Robertson and Plummer).

I. Concerning Virgins (7:25-38)

25 Now concerning the virgins,[32] I have no commandment of the Lord, but I give an opinion as one having received mercy by the Lord to be faithful.

26 I consider therefore this to be appropriate because of the present necessity,[33] that it is fitting for a man to be thus.

27 Are you bound[34] to a wife? Seek not a divorce; are you free from a wife? Seek not a wife.

28 But if even you should marry, you have not sinned; and if the virgin marry, she has not sinned. But such will have tribulation in the flesh, and I am trying to spare[35] you.

29 Now this I say, brothers, the time is shortened;[36] so that from now on those having wives be as those not having *them*,

30 and those weeping as not weeping, and those rejoicing as not rejoicing, and those buying as possessing nothing,[37]

31 and those using the world as not using it up;[38] for the present form of this world is passing away.

---

32. *parthenōn*—From *parthenos*, a maiden, virgin, and also used of men who "abstain from all uncleanness and whoredom attendant on idolatry, and so has kept his chastity" (Thayer).

33. *enestōsan anagkēn*—The word *anagkē* is used "either for external circumstances or inward sense of duty" (Robertson, *Word Pictures*). In Luke 21:23, it refers to the woes that precede the Second Coming of Christ. In 1 Thessalonians 3:7, it is used for Paul's persecutions. There may be a "mingling of both ideas here" (Robertson, *Word Pictures*).

34. *dedesai*—Perfect passive indicative of *deō*, to tie, bind, tie to something, binding a husband to his wife.

35. *pheidomai*—Present middle indicative and possibly conative. In other words, "I am trying to spare you" (Robertson, *Word Pictures*).

36. *sunestalmenos estin*—Perfect periphrastic passive indicative of the old verb *sustellō*, to place together, to draw together. Only here and in Acts 5:6 in the New Testament (Robertson, *Word Pictures*).

37. *mē katechontes*—From *katechō*, to detain, hold back, retain, keep secure, hold fast, keep firm possession of, to possess, as here.

38. *mē katachrōmenoi*—From *katachraomai*, make full use of, misuse, use up, to use much or excessively, to consume by use, or to use up fully.

32   Now I want you to be free from care.[39] The unmarried person is concerned about the things of the Lord, how he may please the Lord;

33   but the married one is concerned[40] for the things of the world, how he may please[41] his wife, and he is divided.

34   And the unmarried woman and the virgin are concerned about the things of the Lord, in order that she may be holy[42] both in the body and in the Spirit; but the married woman is concerned about the things of the world, how she may please her husband.

35   But this for your own benefit I speak, not that I might throw a noose[43] over you, but for your good repute and constant devotion to the Lord without distraction.

36   Now if anyone thinks he is behaving shamefully toward his virgin, if she be passionate, and it ought thus to happen, whatever he wishes he is to do; he commits no sin; let them marry.[44]

37   And whosoever stands firm[45] in his heart, not having necessity, and has dominion concerning his own will, and has decided this in his own heart, to hold back[46] his own virgin, he will do well;

38   so both the one giving his own virgin in marriage does well, and the one not giving in marriage will do better.

---

39.   **amerimnous**—A compound adjective (*a* privative, and *merimna*, anxiety) found only here and in Matthew 28:14 in the New Testament.

40.   **merimnai**—From *merimnaō*, I am anxious, I have anxiety, I am (unduly) concerned, to care for, or be unduly concerned about someone or something.

41.   **aresēi**—From *areskō*, I endeavor to please, I am pleasing, to accommodate (with reference to conduct, activity, often almost serve) (Bauer).

42.   **hagia**—Set apart by (or for) God, hence, holy, sacred.

43.   **brochon**—Noose, such as one would throw, as a lasso, on someone in order to catch him or restrain him (Bauer).

44.   **gameitōsan**—Present active imperative (plural), they are to marry.

45.   **hedraios**—Steadfast, firm, to stand firm. Used of "steadfast in the faith" (1 Pet. 5:9).

46.   **tērein**—A case where the virgin daughter does not desire to marry "and the father agrees with her" (Robertson, *Word Pictures*).

J. Concerning Remarriage (7:39-40)

39   A woman is bound for whatever time her husband lives; but if the husband dies, she is free for whom she wishes to marry, only in the Lord.

40   But she is happier if she remains thus, according to my opinion, and I think I also have the Spirit of God.

CHAPTER 8

III. Idolatry and Spiritual Freedom (8:1 to 11:1)
A. Knowledge and Love (8:1-6)

1   Now concerning the meat sacrificed to idols, we are aware that we all have knowledge.[1] The knowledge puffs up,[2] but the love builds up.

2   If anyone considers[3] himself to have become learned about something, he does not yet know as he ought[4] to know;

3   but if anyone loves God, this one is known[5] by him.

4   Concerning the eating therefore of meat sacrificed to idols, we know that an idol is nothing[6] in the world, that there is no God but one.

---

1. *gnōsin*—Knowledge "as an attribute of God (Rom. 11:33) and of man (1 Cor. 8:1,7,11)" (Bauer).

2. *phusioi*—Puff up, blow up, make arrogant or proud.

3. *dokei*—From *dokeō*, consider, believe, think, suppose (intransitive sense as here).

4. *dei*—Literally it is necessary, one has to, or one must. "Denoting compulsion of any kind" (Bauer).

5. *egnōstai*—Perfect passive indicative of *ginōskō*, come to know, know, learn, comprehend, understand, perceive. An "abiding state of recognition by *(hup')* God" (Robertson, *Word Pictures*).

6. *ouden . . . eidōlon*—In secular Greek, form, shadow, image, phantom (Bauer). Used here of an idol or false god. Here with *ouden* meaning "nothing" in sense of representing God.

5   For if indeed there are [7] so-called[8] gods whether in heaven or on earth, even as there are many gods and many lords,

6   yet for us *there is* one God, the Father, from whom [9] *are* all things and we unto him, and one Lord Jesus Christ, through whom *are* all things and we through him. [10]

B. The Christian's Influence (8:7-13)

7   But not in every person is the knowledge; [11] and some by the custom until now continue to eat—as it were—the sacrificial meat of the idol, and their conscience[12] being weak is defiled. [13]

8   But food will not commend us to God; neither if we do not eat are we worse off, [14] nor if we do eat are we better off. [15]

9   And take care lest this freedom[16] of yours should become a cause of stumbling to the weak.

10   For if anyone should see you, a person having knowledge, [17] dining in an idol's temple, would not his conscience, being weak, be built up to eat the meats sacrificed to idols?

---

7.   *kai gar eiper eisin*—This clause is concessive, a condition of the first class "assumed to be true for argument's sake" (Robertson, *Word Pictures*).

8.   *legomenoi*—"So-called gods, reputed gods" (Robertson, *Word Pictures*).

9.   *ex hou*—Of whom, from whom, indicating the source of their existence.

10. *di'hou . . . di'autou*—Through whom . . . through him. These expressions "point to Jesus Christ as the intermediate agent in creation as in Col. 1:15-20; John 1:3f." (Robertson, *Word Pictures*).

11. *hē gnōsis*—"The knowledge *(hē gnōsis)* of which Paul is speaking" (Robertson, *Word Pictures*).

12. *suneidēsis*—"The innate power to discern what is good, an abiding consciousness bearing witness concerning a man's conduct" (Souter).

13. *molunetai*—From *molunō*, to pollute, stain, defile.

14. *husteroumetha*—In the passive, to go without, lack, be lacking, come short of.

15. *perisseuomen*—To abound, have an abundance, be rich, have more (as of divine approval) (Bauer).

16. *exousia*—Right to make decisions, act, to make choices, to have authority, power. From *exestin*, meaning "a grant, allowance, authority, power, privilege, right, liberty" (Robertson, *Word Pictures*).

17. *gnōsin*—See footnote 11 above.

11   For the weak one is destroyed[18] by your knowledge, the brother for whose sake Christ died.

12   And so, in sinning[19] against the brothers and smiting their weak conscience you sin against Christ.

13   Wherefore if food causes my brother to sin,[20] I will in no wise eat meat forever so that I will not cause my brother to sin.

---

18. *apollutai*—Present middle indicative of *apollumi*, I lose, I destroy, I am perishing, "the resultant death being viewed as certain" (Souter).

19. *hamartanontes*—From *hamartanō*, originally "I miss the mark; hence, I make a mistake, I sin, commit a sin (against God)" (Souter). Here the idea is of sinning against another person.

20. *skandalizei*—From *skandalizō*, a late verb meaning "to set a trapstick" (Matt. 5:29), or "stumbling-block like *proskomma* in verse 9" (Robertson, *Word Pictures*). Hence, fall, cause to be caught, cause to sin (Bauer).

CHAPTER 9

C. Paul's Freedom as an Apostle (9:1-6)

1 Am I not free?[1] Am I not an apostle? Have I not seen Jesus[2] our Lord? Are you not my work in the Lord?

2 If to others[3] I am not an apostle, yet I am to you; for you are the seal[4] of my apostleship in the Lord.

3 This is my reply[5] to those who sit in judgment[6] over me.

4 Have we not freedom[7] to eat and drink?

5 Have we not the right to take along a sister-wife,[8] even as the rest[9]

---

1. *eleutheros*—Not bound, independent, the opposite of one who is a bond servant as in 1 Corinthians 12:13. Here, free from the bondage of Mosaic tradition.

2. *Iēsoun . . . heōraka*—See 1 Corinthians 15:8; Acts 9:17,27; 18:9.

3. *allois*—That is, the Judaizers who disputed his "right to be accounted an Apostle" (Robertson and Plummer).

4. *sphragis*—Signet, seal, "sign or stamp of approval, certificate . . . that which confirms, attests, or authenticates" (Bauer).

5. *apologia*—A defense, as in a court of law; a reply, speech of defense.

6. *anakrinousin*—I examine, question, pledge, call to account, discern.

7. *exousian*—Freedom in the sense of choice, right to decide or to act, ability, might, power, authority, ruling power, absolute power, official power. Authority that is absolute.

8. *adelphēn gunaika*—Literally, sister-believer wife; figuratively, "a sister in the faith, as here."

9. *hoi loipoi*—We do not know who "the other apostles" were, maybe "missionaries in general" (Conzelmann).

of the apostles and the brothers[10] of the Lord—and Cephas?[11]

6   Or do only I and Barnabas have freedom not to work?[12]

D. The Minister's Right to Material Support (9:7-15a)

7   Who serves as a soldier at one's own expense[13] ever? Who plants a vineyard and eats not the fruit of it? Or who herds a flock and eats not from the milk of the herd?

8   Do I speak these things according to[14] human judgment, or does the law also say these things?

9   For in the law of Moses it is written, thou shalt not muzzle an ox that is threshing *the grain*. Is it about the oxen that it is a concern[15] to God,

10   or is he *not* certainly[16] speaking for our sake? For because of us it was written that the one plowing ought to plow in hope, and the one who is threshing in the hope of sharing *the crops*.

11   If we have sown to you spiritual things, is it a great matter if we shall reap from you the material things?[17]

12   If others share your freedom, do we not more? But we have not

---

10.   The names of the brothers of Jesus are given in Matthew 13:55 ff.

11.   *kai Kēphas*—The Hebrew name for *Peter*. According to tradition, John was celibate, but not Peter.

12.   *exousian mē ergazesthai*—To work or not to work in behalf of his support on the mission journey rather than draw on the community for support was the decision that both Paul and Barnabas had every right to make.

13.   *opsōniois*—Literally, money paid to a soldier, hence, pay, wages.

14.   *kata anthrōpon*—According to, by way of. Findlay has "as any man might do."

15.   *melei*—With dative of person, it is a care. It is an object of anxiety (Souter).

16.   *pantōs*—Entirely, to be sure, in any case.

17.   *ta sarkika*—From *sarkikos*, an old adjective, fleshly, carnal, in the manner of the flesh, belonging to the order of earthly things, material, things that minister to the body.

used this freedom, rather we endured[18] all things so that we may cause no hindrance[19] to the gospel of Christ.

13   Do you not know that those performing[20] the temple rites eat sacred things[21] from the temple sacrifice, *that* those who wait on the altar of burnt offerings share with *it*?

14   In the same way the Lord ordered[22] those who proclaim the gospel to live out of the gospel.[23]

15   But I on my part have not made use of[24] any of these.

E. Paul's Course for the Sake of the Gospel (9:15b-23)

On the other hand, I did not write these things that it might be so done in my case,[25] for it is better for me to die or—that no one shall render void my ground of boasting.[26]

16   For if I preach the gospel[27] it is not for me a ground for boasting, for a necessity is laid upon me; for woe is to me if I preach not the gospel.

17   For if of my own free will I do this, I have a reward[28] but if not of my own will, I have been entrusted with a stewardship.

---

18. *stegomen*—Literally, to preserve, protect or keep by covering, to keep secret, conceal, hide, hold out against, bear up against, and thus to endure, forbear, bear.

19. *egkopēn*—Hindrance, cause a hindrance to something, as here.

20. *ergazomenoi*—Do, carry out, accomplish, perform, practice, officiate.

21. *[ta]*—The context implies sacred things sacrificed in the temple.

22. *dietaxen*—From *diatassō*, direct, command, order.

23. *ek tou euaggeliou*—From the gospel, out of the gospel, the gospel being the source of the livelihood.

24. *ou kechrēmai*—From *chraomai*, from *chrē* "necessity," I use, I treat, I employ.

25. *en emoi*—Literally, "in me."

26. *kauchēma*—From *kauchaomai*, boast, what is said in boasting, having a reason for boasting (Bauer).

27. *euaggelizōmai*—Bring or announce good news, hence, preach the gospel.

28. *misthon*—From *misthos*, pay, wages, as for work done.

18   What then is my reward? That as I proclaim the good news, I will set forth[29] the gospel[30] free of charge, so that I might not use to the full my freedom in the gospel.

19   For being free from all things, I made myself a slave[31] to all, that I might gain the more.

20   And I became to the Jews as a Jew,[32] so that I might gain Jews; to those under the law[33] as under the law, although I myself am not under the law, in order that I might gain those under the law.

21   To those without the law[34] as without the law, not being without the law of God but subject to the law of Christ, that I might gain those who are without the law.

22   I became to the weak[35] as one weak in order that I might gain the weak; to all people I became all things so that I might save at least some.

23   But all things I do for the sake of the gospel[36] that I may become a cosharer of it.

---

29. *thēsō*—Future of *tithēmi*, place, put, lay, set up, set forth.

30. *to euaggelion*—Originally "a reward for good news, then simply good news" (Bauer). In the New Testament, as elsewhere, in the specific sense of "God's good news to men, the *gospel*" (Bauer).

31. *emauton edoulōsa*—From *douleuō*, to be a slave, to be subjected as to someone.

32. *hōs Ioudaios*—"As" a Jew, that is "he conformed to Jewish customs and used methods of teaching adapted to them" (Gould). Paul, of course, was a Jew; he sought in every way possible to gain the support of the Jews in his mission.

33. *hupo nomon*—Those who had not been "emancipated from the law as a means of salvation" as Paul had been (Robertson, *Word Pictures*).

34. *anomois*—Literally, disobedient to the law, lawless, but here the "heathen, those outside the Mosaic law (Rom. 2:14)" (Robertson, *Word Pictures*).

35. *tois asthenesin*—Powerless, weak. Figuratively miserable, feeble, weak, as "in faith." Paul's effort to identify with others. Weak "in faith and Christian discernment" (Vincent).

36. *dia to euaggelion*—For the sake of the gospel, on account of the gospel. Paul's burning desire was to see all men saved.

F. Paul's Ascetic Life-Style (9:24-27)

24 Do you not know that those who run in the stadium[37] all indeed run, but one receives the prize; so run that you might get[38] it.

25 On the other hand, everyone who is engaging in a contest exercises self-control[39] in every respect, they indeed therefore that they may receive a perishable crown, but we an imperishable crown.

26 I therefore so run as not *aimlessly,*[40] I so box as not beating the air;

27 rather, I severely discipline[41] my body and enslave it,[42] lest in some way having preached to others I myself become disqualified.

---

37. **stadiōi**—*Stadium, stade, arena,* in which the ancient athletic contests, foot races, etc. were held for the benefit of the public.

38. **katalabēte**—From *katalambanō,* seize tight hold of, arrest, catch, capture, appropriate, attain, make one's own.

39. **egkrateuetai**—A middle dependent verb, abstain, control oneself, "exercise self control in all respects of athletes" (Bauer).

40. **adēlōs**—Uncertainly.

41. **hupōpiazō**—Literally, give a black eye to, strike under the eye; figuratively, torment, maltreat, treat roughly.

42. **doulagōgō**—From *doulagōgeō,* to bring into subjection, enslave, bring under control.

CHAPTER 10

G. The Case of Israel's Backsliding (10:1-5)

1   For I do not want you to be ignorant, brothers, that our fathers[1] all
    were under the cloud[2] and all passed through the sea.

2   And all unto Moses[3] got themselves baptized in the cloud and in
    the sea,

3   and all ate the same spiritual food,[4]

4   and all drank the same spiritual drink; for they continued to drink[5]

---

1. *hoi pateres hēmōn*—Used of the male ancestor (immediate) but also in a
    general way forefather and figuratively of "spiritual fatherhood" (Bauer).

2. *tēn nephelēn*—The pillar of cloud under which the Israelites of the Exodus
    marched by day (Ex. 13:21; 14:19). The cloud which covered the host
    (Num. 14:14; Ps. 105:39). "This mystic cloud was the symbol of the
    presence of the Lord with the people" (Robertson, *Word Pictures*).

3. *eis ton Mōüsēn*—A reference to Moses, the leader of the Israelites during
    the Exodus. Moses as their leader stood somewhat in reference to them as
    Christ is now our leader, but just what Paul had in mind by the figure is not
    clear.

4. *pneumatikon brōma*—Evidently a reference to the manna (Ex. 16:13 ff.)
    which was supernatural in character and, therefore, termed "spiritual" by
    Paul.

5. *epinon*—Imperfect tense indicating "continual access to the supernatural
    source of supply" (Robertson, *Word Pictures*).

from a spiritual rock that followed them; and the rock was the Christ.[6]

5   But not with the most of them was God well pleased for they were scattered on the ground[7] in the wilderness.

H. A Warning Against Idolatry (10:6-14)

6   Now these things became examples[8] for us so that we should not be desirers[9] of evil as they also desired.

7   And stop becoming idolaters, as some of them; even as it is written, the people sat down to eat and drink, and got up to play[10] like children.

8   And let us cease committing sexual immorality[11] as certain of these did and fell in one day 23,000.

9   Neither let us tempt the Lord as some of them did[12] and perished by the serpents.[13]

10   And do not murmur even as certain ones of them murmured, and perished by the destroyer.[14]

---

6.   **ho Christos**—The Christ. A symbolic reference to the preexistent Christ, but certainly Paul did not mean to imply that "'the pre-incarnate Christ followed the march of Israel in the shape of a lump of rock' (Hoffman)" (Robertson, *Word Pictures*).

7.   **katestrōthēsan**—From a compound verb *katastrōnnumi*, to stretch, "spread down as of a couch," lay low, scatter on the ground as a hurricane would scatter.

8.   **tupoi**—Our types, from *tuptō*, strike and leave a mark by the blow as of the print of the nails (John 20:25).

9.   **epithumētas**—From *epithumētēs*, one who desires, a luster after; here, desirous of evil.

10. **paizein**—From *paizō*, to dance, amuse oneself, play with someone.

11. **porneuōmen**—Literally, "to prostitute, practice prostitution, or sexual immorality" in general (Bauer). Specifically, sex outside of marriage.

12. See Numbers 25:9 where 24,000 died in the plague.

13. **opheōn**—From *ophis*, serpent. See Numbers 21:4-6.

14. **tou olothreutou**—A reference to the destroying angel of Exodus 12:23.

11 Now these things[15] came to them as an example[16] and were written for our warning unto whom the ends of the ages[17] have come.[18]

12 Therefore the one who thinks that he stands[19] is to watch out lest he should fall.

13 Temptation[20] has not come upon you except what is common to man;[21] but faithful is God, who will not allow you to be tempted beyond what you are able *to endure,* but will provide with the temptation also the way out[22] *which* you are able to bear up under.

14 For this very reason, my beloved, flee from[23] idolatry.

I. The Cup of the Lord or the Cup of Demons (10:15-23)

15 As to wise men,[24] I speak; consider ye what I say.

16 The cup of the blessing[25] which we bless, is it not a communion[26] of

---

15. *tauta*—The things Paul had been talking about in the preceding verses, that is, death by the fiery serpents.

16. *tupikōs*—"Typologically, as an example or warning" (Bauer).

17. *ta telē tōn aiōnōn*—"The consummation of the ages" (also Matt. 13:40). "The plural seems to point out how one stage succeeds another in the drama of human history" (Robertson, *Word Pictures*).

18. *katēntēken*—It is not clear if Paul was referring here to the second coming of Christ as in 7:26. "In a sense," though, "the ends of the ages like a curtain have come down to all of us" (Robertson, *Word Pictures*).

19. *hestanai*—Perfect active infinitive of *histēmi*. The action took place in the past but still holds.

20. *peirasmos*—Trial, test, temptation, enticement to sin.

21. *anthrōpinos*—Literally, human; used of things belonging to humans, the opposite of divine things, usual among people.

22. *tēn ekbasin*—A way out, end.

23. *pheugete apo*—From *pheugō*, to seek safety in flight, flee, escape. In a moral sense, flee from, avoid, shun.

24. *phronimois*—From *phronimos*, wise, thoughtful, sensible, prudent.

25. *eulogias*—An old word used in the sense of praise, fine speaking, blessing, consecration.

26. *koinōnia*—Fellowship, association, communion, close relationship, "(hence a favorite expr. for the marital relationship as the most intimate betw. human beings Isocr. 3:40)" (Bauer).

the blood of Christ? The loaf we break, is it not a communion of the body of Christ?

17 For one bread, one body are we the many, for we all partake of[27] the one loaf.[28]

18 Look at Israel with respect to the flesh;[29] are not those who are eating the sacrifices partakers[30] of the altar?

19 What then am I saying? That the meat offered to an idol[31] is anything? Or that an idol is anything?

20 Rather *I say* that what they sacrifice, they sacrifice to demons[32] and not to God, and I do not want you to become a partaker of *the altar* of the demons.

21 You are not able[33] to drink the cup of the Lord and the cup of demons; you are not able to partake of the table of the Lord and of the table of demons.

22 Or do we provoke to jealousy[34] the Lord? Are we stronger than he?

23 Everything is possible,[35] but not everything is helpful. Everything is permissible, but not everything builds up.[36]

---

27. **metechomen**—From *metechō*, share, participate, have a share "with gen. of the thing *in* or *of someth*." (Bauer).

28. **henos artou**—The one loaf, the mystical body of Christ.

29. **kata sarka**—According to the flesh, with reference to the flesh.

30. **koinōnoi**—From *koinōnos*, partner, sharer, companion, "one who takes part in someth. with someone" (Bauer), in something.

31. **eidōlon**—"(Fr. Hom. on, in secular Greek) image, form, shadow, phantom" (Bauer). Here, *image, false god, idol*.

32. **daimoniois**—From *daimonion* (neuter substantive of adjective *daimonios*), a divinity, deity, evil spirit, demon. Here, demon or evil spirits.

33. **ou dunasthe**—From *dunamai*, I am able, I can, I have power. Our English word *dynamite* comes from this root.

34. **parazēloumen**—From *parazēloō*, to make jealous, as "someone of someone," to provoke to jealousy.

35. **exestin**—Third singular of *exeimi* (otherwise unused), impersonal verb: it is possible, it is permitted, it is proper.

36. **oikodomei**—From *oikodomeō*, I build, erect, build up, restore, with the resulting idea of benefit, establish, strengthen, edify.

J. Limited Liberty (10:24 to 11:1)

24   No one is to seek[37] his own thing but the welfare of the other.

25   Eat everything offered for sale in the meat market,[38] asking no
     questions for conscience's sake,

26   for the earth is the Lord's[39] and the fullness thereof.

27   If any one of the unbelievers invites[40] you *for a meal* and you desire
     to go, eat everything that is set before you without asking any
     questions because of your conscience.

28   And if anyone says to you, "This is sacrificial meat,"[41] you are not
     to eat *it* for the sake of the one who informed you and for
     conscience's sake—

29   for conscience, I say, not your own but that of the other person.
     For why is my liberty judged by another's scruples?[42]

30   If I eat with thanks, why am I defamed[43] over that for which I give
     thanks?

31   Whether therefore you eat or drink or whatever you do, do
     everything unto the glory of God.

32   And become blameless[44] both to the Jews and to the Greeks and to
     the church of God,

---

37. **zēteitō**—From *zēteō*, to look for, seek, try to obtain, desire to possess,
    aim (at), strive, desire, wish.

38. **makellōi**—From *makellon*, enclosure, grating, an old word found in the
    papyri and inscriptions meaning "the provision market" (Robertson, *Word
    Pictures*). Here, meat market.

39. **tou Kuriou**—The Lord's. A quotation from Psalm 24:1.

40. **kalei**—From *kaleō*, call, call by name, and hence, invite.

41. **hierothuton**—From *hierothutos*, devoted or sacrificed to a divinity, meat
    sacrificed to idols (Bauer).

42. **suneidēseōs**—From *suneidēsis*, consciousness, conscience, moral con-
    sciousness, conscientiousness, scruples.

43. **blasphēmoumai**—Revile, defame, injure the reputation of (people)
    (Bauer).

44. **aproskopoi**—From *aproskopos*, literally not causing to stumble, having
    nothing for one to strike against. Passively, without offense, giving no
    offense, blameless.

33   even as I strive to please all in everything, not seeking my own
          advantage[45] but that of the many, in order that they may be saved.

---

45. *to emautou sumphoron*—Something advantageous, beneficial, profit-
         able, as an advantage, benefit.

CHAPTER 11

1   Keep on becoming[1] imitators of me, just as[2] also I am an imitator of Christ.

IV. Problems Related to Worship and the Church in General (11:2 to 14:40)
A. The Head Dress of Women and Men at Church (11:2-16)

2   Now I praise you because in all things you remember me and hold fast the precepts[3] just as I delivered *them* to you.

3   But I want you to know that the head[4] of every man is the Christ, and the head of a woman is the man, but the head of the Christ is God.

4   Every man praying or prophesying having something on his head[5] dishonors his head;

5   but every woman praying or prophesying with the head uncovered

---

1. *ginesthe*—From *ginomai*, become, come to be, the durative idea. The process is to continue.

2. *kathōs*—In comparisons, just as, as, to the degree that. Corinthians were to imitate Paul in whatever measure he was an imitator of Christ.

3. *paradoseis*—From *paradosis*, a handing down or over, giving over, or giving up, instruction, precepts.

4. *kephalē*—Head, as of the head of a "man or beast." Used widely in this respect in ancient literature.

5. *kata kephalēs echōn*—"Literally, having a veil (*kalumma* understood) down from the head" (Robertson, *Word Pictures*).

dishonors her head; for she is one and the same[6] with her whose head is shaven.

6   For if the woman does not cover her head, she is also to have her hair cut; and if it is a disgrace to a woman to have the hair cut or her head shaved, she is to veil herself.[7]

7   For, indeed, a man is not obligated to have the head covered, he being the image[8] and the glory of God; but the woman is the glory of a man.

8   For man is not from woman,[9] but woman from man;

9   for also man was not created for the sake of the woman but the woman for the sake of the man.[10]

10   For this reason the woman ought to have the symbol of authority[11] over her head because of the angels.

11   Nevertheless, neither is there woman apart from man nor man apart from woman in the Lord;[12]

12   For just as the woman is of the man, so also the man is through the woman;[13] but all things are from God.

---

6. *hen . . . kai to auto*—In breaking the custom, the woman created for herself a problem with both social and religious implications.

7. *katakaluptesthō*—Present middle imperative of *katakaluptō*, used only here in the New Testament. "Let her cover up herself with the veil (down, *kata*, the Greek says, the veil hanging down from the head)" (Robertson, *Word Pictures*).

8. *eikōn*—Likeness, image, form, appearance.

9. *ek gunaikos*—Out of woman. A reference to the creation of woman as recorded in Genesis (2:21-22).

10. *dia ton andra*—Because of, for the sake of the man.

11. *exousian*—A word as used here that has caused much ado among expositors. It seems that Paul merely had in mind here that a woman at worship had a moral obligation to conduct herself in a way as not to shock anyone, even the angels who veiled themselves in the presence of the Lord (Isa. 6:2).

12. *en Kuriōi*—An expression comparable to *en Christōi* which Paul frequently used in his epistles. "In the sphere of the Lord, where Paul finds the solution of all problems" (Robertson, *Word Pictures*).

13. *dia tēs gunaikos*—*Dia* with the genitive *gunaikos*, hence, the woman is the intermediate agent. It is through her that man has his natural birth.

13 Judge ye among yourselves: is it proper[14] for a woman unveiled to offer prayers to God?

14 And does not nature[15] itself teach you that a man if he wear long hair it is a dishonor to him,

15 but if a woman wears the hair long it is a glory to her; because the long hair has been given to her as a substitute for a covering.[16]

16 But if anyone seems to be contentious,[17] we have no such custom, neither do the churches of God.

B. Conduct at the Lord's Supper (11:17-34)

17 But this, in giving my instructions, I do not praise you because you come together not unto the better but unto[18] the worse.

18 First of all, for when you come together in church I hear that there are divisions[19] within you, and in part I believe it.

19 For there must also be factions[20] among you so the approved may also become manifest among you.

20 When you come together therefore at the place, it is not to eat the Lord's Supper,[21]

---

14. *prepon*—From *prepō*, to be suitable, seemly, fitting, proper, right.

15. *phusis*—Nature. Hence, "*natural endowment* or *condition*, inherited fr. one's ancestors" (Bauer), natural disposition or characteristic.

16. *anti peribolaiou*—From *peribolaion*, a wrap, covering, cloak, robe, as of "an article of clothing" (Bauer).

17. *philoneikos*—A compound adjective (*philos, neikos*) "fond of strife. Only here in N. T." (Robertson, *Word Pictures*). Contentious, quarrelsome.

18. *eis to kreisson . . . eis to hēsson*—The meaning of the preposition *eis* and the preposition *en* originally was precisely the same but with a verb of motion more like *eis to oros*, into the mountain.

19. *schismata*—Division, split, dissension, schism. Literally, tear, crack, as a crack in a stone.

20. *haireseis*—Party, sect, dissension, faction, dogma, opinions.

21. *ouk estin kuriakon deipnon phagein*—The Lord's Supper turned out to be, in Paul's view, not the real purpose for the gathering but more like one of Caesar's banquets, their own supper.

21   for in the eating each one takes his own supper[22] beforehand, and
the one is hungry and the other is drunken.

22   For is it that you have not houses in which to eat and to drink? Or
do you care nothing[23] for the church of God, and humiliate[24] those
who have nothing? What shall I say to you? Shall I praise you? In
this I praise you not.

23   For I received from the Lord,[25] that which also I delivered to you,
that the Lord Jesus in the night in which he was betrayed took
bread,

24   and when he had given thanks, he broke it and said, This is my
body which is for you; this keep on doing in remembrance of me.[26]

25   Likewise also the cup after the supper, saying, This cup is the new
covenant[27] in my blood; this continue to do, as often as you may
drink it, in my memory.

26   For as often as you eat this bread and drink the cup, you proclaim[28]
the death of the Lord, until he comes.

27   Consequently, whosoever eats the bread or drinks the cup of the

---

22. *deipnon*—Supper, or dinner, indicated "the main meal (toward) evening."
The word is used also of the "(formal) dinner, banquet" (Bauer).

23. *kataphroneite*—From *kataphroneō*, despise, treat with contempt, scorn.
Look down on, as upon something or someone, disregard, care nothing for.

24. *kataischunete*—From *kataischunō*, to put to shame, humiliate, disfigure,
dishonor, disgrace.

25. *parelabon*—I received from the Lord. "Direct claim to revelation from the
Lord Jesus on the origin of the Lord's Supper" (Robertson, *Word Pictures*).

26. *eis tēn emēn anamnēsin*—"Not my remembrance of you, but your
remembrance of me" (Robertson, *Word Pictures*). Objective use of *emēn*
(possessive pronoun).

27. *kainē diathēkē*—Literally, "new last will and testament." Not the
covenant between God and Israel, but God's new covenant through Christ to
all humanity. "New" not merely in time, but "in the sense unused . . .
something not previously present, *unknown, strange, remarkable*, also with
the connotation of the marvelous or unheard-of" (Bauer).

28. *kataggellete*—From *kataggellō*, to proclaim (solemnly), as to proclaim
the gospel, or the faith, or the second Advent of Jesus.

Lord in an unworthy manner[29] shall be held guilty[30] of the body and of the blood of the Lord.

28 But a man is to test himself,[31] and so he is to eat of the bread and drink of the cup;

29 for the one eating and drinking eats and drinks judgment against himself not discerning[32] the body.

30 Because of this, many among you are feeble and sick and great numbers[33] sleep.

31 But if we discerned ourselves correctly,[34] we would not be judged.

32 But we being judged by the Lord are disciplined[35] so that we may not be condemned with the world.

33 And so, my brothers, in coming together for a meal, wait for one another.[36]

34 If anyone is hungry, he is to eat at home, lest you come together unto condemnation. But the other matters[37] I will set in order whenever I arrive.

---

29. *anaxiōs*—"In an unworthy or careless manner" (Bauer). The idea is not that a participant in the Lord's Supper must be "worthy." The emphasis here is only on the manner of the observance.

30. *enochos*—Frequently used as a legal term, liable, guilty, answerable.

31. *dokimazetō*—From *dokimazō*, to examine, put to the test, prove by testing, prove, accept as proved (Bauer).

32. *mē diakrinōn*—From *diakrinō*, to differentiate, make a distinction, discriminate, pass judgment on, judge correctly, render a decision (Bauer), discern.

33. *hikanoi*—From *hikanos*, adequate, sufficient, large enough, also in the sense of "large, much of number, quantity" (Bauer).

34. *heautous diekrinomen*—See footnote 32.

35. *paideuometha*—From *paideuō*, to train, educate, instruct, bring up, give guidance in the practice of discipline.

36. *allēlous ekdechesthe*—From *ekdechomai*, to wait (for someone), expect. This is exactly what the Corinthians had not been doing when they gathered to observe the Lord's Supper.

37. *ta . . . loipa*—From *loipos*, literally the remaining, the rest, the other things, in addition to. Evidently there were other matters which Paul needed to deal with but he would wait for that until he could see them face-to-face.

CHAPTER 12

C. Spiritual Gifts (12:1-11)

1   Now concerning the spiritual gifts,[1] brothers, I do not want you to be ignorant.

2   You know that when you were Gentiles you were led away[2] to the dumb idols,[3] even as often as you were led.

3   Therefore I make known to you that no one speaking in the Spirit of God says, Anathema Jesus,[4] and no one is able to say Lord Jesus except in the Holy Spirit.

4   Now there are allotments[5] of spiritual gifts, but the same Spirit;

5   and there are allotments of service,[6] and the same Lord;

---

1. *peri . . . tōn pneumatikōn*—*Spiritual gifts.* Obviously other questions (even as the problem of sacrificial meats) were raised in the letter to Paul (see 8:1).

2. *apagomenoi*—From *apagō*, lead away, as a condemned prisoner (periphrastic imperfect passive, but without the copula *ēte*—a common elipsis).

3. *ta aphōna*—From *aphōnos*, silent, incapable of speech, dumb.

4. *Anathema Iēsous*—Anathema is used of a votive offering in the Temple, also of that which is "devoted to the divinity," whether "consecrated" or "accursed." Here the meaning seems to be that of "object of a curse" as "Jesus be cursed" (Bauer).

5. *diaireseis*—Division, apportionment, allotment, variety, difference (Bauer).

6. *diakoniōn*—Service, as of the "office of the prophets and apostles" and "of the office of a deacon (Romans 12:7)" (Bauer).

6   and there are allotments of activities,[7] but the same God, the one
         who energizes the all in all.

7   To each one is given the manifestation[8] of the Spirit that is
         appropriate.

8   For indeed to one through the Spirit[9] is given speech[10] of wisdom,
         and to another speech of insight according to the same Spirit,

9   to another faith in the same Spirit, and to another acts of
         healings[11] in the one Spirit,

10   and to another activities[12] of powers, and to another prophecy,
         and to another the ability to distinguish between spirits,[13] to
         another kinds of tongues, and to another interpretation of
         tongues,

11   but the one and the same Spirit energizes all these things,
         distributing to each one individually just as he desires.[14]

D. The Unity of the Body of Christ (12:12-31)

12   For even as the body[15] is one and has many members, and all the

---

7. **energēmatōn**—From *energēma* (from *energeō*), operation, wrought,
   workings, activities.

8. **phanerōsis**—From *phaneroō*, to make manifest *(phaneros)* (Robertson,
   Word Pictures).

9. **dia tou pneumatos**—The Spirit is the intermediate agent of God's
   allocations of the nine manifestations of the work of the Spirit found in verses
   8-10.

10. **logos**—An old word for reason and then speech.

11. **iamatōn**—From *iama*, healing; here (spiritual) gifts of healing (Bauer).

12. **energēmata**—Effect, thing wrought, operation, in the plural "workings"
    (Thayer).

13. **diakriseis pneumatōn**—Help was needed in Corinth to tell whether the
    so-called "gifts" stemmed from the Holy Spirit "or merely strange though
    natural or even diabolical (I Tim. 4:1; I John 4:1f.)" (Robertson, *Word
    Pictures*).

14. **bouletai**—From *boulomai*, want, wish, desire as in "decisions of the will
    after previous deliberations" (Bauer).

15. **sōma**—Originally body (of an animal or a person) but here the church, the
    body of believers of which Christ is the head.

members of the body, being many, are one body, so also the Christ.

13 For we all in one Spirit were baptized into one body whether Jew or Greek,[16] whether bond servants or freemen, and we all drank of one Spirit.

14 For the body also is not one member but many.[17]

15 If the foot say, because I am not a hand, I am not of the body, it is not therefore not[18] of the body;

16 and if the ear say, because I am not an eye I am not of the body, it is not therefore not[18] of the body.

17 If the whole body were an eye,[19] where the faculty of hearing; if the whole body were hearing, where the sense of smell?

18 But now God has arranged[20] the members, each one of them, in one body just as he willed.

19 But if they all were one member, where the body?[21]

20 But now there are, indeed, many members, but one[22] body.

---

16. *eite Ioudaioi eite Hellēnes*—The salvation experience is the same for all the peoples of the world. Ethnic divisions have no room at the foot of the cross.

17. *polla*—Robertson calls these words "the key to the whole problem of church life both local and general" (*Word Pictures*).

18. *ou para touto ouk*—Paul's use of the double negative here presents an unusual bit of syntax, but the negatives do not cancel each other; rather each one retains "its full force" (Robertson, *Word Pictures*).

19. *ophthalmos*—"Eye, the organ of sight, but also organ of sense perception" (Bauer). From this word we get *ophthalmologist*.

20. *etheto*—From *tithēmi*, to place, put, lay, establish, make someone or something of someone. Here the idea of "arranged" emerges.

21. *pou to sōma*—Where the body? Where would the body be? In essence, the question here suggests its own answer: there would be no body! In such a case the body, as we think of it, would no longer exist.

22. *polla men*—In the closing verse, Paul reverted to his favorite idea of unity, even as the prayer of Jesus was that all might be "one" (John 17:11). Compare footnote above.

21   And the eye cannot say[23] to the hand, I have no need[24] of you or again the head to the feet, I have no need of you.

22   On the contrary, by much more the members of the body which are considered to be less important[25] are necessary,

23   and those members of the body which we consider to be less esteemed[26] we put about these greater value and our unseemly parts[27] have a more honorable position, and our seemly parts have no need.

24   But God united[28] the body, giving to the inferior[29] part more abundant honor,

25   in order that there should be no division[30] in the body, but that the members may have the same concern[31] for one another.

26   And if one member suffers, all the members suffer together;[32] and if a member is honored, all the members rejoice with it.

---

23. *dunatai*—From *dunamai* (passive deponent) meaning I am able, I can; *ou dunatai eipein*, literally, is not able to say, cannot say.
24. *chreian*—Necessity, need, lack.
25. *asthenestera*—From *asthenēs*, powerless, weak, used in the literal sense of ill or sick and figuratively feeble, miserable, with the resultant idea here of "less important" (Bauer).
26. *atimotera*—From *atimos*, dishonored, unhonored, unesteemed, insignificant, less honorable.
27. *aschēmona*—From *aschēmōn*, unpresentable, shameful, indecent, (that is, private parts, Bauer).
28. *sunekerasen*—From *sugkerannumi*, mix (together), unite, blend.
29. *husteroumenōi*—From *hustereō*, come too late, lack, be in need of, be less than, inferior to, be lacking, come short of (Bauer).
30. *schisma*—Division, split, dissension.
31. *merimnōsin*—From *merimnaō*, to be over anxious, have anxiety, be (unduly) concerned, be concerned about something, care for.
32. *sumpaschei*—From *sumpaschō*, a compound word meaning to suffer along with or suffer together with. Used also in the sense of "to have sympathy."

27   Now you are a body[33] of Christ and members individually.

28   And those whom God placed in the church are: first apostles, secondly prophets, thirdly teachers, then miraculous powers, then gifts of healing, helpful deeds,[34] acts of administrations,[35] kinds of tongues.

29   Are all apostles? Are all prophets?[36] Are all teachers? Have all miraculous powers?

30   Have all gifts of healing? Do all speak in tongues? Do all interpret?[37]

31   But strive earnestly[38] for the greater gifts.

---

33.   *sōma*—Here we have the figure of the body which Paul dealt with (vv. 14-26) "now applied in detail to the Church" at Corinth (Findlay) and "the same solidarity of manifold parts and powers."

34.   *antilēmpseis*—From *antilēmpsis,* from *antilambanō* ("to lay hold of, to hold fast to"), hence, helpful deeds.

35.   *kubernēseis*—Akin to *kubernētes,* steersman, captain, pilot. Hence, "Administration; the plural indicates proofs of ability to hold a leading position in the church" (Bauer).

36.   *prophētai*—From *prophētēs,* prophet "as proclaimer and interpreter of the divine revelations." "For speakers for God and Christ" (Robertson, *Word Pictures*).

37.   *diermēneuousin*—From *diermēneuō,* to translate, interpret or explain something as "ecstatic speech."

38.   *zēloute*—From *zēloō,* to strive "in a good sense, exert oneself earnestly in behalf of something, manifest zeal, etc."

CHAPTER 13

E. The Superlative Way—The Love (13:1-13)

1 And still I point out to you the superlative[1] way:

1. The Necessity for the Love (13:1b-3)

if I speak with the tongues of men and of angels but have not *the* love,[2] I am already become a noisy gong or a clanging cymbal.

2 And if I have the gift of prophecy[3] and know all the mysteries[4] and all the knowledge,[5] and if I have all the faith so as to remove mountains, and have not *the* love, I am nothing.

---

1. *huperbolēn*—From *huperballō*, to surpass, go beyond, outdo. Hence, something of extraordinary character or quality, a far better way.
2. *agapēn*—Love, a word used widely by Christians "as opposed to *erōs* (sexual love)" (Robertson, *Word Pictures*). A word used extensively by early Christians to express God's love for humanity, humanity's love for God, and human love for others as a result of the divine love of God.
3. *prophēteian*—Prophetic activity, the gift of prophesying, of prophecy, the utterance of the prophet, prophetic word, saying, prophecy (Bauer). Here, speaking for God.
4. *mustēria*—A secret teaching, rite, secret. Used widely by Paul for God's plan of worldwide redemption, through Christ, which in other generations was not made known until after the Advent of Christ. A term widely used in the mystery religions but with an altogether different meaning.
5. *gnōsin*—Used widely of knowledge as one of God's attributes, of Christian knowledge, and of the "heretical" knowledge (*gnosis*—Gnosticism).

3   And if I dole out all my belongings, bit by bit,[6] and if I give up my
          body that I may boast,[7] but have not *the* love, I am helped in no
          way.[8]

2. The Character of the Love (13:4-7)

4   The love has patience,[9] the love is usefully kind,[10] is not filled with
          jealousy;[11] the love does not brag, does not put on airs,[12]

5   does not behave disgracefully,[13] strives not for its own advantage,
          is not habitually irritable,[14] does not place evil to its account,[15]

6   rejoices not in unrighteousness,[16] but rejoices with others in the
          truth;

---

6. ***psōmisō***—From *psōmos*, "a bit, morsel." To feed, "by putting a bit or
    crumb (of food) into the mouth" of an infant or young animal (Thayer).
    Hence, to feed someone or to "give away all one's property bit by bit, dole
    it out" (Bauer).

7. ***kauchēsōmai***—To glory, pride oneself, boast, boast about, mention in
    order to boast of, be proud of (Bauer).

8. ***ouden ōpheloumai***—Literally, "I am helped nothing."

9. ***makrothumei***—From "*makros*, long, *thumos*, passion, ardour" (Robert-
    son, *Word Pictures*).

10. ***chrēsteuetai***—From *chrēstos*, gracious, useful, kind, and that in turn from
    chraomai "to use." Paul may have coined this word (Findlay).

11. ***zēloi***—From *zēloō* (present active indicative), to desire, strive, exert oneself
    earnestly; in a bad sense, "be filled with jealousy, envy, *tina* toward
    someone" (Bauer).

12. ***ou phusioutai***—From *phusioō*, puff up, blow up, make arrogant or proud
    because of something. The passive "become puffed up or conceited, put on
    airs" (Bauer).

13. ***aschēmonei***—To behave indecently, dishonorably, disgracefully.

14. ***paroxunetai***—To provoke to wrath, to urge on, stimulate, irritate. In the
    passive sense, become irritated, angry (Bauer).

15. ***ou logizetai to kakon***—A sort of marketplace term, "account, take into
    account." Here, take evil into account, that is, does not have any dealings
    with that which is evil.

16. ***adikiai***—Wrongdoing, misdeeds, wickedness, injustice, unrighteousness.

7   continues to bear[17] all things, continues to have faith in spite of all things, continues to hope in the face of all things, keeps on enduring[18] all things.

3. The Permanency of the Love (13:8-13)

8   The love never comes to an end.[19] But whether gifts of prophecy, they shall pass away;[20] whether tongues, they shall cease; whether knowledge, it shall be set aside.[21]

9   For we know in part[22] and we prophesy in part;

10   but when the mature stage comes,[23] that which is of a part shall be done away.[24]

11   When I was a child, I kept talking[25] as a child, I kept thinking as a child, I kept reasoning as a child; now that I have become a man, I have set aside[26] the things of the child.

---

17. *stegei*—From *stegō* which comes in turn from *stegē*, roof. Love "covers, protects, forbears" (Robertson, *Word Pictures*). See 1 Peter 4:8, "for love covers a multitude of sins."

18. *hupomenei*—"*Remain or stay (behind)*, while others go away" (Bauer), remain (instead of fleeing), hold out, abide, stand one's ground, "endure in trouble, affliction, persecution" (Bauer).

19. *piptei*—From *piptō*, fall (down) from a higher point, fall to pieces, fall down (violently), fall to the ground, come to an end, become invalid, fail (Bauer).

20. *katargēthēsontai*—From *katargeō*, to make powerless, ineffective, idle, wipe out, abolish, set aside something.

21. See footnote 20 for same verb.

22. *ek merous*—Part of something "in contrast to the whole" (Bauer).

23. *to teleion*—From *teleios*, perfect, complete, "having attained the end or purpose" (Bauer). As a substantive (*to teleion*), what is perfect. Mature, full-grown, adult.

24. See footnote 20 above.

25. *elaloun*—From *laleō*, of persons. Speak, express oneself in words, say something, talk. Imperfect active of *laleō*. Linear action in the past. So of the verbs *ephronoun* and *elogizomēn* (imperfect middle).

26. *katērgēka*—Perfect active indicative of *katargeō*. See footnote 20 above.

12   For the present we see by means of a mirror[27] dimly,[28] but then face-to-face; now I know in part, but then I shall know fully[29] just as I am fully known.

13   And now abide[30] faith, hope, *the* love, these three; but the greatest[31] of these is *the* love.

---

27. ***di'esoptrou***—From *esoptron*, mirror. With *dia*, as here, "by means of a mirror."

28. ***en ainigmati***—From *ainigma*, literally, riddle. Then indirect or indistinct image seen by a dim reflection in a mirror (Bauer).

29. ***epignōsomai***—From *epignōskō*, future, to know completely, exactly, "through and through something" (Bauer). Knowledge by experience that is total, complete, not lacking.

30. ***menei***—Third person singular, in agreement with faith *(pistis)* first in the triad. From *menō*, to stay, remain, live, lodge, dwell, continue, abide, remain.

31. ***meizōn***—A predicate adjective, hence, no article. The adjective is in the comparative form but "used as superlative, for the superlative form *megistos*" (Robertson, *Word Pictures*). *Megistos* was rarely used in the *Koine* (Robertson).

CHAPTER 14

F. The Spiritual Gifts of Tongues and Prophecy (14:1-40)
1. Tongues and Prophecy (14:1-3)

1   Pursue[1] the love, and strive earnestly for the spiritual gifts, but rather that you may keep on prophesying.

2   For the one speaking in a tongue speaks not to men but to God, for nobody hears with understanding, for he is speaking mysteries[2] in the spirit;

3   but the one prophesying to men speaks edification[3] and exhortation and encouragement.

2. The Principle of Edification (14:4-13)

4   The one speaking in a tongue builds up[4] himself; but the one prophesying builds up the church.

5   Now I want you all to speak in tongues, but rather that you should keep on prophesying. For better is the one prophesying than the

---

1. *diōkete*—From *diōkō*, pursue, run after, hasten, press on, strive for, aspire to, seek after (Bauer).

2. *mustēria*—From *mustērion*, secret, secret teaching, secret rite (as in the mystery religions). Here, and in Paul's usage, God's plan of redemption for the whole world as projected in Jesus Christ. "Truth about God, once hidden, but now revealed" (Robertson and Plummer).

3. *oikodomēn*—From *oikodome*, building, (as a process), construction (Bauer). Figuratively, building up, edifying, edification.

4. *oikodomei*—From *oikodomeō*, build, as in the erection of real buildings. Here in the sense, to "edify," strengthen.

one speaking in tongues, unless he interpret,[5] so that the church may receive edification.

6   But now, brothers, if I come to you speaking in tongues, what shall I benefit[6] you unless I should speak to you either in revelation[7] or in knowledge or in prophecy or in teaching?

7   Nevertheless, the lifeless[8] things giving sound, whether flute or harp, if it gives not a difference[9] in the tones how shall what is played on the flute or what is played on the harp be known?

8   For even if the trumpet gives an indistinct[10] sound, who shall prepare himself for battle?

9   Thus also if you through the tongue do not utter intelligible speech, how shall that which is spoken be known?[11] For you will be talking into the air.[12]

10 If it should happen that there are ever so many kinds of languages in the world, and no one of them without meaning,[13]

11 if I therefore should not know the meaning[14] of the language, I will be to the one speaking a babbler and the one speaking with me a babbler.[15]

12 Thus also ye, since you are eager for spiritual gifts,[16] strive that

---

5. *diermēneuēi*—From *diermēneuō*, translate, interpret, explain.

6. *ōphelēsō*—From *ōpheleō*, benefit, aid, help, be of use (to) (Bauer).

7. *apokalupsei*—From *apokaluptō*, reveal, uncover, bring to light, disclose, "especially of divine revelation of certain supernatural secrets" (Bauer).

8. *apsucha*—Inanimate, lifeless, literally without a soul.

9. *diastolēn*—Difference, distinction, as between a Jew and a Gentile.

10. *adēlon*—From *adēlos*, unseen, not clear, indistinct, intelligible, unmarked.

11. *eusēmon*—Clear, distinct, easily recognizable.

12. An ancient proverb common in Paul's day.

13. *aphōnon*—From *aphōnos*, literally without a voice, voiceless, soundless, dumb; hence, "incapable of conveying meaning."

14. *tēn dunamin*—Literally the power, might, strength. Figuratively meaning when used of language as here.

15. *barbaros*—An onomatopoetic word used by the Greeks for those who spoke a language other than Greek. Hence, a "babbler," as here.

16. *zēlōtai este pneumatōn*—Literally, zealous for spirits. Here the context suggests spiritual gifts as the meaning.

you may abound for the edification[17] of the church.

13 Wherefore the one speaking in a tongue is to pray that he may interpret.[18]

3. The Role of the Mind (14:14-20)

14 For if I pray in a tongue, my spirit is praying, but my mind is unfruitful.[19]

15 What is it then? I will pray with the spirit, but I will also pray with the mind;[20] I will sing with the spirit, but I will also sing with the mind.

16 Otherwise if you give thanks and praise with the Spirit, the one filling up the place of the layman[21] how will he say the amen[22] at your prayer of thanksgiving, since he does not know what you are saying?

17 For you, indeed, give thanks well,[23] but the other person is not being built up.

18 I thank God I speak in tongues more than you all,

19 but in the church I would rather speak five words with my mind, that I may instruct[24] others, than ten thousand words in a tongue.

---

17. *oikodomēn*—From *oikodomē*, building, building as a process, spiritual strengthening, hence, building up, edification. "Purpose clause with the object by prolepsis stated beforehand" (Robertson, *Word Pictures*).

18. *diermēneuēi*—See footnote 5.

19. *akarpos*—Literally without fruit, fruitless, unfruitful, figuratively useless, unproductive (Bauer).

20. *tōi noi*—From *nous*, the mind, the understanding.

21. *ton topon tou idiōtou*—From *idiōtēs*, amateur, lay person, untrained, or unskilled. The lay person had a place at a gathering just as the believer had a place.

22. *amēn*—An old Hebrew word meaning firm (Gould). The term is used to express assent of what another has just said. The word carries the general meaning of truly, so let it be.

23. *kalōs*—Fitly, in the right way, beautifully, well, commendably, ably, rightly, correctly.

24. *katēchēsō*—From *katēcheō*, I make myself understood, with the resultant idea of teach, instruct someone as here.

20   Brothers, cease becoming children[25] in understanding—rather, be
as a child with respect to wickedness—and keep on becoming
mature[26] in discernment.

4. The Effect of Tongues on Unbelievers (14:21-25)

21   In the law it is written[27] that in other tongues and with the lips of
others I will speak to this people, and not even under these
circumstances will they hear me, saith the Lord.

22   Therefore the tongues are for a sign,[28] not for the believers but for
the unbelievers, but the prophecy is not for the unbelievers but for
the believers.

23   If therefore the entire church comes together for the same purpose
and all speak in tongues, and the unlearned or unbelievers come
in, will they not say that you are out of your mind?[29]

24   And if all prophesy, and some unbeliever or unlearned person
should enter, he is convicted[30] by all, he is called to account by all.

25   And the secrets[31] of his heart become manifest, and thus having
fallen upon his face he will worship God, confessing[32] that God is
really among you.

---

25. *paidia*—See Hebrews 5:11-14 for an example of intellectual immaturity on
the part of adult believers.

26. *teleioi*—Complete, perfect, full-grown, adult, mature.

27. A reference to Isaiah 28:11 ff.

28. *sēmeion*—Token, indication, or "the sign or distinguishing mark by which
something is known." The sign may be something in the character of a
miracle or wonder, "an event that is contrary to the usual course of nature"
(Bauer).

29. *mainesthe*—From *mainomai*, to be out of one's mind, be mad, insane, and
hence, as a result, have no control over oneself.

30. *elegchetai*—From *elegchō*, to expose, bring to light, convince or convict
"someone of something," correct, reprove.

31. *ta krupta*—From *kruptō*, to conceal, hide, cover, keep secret.

32. *apaggellōn*—Announce, report, tell, proclaim, confess.

5. Some Final Instructions (14:26-40)

26   What then is *the conclusion*, brothers? Whenever you assemble, each one has a psalm, has a teaching, has a revelation, has a tongue, has an interpretation; everything is to take place[33] for the purpose of edification.

27   Whether anyone speaks in a tongue, by two or at the most three, and in turn,[34] one also is to interpret;

28   But if there be no interpreter, he is to keep silent in the church,[35] but he is to talk to himself and to God.

29   But two or three prophets are to speak, and the others are to examine[36] the prophecy;

30   And if a revelation[37] is made by another person sitting *there*, the first one is to be silent.

31   For you can all prophesy one by one, that all may learn and all may become encouraged.[38]

32   And the spirits of the prophets are subject to[39] the prophets;

33   for God is not a *God* of disorder[40] but of peace.

34   As in all the churches of the saints, the women in the churches are

---

33. *ginesthō*—From *ginomai*, to become, come to be, originate, come about, be made, create, be created, happen, take place.

34. *kai ana meros*—"One at a time" and, "not over three in all" (Robertson, *Word Pictures*).

35. *en ekklēsiai*—That is, in the assembly of believers, the gathering of believers at an appointed place.

36. *diakrinetōsan*—To separate, arrange something, differentiate, make a distinction, judge, render a decision, pass judgment (on).

37. *apokaluphthēi*—From *apokaluptō*, to reveal, bring to light, disclose, uncover, reveal.

38. *parakalōntai*—From *parakaleō*, literally, to call to one side, summons as for help; exhort, urge, appeal to, encourage, cheer up, comfort.

39. *hupotassetai*—From *hupotassō*, to subject, put in lower rank.

40. *akatastasias*—Disorder, disturbance, unruliness.

to keep silent, for it is not permitted[41] for them to speak; rather they are to subordinate[42] themselves just as the law says.

35   But if they want to learn something, they are to ask their own husbands at home; for it is shameful[43] for a woman to talk in church.

36   What? Was it from you[44] that the word of God went out, or unto you[44] only has it come down?

37   If anyone thinks that he is a prophet or a spiritual person,[45] he is to know that what I write to you is a commandment of the Lord.

38   If anyone fails to understand *this*, he is ignorant.[46]

39   So my brothers continue to seek the gift of prophecy, and forbid not[47] the speaking in tongues;

40   but everything is to be done respectably[48] and in an orderly way.

---

41. *epitrepetai*—From *epitrepō*, permit, allow. Literally with *ou*, it is not permitted.

42. *hupotassesthōsan*—From *hupotassō*, to subordinate, subject, subject oneself, become subject, or subordinate, obey.

43. *aischron*—From *aischros*, base, shameful, disgraceful.

44. *aph'humōn . . . eis humas monous*—From you . . . unto you. In other words, are you claiming that you are the source of the word of God . . . that you are the only one that the word came to?

45. *pneumatikos*—Pertaining to the spirit, spiritual, one who possesses the Spirit.

46. *agnoeitai*—From *agnoeō*, to be ignorant of a fact or thing, not to know.

47. *kōluete*—From *kōluō*, with reference to persons, prevent, forbid, hinder.

48. *euschēmonōs*—A compound word from *eu* and *schēma* (the figure), shapely, of elegant figure, graceful, comely, "bearing oneself becomingly in speech or behavior," properly, decently.

CHAPTER 15

V. The Resurrection of the Dead (15)
A. The Fact of Christ's Resurrection (15:1-11)

1 Now I make known to you, brothers, the gospel[1] which I preached to you, which you also received, and in which you stand,[2]

2 through which[3] also you are saved, if you continue to hold fast to whatever word I preached to you, unless you believed to no purpose.[4]

3 For I delivered to you, among first things,[5] that which I also received, that Christ died for our sins according to the Scriptures,

4 and that he was buried, and that he has been raised up on the third day according to the Scriptures.[6]

---

1. **to euaggelion**—A compound word meaning good announcement, good news, gospel, the good news as it pertains to the Savior and his redeeming mission in behalf of sinful people.

2. **en hōi kai hestēkate**—From histēmi, intransitive as here, stand still, appear, come up, stand, stand up firmly, stand firm.

3. **di'hou**—Through which, that is the gospel Paul preached to them, and which became the intermediate agent through which the Corinthians were saved.

4. **mē eikē**—Without cause, to no avail, in vain, without due consideration, in a haphazard manner (Bauer).

5. **en prōtois**—From prōtos, "Among first things," that is, with reference to importance—not time (Robertson, *Word Pictures*).

6. **kata tas graphas**—According to the Scriptures: Acts 13:32 ff.; 17:3; 26:22 ff.; Romans 1:2 ff.

5   And that he appeared[7] to Cephas, thereafter to the twelve;

6   thereupon he appeared to more than five hundred brothers at once, the majority of whom remain until now, but certain ones fell asleep.[8]

7   Then he appeared to James,[9] then to all the apostles;

8   last of all as though to one in untimely birth,[10] he appeared to me.

9   For I am the least[11] of the apostles, who am not fit to be called an apostle, because I persecuted[12] the church of God.

10   But by the grace[13] of God I am what I am, and his grace that was manifested unto me was not in vain,[14] rather I labored more abundantly than they all, but not I but the grace of God that was with me.

11   Whether I therefore or whether they,[15] thus we preach and thus you believed.

---

7. *ōphthē*—From *horaō*, transitive, to notice, see, catch sight of. In the passive sense, to appear, become visible to someone.

8. *ekoimēthēsan*—From *koimaomai* (only in passive) to fall asleep, sleep. Figuratively to die, pass away, fall asleep in "the sleep of death" (Bauer).

9. *Iakōbōi*—James, Jesus' brother (Gal. 1:19). James appears to have been the "foremost" of the brothers of Jesus, and this special appearance to James may have had an important bearing on his subsequent relationship to the churches. He was not only the brother of Jesus but also one who had witnessed to his living presence following the resurrection.

10. *ektrōmati*—Miscarriage, untimely, premature birth. Hence, "untimely birth." A compound word from *ektitrōskō*, to cause or suffer abortion.

11. *ho elachistos*—Used as a superlative form of the adjective *mikros*, least, smallest, very small, insignificant, quite unimportant.

12. *ediōxa*—From *diōkō*, run, press on, hasten, persecute, pursue.

13. *chariti*—"A lovely, unmerited, God-given experience of his favoring presence felt in the life of man. One can have peace only after he has received grace" (Caudill, *Ephesians*).

14. *kenē*—From *kenos*, feminine of the adjective agreeing with *hē charis*, without profit, without result, without effect, without reaching its goal (Bauer).

15. *eite oun egō eite ekeinoi*—No matter who labored "more abundantly," the result is one and the same. The gospel is preached, and the hearers believe.

B. The Hopelessness of Life Apart from Resurrection (15:12-19)

12 Now if Christ is being preached that he has been raised from the dead,[16] how do some among you keep on saying that there is no resurrection of the dead?

13 But if there is no resurrection of the dead, neither has Christ been raised up;[17]

14 and if Christ has not been raised up, then also our preaching is senseless[18] and your faith is vain.

15 And we are also found to be false witnesses of God because we testified against God that he raised up Christ whom he raised not up if indeed therefore the dead are not raised;[19]

16 for if[20] the dead are not raised, neither has Christ been raised.

17 And if Christ has not been raised, your faith is futile, you are yet in your sins.[21]

18 Then also those who have fallen asleep[22] in Christ are lost.[23]

19 If only in this life we have hope[24] in Christ, we are of all men the more pitiable.[25]

---

16. **ek nekrōn**—Literally, from the dead ones, from among the dead.

17. **oude . . . egēgertai**—Perfect indicative of egeirō, to arouse, cause to rise. The perfect tense represents action that took place in the past and still holds.

18. **kenon**—Empty, hence figurative of things without any basis, without truth, power, and result, profit, effect, "without reaching its goal," vain (Bauer).

19. **ouk egeirontai**—That is, if there is no such thing as a resurrection of dead ones.

20. **ei gar**—Paul here reaffirmed what he said in verse 13.

21. **en tais hamartiais humōn**—Apart from the resurrection of Christ, there would be no basis for the hope of forgiveness of sins. All would be without a Savior.

22. **koimēthentes**—From koimaō, fall asleep, pass away, die, as here.

23. **apōlonto**—Second aorist middle indicative of apollumi, to destroy. Here, in the middle to perish, did perish.

24. **ēlpikotes**—Periphrastic perfect active indicative. "Hope limited to this life even if 'in Christ'" (Robertson, Word Pictures).

25. **eleeinoteroi**—Comparative (not superlative) of eleeinos, pitiful, to be pitied. Hence, more pitiable of all men, then figuratively, the most pitiful.

C. Christ the Firstfruits of the Resurrection (15:20-28)

20   But now Christ has been raised from the dead ones, the firstfruits[26] of them that sleep.

21   For since through a man[27] *came* death, also through a man *will be* the resurrection of the dead.

22   For just as in the case of Adam all die, thus also in the Christ all will be made alive.[28]

23   But each in his own turn;[29] Christ the firstfruits,[30] thereafter those of the Christ at his coming;

24   then the end, whenever he shall deliver the kingdom to the God and Father, whenever he shall abolish[31] all rule and all authority and power.

25   For he must[32] reign until he put all the enemies under his feet.

26   *Then* the death, the last enemy, is done away with;[33]

27   for he hath subordinated[34] all things under his feet. And whenever

---

26. *aparchē*—A sacrificial term pertaining to "first-fruits of any kind . . . which were holy to the divinity and were consecrated" (Bauer). Figuratively, of persons, "first-fruits of Christians" (Bauer).

27. *di'anthrōpou*—Through the man Adam, the antitype of Christ.

28. *zōiopoiēthēsontai*—First future passive indicative of *zōopoieō*, to make alive, give life to, keep or preserve alive. The words "all [*pantes*] will be made alive" do not refer to the whole human race, but rather to the dead in Christ, whereas the "all" (*pantes*) in the first clause apparently means "the whole human race."

29. *tagmati*—From *tagma*, that which is ordered, as of the arrangement of military troops into groups, divisions. Hence, order, arrangement, turn (Bauer).

30. See footnote 26.

31. *katargēsēi*—From *katargeō*, to render ineffective, idle, powerless, wipe out, abolish, bring to an end.

32. *dei*—It is necessary, inevitable.

33. *katargeitai*—See footnote 31.

34. *hupetaxen*—From *hupotassō*, subordinate, subject, to bring someone to subjection, subordinate (Bauer).

he shall say that all things have become subordinate,[35] it is plain that he is excepted who did subject all things to himself.

28 And whenever the all things are subjected to him,[36] then even the Son himself shall subordinate himself to him who subjects[37] all things to himself, in order that God may be the all in all.

D. An Appeal to Reason (15:29-34)

29 Otherwise what are they doing—those being baptized[38] for the dead ones? If dead persons actually are not raised, why are they being baptized for them?

30 And why are we in danger[39] every hour?

31 Daily I die, by the pride[40] over you, brothers, that I have in Christ Jesus our Lord.

32 If according to man I fought[41] with beasts in Ephesus, what good is it to me? If dead persons are not raised,

Let us eat and drink[42]
for tomorrow we die.

33 Do not be misled;[43] bad company corrupt morally good habits.[44]

34 Come to your senses[45] righteously and stop sinning, for some have an ignorance[46] of God; I say this to put you to shame.

---

35. See footnote 34.
36. *autōi*—That is, to God.
37. See footnote 34.
38. *baptizomenoi*—From *baptizō*, immerse, dip, plunge under the water.
39. *kinduneuomen*—From *kinduneuō*, run the risk, be in danger, in peril.
40. *kauchēsin*—Boasting; exultation, glorying.
41. *ethēriomachēsa*—From *thēriomacheō*, I fight with wild beasts.
42. *phagōmen kai piōmen*—Let us eat and drink, the motto of the Epicureans. See Isaiah 22:13.
43. *planasthe*—From *planaō*, mislead, lead astray, cause to wander, deceive.
44. *ēthē*—From *ethos*, usage, habit, custom, those of the fathers, of the country, of the Jews.
45. *eknēpsate*—From *eknēphō*, come to one's senses, become sober as from drunkenness.
46. *agnōsian*—Ignorance, lack of spiritual understanding, lack of knowledge of God.

E. The Manner of the Resurrection (15:35-49)

35   But someone will say, How are the dead raised up; and with what sort of body[47] do they come?

36   Foolish one, that which you sow is not made alive[48] except it die.

37   And that which you sow, you sow not the body that is to be but a naked[49] seed perhaps of wheat or of some of the rest;

38   but God gives to it a body according as he willed,[50] and to each of the seeds its own body.

39   Not every kind of flesh[51] *is* the same flesh, rather but *there is* a different *flesh* of men, and a different flesh of animals, and a different flesh of birds, and different *flesh* of fishes.

40   And bodies heavenly,[52] and bodies earthly; but the glory of the heavenlies is of one kind, and the *glory* of the earthlies is of another kind.

41   *There is* one glory[53] of the sun, and another glory of the moon, and another glory of the stars; for a star differs from *another* star in glory.

42   Thus also the resurrection of the dead. It is sown in perishability,[54] it is raised up in imperishability;

---

47.   **sōmati**—From *sōma*, body, whether human or animal.

48.   **zōiopoieitai**—From *zōiopoieō*, give life to, make alive.

49.   **gumnon**—From *gumnos*, stripped, bare, without an outer garment, naked, uncovered.

50.   **ēthelēsen**—From *thelō*, to purpose, resolve, be resolved or determined, to will (have in mind), intend (Thayer).

51.   **sarx**—Literally, "of the material that covers the bones of a human or animal body," the body itself (Bauer).

52.   **epourania**—From *epouranios*, in reference to heaven, "the place where God dwells, with the beings and things that pertain to him; they may actually be there with him, or they may belong there by nature, or come from there, etc." (Bauer). Also applied to "the heaven" where "the sun, moon, and stars are located." As a substantive, used of "things in heaven."

53.   **doxa**—Splendor, glory, grandeur, manifest presence of God, as the "pillar of fire" of witness in the wilderness.

54.   **phthorai**—Destruction, ruin, deterioration, corruption, disillusion, perishableness, rottenness, corruption, decay, decomposition.

43   it is sown in dishonor,[55] it is raised in glory; it is sown in weakness, it is raised in power;

44   it is sown a physical body,[56] it is raised a spiritual body. If there exists a physical body, there exists also a spiritual body.

45   So also it has been written, the first man Adam became a living soul,[57] the last Adam a life-giving spirit.[58]

46   But not first is the spiritual but the physical,[59] thereafter the spiritual.

47   The first man is out of the earth, made of dust,[60] the second man is out of heaven.

48   As is the earthly, such are also the earthlies and as is the heavenly,[61] such also are the heavenlies.

49   And just as we bore[62] the likeness of the earthly, we shall also bear the likeness of the heavenly.

F. The Final Victory over Death (15:50-58)

50   Now this I say, brothers, that flesh and blood cannot inherit[63] the kingdom of God, neither does the perishable inherit the imperishable.

---

55. **atimiai**—Disgrace, dishonor, shame; from *time* (honor), with alpha privative.

56. **sōma psuchikon**—As a substantive, the physical (body) in contrast to *to pneumatikon*, as here (Bauer).

57. **eis psuchēn zōsan**—*Eis*, here in predicate use, as in LXX is Hebraistic. "God breathed a soul *(psuchē)* into 'the first man'" (Robertson, *Word Pictures*).

58. **pneuma zōiopoioun**—From *zōiopoieō*, give life to, make alive. See footnote 48.

59. **alla to psuchikon**—From *psuchikos*, that which relates to "the soul or life" in regard to the natural world and "in contrast to the supernatural world" (Bauer).

60. **choïkos**—Earthy, made of earth or dust (Bauer).

61. See footnote 52.

62. **ephoresamen**—From *phoreō*, bear, carry, (in contrast to *pherō*) "for a considerable time or regularly, hence *wear*" (Bauer).

63. **klēronomēsai**—From *klēronomeō*, obtain, acquire, come into possession of something, inherit, be an heir.

51   Behold I tell you a mystery; we all shall not sleep,[64] but we all shall
be changed.[65]

52   In a split second,[66] in the flash of an eye,[67] at the sound of the last
trumpet;[68] for the trumpet will sound, and the dead ones will be
raised up imperishable, and we shall be changed.

53   For it is necessary for this perishable[69] to put on[70] the imperishable[71] and this mortal to put on immortality.

54   And whenever this perishable shall put on[72] the imperishable, and
this mortal shall put on immortality, then shall come to pass the
word that has been written,[73]

55   the death is swallowed up in victory. Where, O death, *is* your
victory? Where, O death, *is* your sting?

---

64. *koimēthēsometha*—From *koimaō*, literally, fall asleep, sleep; used figuratively of the sleep of death; hence, fall asleep, die, or pass away.

65. *allagēsometha*—From *allassō*, alter, change.

66. *atomōi*—From *temnō* with a privative meaning; to cut. Our word *atom*
comes from this word. The particle of time was so instantaneous that it was
considered indivisible. Hence, our *split second.*

67. *hripēi*—Used only here in the New Testament. Originally it meant *"the
swing or force with which a thing is thrown; a stroke or beat.* Used in the
classics of *the rush* of a storm, *the flapping* of wings; *the buzz* of a gnat; *the
quivering* of a harp string; *the twinkling* of the stars"* (Vincent). The word was
used "generally of any rapid movement, as of the feet in running, or the
quick darting of a fish" (Vincent).

68. *eschatēi salpiggi*—An eschatological symbol that signals the end of
earthly things and the resurrection that is to follow.

69. *phtharton*—From *phthartos*, subject to decay, or destruction, perishable
(Bauer).

70. *endusasthai*—From *endunō*, in the active, dress, clothe; in the middle, put
on, clothe oneself, put on, wear something.

71. *aphtharsian*—The oppositive of *phtharton* (footnote 69), incorruptability,
hence, immortality.

72. *endusētai*—First aorist middle subjunctive used with *hotan*, (whenever)
indicating "merely indefinite future" (Robertson, *Word Pictures*). The verb
means to put on as one would put on a garment.

73. *ho gegrammenos*—See Isaiah 25:8; Hosea 13:14.

56 Now the sting of the death *is* the sin,[74] but the power of the sin is the law;

57 but thanks *be* to God who is giving us the victory[75] through our Lord Jesus Christ.

58 Therefore, my beloved brothers, keep on becoming steadfast,[76] immovable, always abounding in the work of the Lord, knowing that your labor is not in vain in the Lord.

---

74. *hamartia*—Sin, missing God's mark, falling short of God's purpose for the life of the believer, any action that marks a "departure from the way of righteousness, both human and divine" (Bauer), disobedience to God's divine law, lawlessness.

75. *to nikos*—Late form for *nikē*, victory (Robertson, *Word Pictures*).

76. *hedraioi*—From *hedraios*, from *hedra*, seat, chair. Hence, sedentary, sitting, firm, steadfast, immovable.

CHAPTER 16

VI. Some Final Instructions, Announcements, and Greetings (16)
   A. Personal and Practical Matters (16:1-18)

1   Now concerning the collection[1] for the saints,[2] even as I made specific arrangements with the churches of Galatia, thus also do ye.[3]

2   Every first day of the week[4] each one of you is to have the habit of laying away[5] by himself (treasuring) whatsoever he may be prospered[6] in, so that whenever I may have come, there may be no collections going on then.

3   Whenever I arrive, those whom you may approve[7] through *your* letters, these I will send to bear away your gift[8] to Jerusalem.

---

1. *logeias*—From *logeia*, a word frequently used in the papyri for the collection of money but especially "for religious purposes" (Bauer).
2. That is, the saints in Jerusalem. See 2 Corinthians 8 and 9.
3. *houtōs kai humeis*—The same order as given to the churches of Galatia is now given to the Corinthians.
4. *kata mian sabbatou*—For similar use of *sabbatou* see Mark 16:9.
5. *thēsaurizōn*—From *thēsaurizō*, save, gather, store up in keeping with one's gains (Bauer).
6. *euodōtai*—From *euodoō*, prosper, succeed, get along well; in passive, as here (Bauer).
7. *dokimasēte*—From *dokimazō*, test, hence, approve. Used with the indefinite relative and *ean* with the aorist subjunctive.
8. *charin*—From *charis*, a word with varied meanings: favor, gracious care, or help, favor, goodwill, attractiveness, graciousness, gracious deed, benefaction, or gift, as here.

4　　If it be fitting[9] also for me to go, they will go with me.

5　　But I will come to you whenever I have gone through Macedonia, for I am going through[10] Macedonia:

6　　but with you perhaps I will stop awhile or even spend the winter, in order that you may help me on my way[11] wherever I may go.

7　　For I will not see you just now in a side journey, for I hope to remain for some time with you if the Lord permits.[12]

8　　And I may remain in Ephesus until Pentecost;[13]

9　　for a great and effectual door stands wide open for me, and the adversaries[14] are many.

10　　But if Timothy come, see that he is with you without cause to be afraid,[15] for he is working the work of the Lord as I also.

11　　Let no one, therefore, treat him with contempt but send him[16] on his way in peace that he may come unto me, for I am waiting for him with the brothers.

12　　And concerning the brother Apollos, I encouraged him much that he come to you with the brothers; but it was not at all his will that

---

9.　*axion*—From *axios* "of things, in relation to other things, corresponding, comparable, worthy" (Bauer). When used of persons, fit, worthy, as here.

10.　*gar dierchomai*—Futuristic use of the present indicative. Paul had a definite plan "to go through" Macedonia.

11.　*me propempsēte*—From *propempto*, escort, accompany, help one on his way "with food, money" (Bauer).

12.　*epitrepsēi*—From *epitrepō*, permit, allow, give permission.

13.　*pentēkostēs*—Literally *Pentecost*, the festival celebrated on the fiftieth day after the Passover and one of the three great festivals of the Jews which were celebrated annually at Jerusalem "in grateful recognition of the completed harvest" (Ex. 23:16; Lev. 23:15 ff.; Deut. 16:9 ff.).

14.　*antikeimenoi*—From *antikeimai*, be in opposition to, opposed to someone or something. Hence, opponent, enemy as in the participial use here.

15.　*aphobōs*—An old adverb, fearlessly, without fear, "without cause to be afraid" (Bauer).

16.　*propemsate*—See footnote 11.

he should come now, but he will come whenever he finds a favorable opportunity.[17]

13 Stay on the alert,[18] stand fast in the faith, act like men, become strong;

14 all your doings[19] are to be in love.

15 Now I appeal to you, brothers; you know the household[20] of Stephanas, that he is the firstfruits of Achaia and that they have established[21] themselves in a ministry to the saints.

16 That you also submit yourselves[22] unto such and to everyone who is hard working and striving together with us *in the work.*

17 But I rejoice at the coming[23] of Stephanas and Fortunatus and Achaicus, for they made up for that which was lacking on your part.

18 For they have refreshed[24] my spirit and yours. Recognize fully,[25] therefore, such men as these.

---

17. *eukairēsēi*—From *eukaireō,* have leisure, opportunity, (a favorable) time (Bauer).

18. *Grēgoreite*—From *grēgoreo,* be or keep awake, be watchful, be on the alert (our "keep your eyes open").

19. *panta humōn*—Literally, all your things or everything of yours or you.

20. *oikian*—From *oikia,* literally a house or building as in Matthew 2:11; 7:24-27. Hence, household, family.

21. *etaxan*—From *tassō,* place or station a person or thing in a fixed spot, appoint to or establish in an office, put someone over or in charge of someone or something, determine, fix, order, appoint (Bauer).

22. *hupotassēsthe*—From *hupotassō,* I rank under, I put in a lower rank, (pass.) I subordinate myself (a military term).

23. *parousiai*—Coming, presence, advent.

24. *anepausan*—From *anapauō,* transitive as here, give (someone) rest, refresh, cause to rest, revive.

25. *epiginōskete*—From *epiginōskō,* literally understand, know, recognize. Hence, know completely, exactly, through and through, notice, perceive, turn about, learn to know; hence, come to know well.

B. Closing Salutation (16:19-24)

19   The churches of Asia send[26] you greetings. Aquila and Priscilla with
the church that is in their house greet you earnestly in the Lord.

20   The brothers all greet you. Greet one another with a holy kiss.[27]

21   The greeting of Paul (is) with my own hand.[28]

22   If anyone does not love[29] the Lord, he is to be accursed.[30] May our
Lord come.[31]

23   The grace[32] of our Lord Jesus Christ (be) with you.

24   My love (be) with all of you in Christ Jesus.[33]

---

26. ***Aspazontai***—From *aspazomai*, literally greet, salute, welcome, as salutations are commonly given to those entering a house or taking leave from one another.

27. ***philēmati hagiōi***—In the synagogue the men kissed each other and the women kissed each other, and this form of greeting came to be a Christian custom.

28. ***tēi emēi cheiri***—A priceless autograph, if it could only have been preserved for us until this day.

29. ***philei***—From *phileō*, have affection for, like, love. A type of love that is not so lofty as the *agape* love.

30. ***anathema***—Properly, "a thing set up or laid by in order to be kept," as a votive offering. Later used of "a person or thing doomed to destruction . . . a thing abominable and detestable" and hence, "accursed," as here (Thayer).

31. ***Marana tha***—An old Aramaic imperatival form apparently used by the earliest church in Palestine "as part of its Lord's Supper liturgy—a prayer for the realization that Jesus' words 'until I drink it anew' will be realized" (Polhill).

32. ***charis***—See footnote 8.

33. ***en Christōi Iēsou***—One of Paul's favorite expressions, and frequently used in the epistle to the Ephesians.

EXPLANATORY NOTES

CHAPTER 1

● 1   In verses 1-3, Paul followed his usual form in the salutation, dividing it into three parts: (1) the sender, (2) those to whom the epistle was addressed, and (3) the warmhearted greeting. Paul emphasized his apostleship by referring to himself as "a called apostle," not one "called to be" an apostle for he was already serving in that capacity. Apparently the use of the word *apostle* was not yet confined to the "twelve." Paul did not refer to his experience on the Damascus road, only to the fact that he was "called" *(klētos)*. Paul linked Christ with God in the matter of his call, for "it takes place through Christ according to the will of God."[1] Sosthenes, to whom Paul referred, may have been the Sosthenes who got the beating in Corinth that was intended for Paul (Acts 18:17). There is nothing to suggest that Sosthenes was a coauthor of the epistle.

● 2   Paul's words "church of God" may have been a veiled protest (Chrysostom) against the "party-spirit" that was rife in the Corinthian church. This could have been Paul's way of saying that the church does not belong to people but to Christ.

The expression "sanctified in Christ Jesus" emphasizes the locus or sphere of the act of consecration. The expression "with all that call upon the name of our Lord Jesus Christ (theirs and ours) in every place" presents the Corinthian Christians with "a picture of their close unity with the brotherhood everywhere through the common bond of faith."[2] The words "call upon the name of our Lord Jesus Christ" constitute "a plain and direct reference to the Divinity of our Lord."[3]

● 3   The language of verse 3 is identical with that of 2 Thessalonians 1:2, except that the word "our" *(hēmōn)* is missing. Paul's "peace" greeting echoes the Hebrew form of greeting, but here the peace stems jointly from God the Father and the Lord Jesus.

● 4   Paul's continual thanksgiving to God rested upon "God's grace, not in general, but specifically given . . . in the sphere of . . . Christ Jesus."[4]

● 5-6   The expression "enriched in him" is "one of Paul's pregnant phrases full of the truest mysticism."[5] The Christian finds his riches not in material things, not in the things "of this world," but from the union that is his in Christ. This enrichment finds expression both in *knowledge* and in *utterance*. The church at Corinth was obviously plagued with divisive perversions but had nevertheless been graciously endowed. After all, the real trouble of the church at Corinth lay in a minority of the Corinthian body. So often a church experiences strife brought on by a handful of self-appointed troublemakers. Moreover, the testimony of Paul's preaching concerning Christ had found its mark among the Corinthians, for many of them had been stabilized and made "to stand" in spite of the pressure of the handful of detracters who stirred up trouble.

● 7-8   All the while the believers were encouraged by Paul to be aware of the fact that they were "not lacking in any gift" as they contemplated, and eagerly awaited, the second advent of the Lord Jesus. As Robertson noted, however, Paul later "will have to complain that they have not paid their pledges for the collection, pledges made over a year before, a very modern complaint" (2 Cor. 8:10).[6] It is worthwhile to note that Paul here paid tribute to the "attitude of expectation" in the posture of the Christian as he awaits the return of the Lord, who at "the end" will confirm the faithful ones "blameless in the day of our Lord Jesus Christ." Here is a ringing note on the doctrine of the "final preservation of the saints," for in that day the saints will be "unimpeachable . . . (Rom. viii.33; Col. i.22,28)."[7]

● 9   As if to accent the fidelity of God, Paul began verse 9 with the word *faithful (pistos)*: "Faithful is God through whom you were called into a fellowship of his Son." "His gifts are bestowed on a wise and settled plan" and "His *word,* with it His character, is pledged to the salvation of those who believe in His Son."[8] This fellowship, therefore, is unending, for it "exists now and extends to eternity: it is affected by and in the Spirit (Rom. viii.9f.)."[9]

● 10   Commencing with verse 10 and continuing through chapter 4, verse 21, Paul moved quickly to the dissensions *(schismata)* that afflicted the Corinthian church. Paul began his appeal (verse 10) with affectionate use of the word "brothers" *(adelphoi)* and made his appeal not "for the sake of the name," but "through the name of our Lord Jesus Christ." (The word *onomatos* is genitive, not accusative case.) In his appeal to the name of Jesus, Paul indirectly condemned "the various party-names."[10] The expression "speaking the same thing" is found in the Greek political life of Paul's day with the meaning "'be at peace' or (as here) 'make up differences.'"[11] Paul was aware of the need for absolute harmony in the church and earnestly pleaded for it. After all, a house "divided against itself shall not stand" (Matt. 12:25, KJV). "The word *schismata,* 'divisions,' implies in itself merely a neutral statement of the existence of divisions. It does not mean the existence of different systems of doctrine. Paul indeed hopes that unity will be restored as a result of his exhortation."[12] Of course, the community had not yet "fallen apart" in the extreme sense of the word, for the fellowship, divided as it was—that is, the haves and the have nots— after a fashion, still observes the supper of our Lord (11:17 *ff.*). Conzelmann holds that the meanings of *nous* (mind) and *gnōmē* (conviction) differ not in meaning.[13]

- 11   Who Chloe's people were, no one knows. Were they her children? Members of her own family? Neither do we know, from Paul's words, where Chloe lived.
- 12   In verse 12, the core of the disputes is laid bare. "These are not cases of personal quarrels but of differences in the attitude of the individual to the community."[14] The passage deals not with theological matters, for there is no explanation by Paul of any theological differences that might have existed between the party heads. The issue is that of relationships. And nothing is said about how the groups arose.
- 13   Paul drove to the heart of the problem with biting words: "Is Christ divided; was Paul crucified in behalf of you, or were you baptized in the name of Paul?" Conzelmann thinks that there may have been in Corinth "a widely adopted view of baptism, namely, that baptism is the ground of a relationship between baptizer and baptized similar to that established in the mysteries." See verse 16. Is there here a possible implication of a hero cult—another form of idolatry? The words *in the*

name of, as used in Christian baptism, usually were commonly understood to signify a committal to the ownership of Christ, subject to the lordship and his protection.[15]

● 14-15   Crispus, whom Paul baptized, was the synagogue ruler in Corinth on Paul's first visit there. His conversion is told in Acts 18:8. He, along with Gaius, was apparently among Paul's earliest converts there. This may have been why Paul baptized them himself. Gaius may have been the one referred to by Paul in Romans 16:23. If so, he was Paul's host while in Corinth. Some think that Gaius was the *Titius Justus,* the Corinthian "God-fearer" who was the next-door neighbor to the synagogue and who became Paul's host when he was no longer able to preach in the synagogue (Acts 18:7). Paul's reason for not baptizing is plainly stated here. He would do nothing to encourage "the cult of personality."[16] "It is not that baptism was unimportant to him, but . . . was equally valid" when administered by others.[17] Paul felt that his call was to evangelize the lost and to leave the matter of baptizing to his colleagues.

● 16   The use of the expression "household" (of Stephanas) finds its pattern in the Old Testament.[18] See Acts 11:14; 16:15,32,34; 18:8 for its frequent use in the New Testament. The term, however, throws no light upon the persons who compose Chloe's household, nor upon the age of the persons baptized (v. 16). If Paul baptized any others, he did not recall it.

● 17   After all, said Paul, "Christ did not send me to be a baptizer but to evangelize, not in wisdom of speech, lest the cross of the Christ be made ineffective." The issue was clearly drawn by Paul, and it was up to the Corinthians to make their choice. They must choose between the "wisdom" of the world and the "cross" *(stauros)* of the Christ. And Paul wanted all to remember that the "criterion" is the cross.[19]

● 18   In verse 18, Paul contrasted, sharply, the response of believers and unbelievers to "the word of the cross." To one group the talk about the cross is regarded as "foolishness," while to believers it is regarded as "the power of God." Lightfoot rightfully says, "in the language of the New Testament salvation is a thing of the past, a thing of the present, and a thing of the future. Saint Paul says sometimes 'ye were saved' (Romans 8:24), or 'ye have been saved' (Ephesians 2:5,8), sometimes 'ye are being saved' (I Corinthians 15:2) and sometimes 'ye shall be saved' (Romans 10:9,13). It is important to observe this, because we are thus taught that *soteria* (salvation) involves a moral condition which must have begun already, though it will receive its final accomplishment hereafter."[20] The saved person, who is forever a child of the King by adoption, is to grow in knowledge and in his likeness to Christ, while all the time looking forward to the ultimate realization of the saved estate at the last day. The real "antithesis," however, in verse 18, lies not "between *mōria*, 'foolishness,' and *sophia*, 'wisdom,' but between *mōria* and *dunamis theou*, 'the power of God.' "[21]

● 19   In verse 19, Paul drew "a powerful warning from the sacred history."[22] By appealing to Isaiah 29:14 as it is rendered in the Septuagint text, Paul presented "Scripture proof" of his thesis in verse 18. There is no indictment here of mere wisdom or understanding about practical matters. "It has its place in the mind that is informed by the Spirit of God (Coi. i.9), and the absence of it is a calamity (Rom. i.21,31)."[23] But there is utterly no place for "worldly cleverness in dealing with the things of God."[24]

● 20   Here Paul alluded to Isaiah 33:18 but "without exact quotation."[25] The portrayal in Isaiah of the destruction of Sennacherib, together with his officers, is seen on the tablet of Shalmaneser in the Assyrian Gallery of the British Museum.[26] "The wise" in verse 20 apparently "refers to the Greek philosopher, *grammateus* to the Jewish scribe and *sunzētētēs* suits both the Greek and the Jewish disputant and doubter (Acts 6:9; 9:29; 17:18; 28:29)."[27] If all were put together, the wise, the scribe, the disputer "of this age," they would fail to stand the test in the light of God's wisdom—the premise of the spirit. "Paul does not say, 'God shows that the world is foolish,' but 'God makes its wisdom foolish.' . . . 'Wisdom' is not primarily a piece of knowledge, but an attitude. It cannot be abstracted from its bearer."[28]

● 21   Here Paul contrasted "the two wisdoms" clearly: God's wisdom, the wisdom of the cross and man's wisdom, the false wisdom of the Greeks—a self-saving trust in ceremony and ritual. The main thought of verse 21 has to do with "God's refutation of the world's wisdom by means of what the world holds to be folly, viz. the word of the Cross."[29] The Greek philosopher (and Pharisee) "had a *sophia* [wisdom] of his own, which stood between his heart and the knowledge of God (Lightfoot)."[30] "Proclamation" is likely the idea Paul had in mind in his use of the word *preaching*. He was not speaking so much of "the act of heralding" *(kēruxis)* as "the message heralded or the proclamation as in verse 23 *{kērugma}*."[31] "The foolishness of preaching is not the preaching of foolishness."[32] The salvation of those who keep on believing "is the heart of God's plan of redemption, the proclamation of salvation for all those who trust Jesus Christ on the basis of his death for sin on the Cross. The mystery-religions all offered salvation by initiation and ritual as the Pharisees did by ceremonialism. Christianity reaches the heart directly by trust in Christ as the Saviour. It is God's wisdom."[33]

The meaning of the expression *en tēi sophiai tou Theou,* "in the wisdom of God," is an occasion of much dispute. Chrysostom and others held that the wisdom of God was "displayed in His works"[34] (Rom. 1:20; Acts 14:17). I would say with Conzelmann that "wisdom comes to man only from God. . . . The possibility of knowing God does not belong essentially to man (as a 'property'); it is bestowed on him by revelation."[35]

● 22-23   Paul's classification of humanity is the "Jewish equivalent for the Greek classification 'Greeks and barbarians.'"[36] In the classification, Paul simply had in mind the response of the Greeks and the Jews to the preaching of the gospel. Both parties had set themselves up as self-appointed judges with an authority that was capable of passing judgment upon God.

● 24-25   Notice that no article is used with Christ in verse 24 and that it is also in the accusative case (as in v. 23) because it is the object of *kērussomen*. No article is needed with the second mention of Christ, however, because its use with the genitive *(Theou)* makes it definite. "Christ crucified is God's answer to both Jew and Greek and the answer is understood by those with open minds."[37]

● 26   In diatribe style, Paul called upon the Corinthians to consider themselves. His use of the word *dunatos* emphasizes "the political aspect," while *eugenēs* (illustrious, highborn) refers to the social aspect or the group that is made up of the "educated, the influential, the people of distinguished family."[38] Paul was not presenting poverty as an ideal for the followers of Christ, and this is "shown at once by the form of expression 'not many.' The rich are not excluded as such."[39] *"The weak act of God,* as men think, *is stronger (ischuroteron)"* than the greatest strength of men.[40]

Among the converts at Corinth, of course, there were people of prominence.

● 27-29   The "three catchwords" of verse 26[41] are reintroduced and dealt with at some length. In doing so, Paul dealt "strictly an interpretation of the event of salvation. . . . that faith becomes the receiver of salvation regardless of its worldly standing."[42]

The verb *katargēsēi* (v. 28) means "'to reduce a person or thing to ineffectiveness,' 'to render *workless* or inoperative,' and so 'to bring to nought.' It is thus a stronger word than *kataischunēi* and is substituted for it to match the antithesis between *onta {being}* and *mē onta {not being}*."[43]

● 30   Paul reminded the Corinthians that it is out of him (out from God) that they were chosen, and the choice was made in the sphere of Christ Jesus "who became wisdom to us from God." "Christ is the wisdom of God (Col. 2:2f.) 'both righteousness and sanctification and redemption.'"[44] In truth, "all the treasures of wisdom and knowledge" are found in Christ Jesus. It is in him that we become righteous and holy and redeemed.[45] Verse 30 amounts to "an interpretation of the being of the crucified Lord. It was said above that he is God's *dunamis,* 'power,' and *sophia,* 'wisdom.' Now it is said that he was made such, by God. This points to the origin and direction of the event of salvation: from God, 'in Christ,' to us. And it shows that here we have not to do with general definitions of the being of Christ (in the sense of a speculation on hypostases), but with the exposition of the cross. This explains our existence in the world; we possess God's wisdom 'in Christ,' i.e., as an 'alien' wisdom."[46]

● 31   An allusion to Jeremiah 9:22 *ff.* "The sense depends on the emphasizing of *en kuriō*."[47]

Notes

1. Hans Conzelmann, James W. Leitch, trans., *A Commentary on the First Epistle to the Corinthians,* *Hermeneia* Series (Philadelphia: Fortress Press, 1975), p. 20.
2. A. T. Robertson, *Word Pictures in the New Testament* (Nashville, Tennessee: Sunday School Board of the SBC, 1931), p. 69.
3. Ellicott, as quoted by A. T. Robertson in *Word Pictures,* p. 69.

4. Ibid., p. 70.

5. Ibid.

6. Ibid., p. 71.

7. Archibald Robertson and Alfred Plummer, "A Critical and Exegetical Commentary on the First Epistle of St. Paul to the Corinthians," *International Critical Commentary* (New York: Charles Scribner's Sons, 1911), p. 7.

8. G. G. Findlay, "St. Paul's First Epistle to the Corinthians," *The Expositor's Greek Testament*, Vol. 3 (Grand Rapids, Michigan: William B. Eerdmans Publishing Co., [n.d.]), p. 761.

9. Robertson and Plummer, p. 8.

10. Ibid., p. 10.

11. Ibid.

12. Conzelmann, p. 32.

13. Ibid.

14. Ibid., p. 32 *ff*.

15. Ibid., p. 35.

16. F. F. Bruce, *New Century Bible*, "I and II Corinthians" (London: Oliphants, 1971), p. 34.

17. Ibid.

18. Conzelmann, p. 36.

19. Ibid., p. 37.

20. J. B. Lightfoot, *Notes on Epistles of St. Paul* (New York: Macmillan and Company, 1895), p. 157.

21. Conzelmann, p. 41.

22. Findlay, p. 767.

23. Robertson and Plummer, p. 19.

24. Ibid., p. 18.

25. Robertson, *Word Pictures*, p. 78.

26. Ibid.

27. Ibid.

28. Conzelmann, p. 43-44.

29. Robertson and Plummer, p. 20.

30. Ibid., p. 21.

31. Robertson, *Word Pictures*, p. 78.

32. Ibid.

33. Ibid, p. 79.

34. Robertson and Plummer, p. 20 *ff*.

35. Conzelmann, p. 46.

36. Ibid.

37. Robertson, *Word Pictures*, p. 79.

38. Conzelmann, p. 50.

39. Ibid.

40. Robertson, *Word Pictures*, p. 80.

41. Conzelmann, p. 50.

42. Ibid., p. 51.

43. Robertson and Plummer, p. 26.

44. Robertson, *Word Pictures*, p. 81.

45. Ibid.

46. Conzelmann, p. 51 *ff*.

47. Ibid., p. 52.

CHAPTER 2

● 1   In chapter 2, verse 1, Paul made the transition from his discussion of the attitude of the Corinthian community in relation to "the word of the cross." He began with an evaluation of his approach as a preacher—a good thing for any minister to do now and then. Hence, "vv 1 and 2 show the unity between the form and the content of the preaching, vv 3-5 the unity between the preaching and the existence of the preacher."[1] Paul reminded the Corinthians that he came "not in the way of excellence . . . not with the bearing of a man distinguished for these accomplishments, and relying on them for his success."[2] "Everything is discarded which could provide additional human support for the message. For otherwise the latter would be subjected to human criteria and would no longer be revelation (cf. v 5)."[3]

● 2   Paul's resolve in verse 2 "is not arbitrary; it is reached on the ground of his understanding of the message, on the ground of the cross."[4] Paul's word *eidenai* (know) has to do not with "knowledge in general, but theological knowledge."[5]

● 3   Paul's words in verse 3 amount to a brief portrait of his own self as a preacher, characterizing himself by timidity, fear, and trembling. Truly his humanity shines through his words here with clearness. Conzelmann takes Paul's threefold characterization of himself here "in a strictly theological sense"; but I prefer to take his words to reflect the way he felt mentally and emotionally as he faced the terrible situation he found at Corinth. Did he have a form of illness, at this particular time, which induced a measure of timidity and fear and trembling that apparently did not characterize his approach at other times? At any rate, "God brings him outwardly and inwardly into conformity with his preaching,"[6] in sharp contrast to "the veneer of false rhetoric and thin thinking" in Corinth.[7]

Maybe Paul was "contrasting his recognition of his limitations with the pride and arrogance of some at Corinth."[8]

● 4   The demonstration of the Spirit and power stood in bold contrast to the plausible words of wisdom which must have marked some of the pulpiteers in Corinth.

● 5   Conzelmann thinks Paul's use of the genitive *anthrōpōn*, "of men," "contains a barb directed against 'human' party slogans."[9] Nevertheless the antithesis is there concerning human and divine wisdom and human and divine power. For the believer, the wisdom is "Christ" (1:24) and his wisdom "confounds all mere human wisdom."

● 6   Paul's word *teleiois* was used by the Gnostics for those initiated into their fellowship, but Paul used the word merely to differentiate between "babes" (3:1) and adults. The word, commonly implying relative perfection, was used by Paul for adults as in 1 Corinthians 14:20; Ephesians 4:13; Philippians 3:15. See also Hebrews 5:9. Some of the "babes" were "simply old babes and unable in spite of their years to digest solid spiritual food."[10] The wisdom *(sophian)* of which Paul spoke is not mere human wisdom but the wisdom that is from above, the wisdom of God that embraces an understanding not only of divine things but of the practical matters of earth.

The understanding of verse 6, of course, depends upon one's interpretation of the words *sophian* and *teleiois*. It seems from the Greek that Paul was not speaking of believers who may be categorically defined as in separate groups, beyond the fact that some converts are less mature in their concepts of truth and duty and less able to perceive the full scope of the *kērugma*. In the strict sense of perfection, the full scope of Paul's words here and elsewhere in his epistles hardly indicates that he expected to find perfection among any of the Christians in Corinth or elsewhere. Perhaps too much theological hairsplitting is made at this point.

● 7   Paul's use of the word *mystery (mustērion)*, here and elsewhere, "refers to the fact that the Gentiles as well as the Jews are included in the scope of God's redemptive purpose in Christ Jesus. Previously this fact was not known."[11] The prevalent use of the word among the mystery religions of Paul's day is obvious to all scholars, but the meaning of Paul's use of the word becomes crystal clear in Ephesians and Colossians "where it refers to

God's Plan for the ages and Paul's role in this as apostle to the Gentiles."[12]

● 8   As G. G. Findlay notes, the world rulers of Paul's day "showed themselves miserably ignorant of God's plans and ways in dealing with the world they ruled."[13] Else, why did they crucify "the Lord of glory"? This seems to be the literal meaning of verse 8. If so, the measure of "indefiniteness" that some note in the verse, and any so-called "contradictions," hardly seem to remain. "The world's 'wisdom' is built around selfishness. Those who crucified Jesus thought that they would serve themselves. The Corinthians need to know that the cross is true wisdom. We live by dying, not by killing, by giving, not by taking."[14]

● 9   The quotation in verse 9 has not been located "either in the Old Testament or in extracanonical Jewish writings."[15] Passages reflecting some similarities, however, have been found in the Old Testament (as Ps. 31:20; Isa. 64:4) and also in rabbinical literature and apocalyptic writings. The thrust of the passage, however, seems to emphasize that the blessings of salvation are God's work. All the blessings come from him. They are his gift for those who come to him by faith.

● 10   The revelation to which Paul referred "took place, at 'the entry of the Gospel into the world,' not 'when we were admitted into the Church, when we were baptized' as Lightfoot interprets it."[16] The agent of the revelation, of course, is the Holy Spirit, who gives the individual believer the ability to perceive and the capacity to translate spiritual knowledge into the personal human relations.

● 11   "The Spirit is the organ of mutual understanding between man and God."[17] The commentators have wrestled with the problem of the unity "between the metaphysical and anthropological senses of *pneuma*, 'spirit,' . . . and with it the affinity between *pneuma* and *sophia*."[18] From Paul's words, it seems clear that he was dealing with the revelations of God's Spirit, the God who "searches all things, even the deep things of God" (2:10). The word *eraunāi* (explore) is found in wide use in "classical Greek" both in philosophical and religious contexts.[19] And incidentally, as Dr. W. H. Davis used to point out, in searching the Scriptures one must have not only the aid of every facet of linguistic study but also the aid of the Holy Spirit.

To understand accurately Paul's use of *pneuma*, the reader must have "an adequate knowledge of his theology, and psychology. But the point here is plain. God's Holy Spirit is amply qualified to make the revelation claimed here in verses 6-10."[20]

● 12   In verse 12 is "a distinct claim of the Holy Spirit for understanding (illumination) the revelation received. It is not a senseless rhapsody or secret mystery, but God expects us to understand 'the things that are freely given us by God.' . . . The tragic failures of men to understand clearly God's revealed will is but a commentary on the weakness and limitation of the human intellect even when enlightened by the Holy Spirit."[21]

● 13   Verse 13 has difficulties for the translator since there is no way to determine for certain whether Greek *pneumatikois* is neuter or masculine. The larger context favors the neuter. Hence, "combining spiritual matters [things] with spiritual terms."

● 14   Here again we have the physical person's inability to understand spiritual things. He does not understand them because he has not come to have an experiential relationship with Jesus Christ and consequently the things of the Spirit. Spiritual wisdom to him is foolishness. The only wisdom he knows is human wisdom. "The *psuchikos* man is the unregenerate man while the *pneumatikos* man is the renewed man, born again of the Spirit of God."[22] For this reason he rejects, refuses to accept the spiritual things, the things of God. "Certainly the initiative comes from God whose Holy Spirit makes it possible for us to accept the things of the Spirit of God."[23]

● 15   "There is a great lesson for Christians who know by personal experience the things of the Spirit of God. Men of intellectual gifts who are ignorant of the things of Christ talk learnedly and patronizingly about things of which they are grossly ignorant. The spiritual man is superior to all this false knowledge."[24] What is more, the spiritual person is "judged by no one."

● 16   Paul concluded his argument in the preceding verses with a reference to Isaiah 40:13 and continued in verse 16 to project the clear line of demarcation between the *pneumatikos* person and the *psuchikoi*. People of spiritual wisdom are superior to people of only earthly wisdom in dealing with spiritual matters. For that matter, their wisdom is superior in general because they have the *sophia* (the wisdom) of God. And this wisdom extends beyond mere spiritual things to practical aspects of life. They are in better position to make decisions, for they have the counsel of God. Paul's faith was unshakable for he could say, "I know him whom I have believed" (2 Tim. 1:12).

Notes

1. Hans Conzelmann, James W. Leitch, trans., *A Commentary on the First Epistle to the Corinthians,* Hermeneia Series (Philadelphia: Fortress Press, 1975), p. 53 *ff.*

2. G. G. Findlay, "St. Paul's First Epistle to the Corinthians," *The Expositor's Greek Testament,* Vol. 3 (Grand Rapids, Michigan: William B. Eerdmans Publishing Co., [n.d.]), p. 775.

3. Conzelmann, p. 54.

4. Ibid.

5. Ibid.

6. Ibid.

7. A. T. Robertson, *Word Pictures in the New Testament* (Nashville, Tennessee: Sunday School Board of the SBC, 1931), p. 83.

8. Personal correspondence with Dr. Frank Stagg.

9. Conzelmann, p. 55.

10. Robertson, p. 84.

11. R. Paul Caudill, *Ephesians: A Translation with Notes* (Nashville, Tennessee: Broadman Press, 1979), p. 24.

12. Personal correspondence with Dr. John Polhill.

13. Findlay, p. 779.

14. Dr. Frank Stagg.

15. Conzelmann, p. 63.

16. Robertson, p. 86.

17. Findlay, p. 781.

18. Conzelmann, p. 65.

19. Ibid., p. 66.

20. Robertson, p. 87.

21. Ibid.

22. Ibid., p. 89.

23. Ibid.

24. Ibid, p. 90.

CHAPTER 3

● 1   There is nothing wrong in being a babe in Christ. That is not the point here. It is the stage of the development of the growing Christian that Paul had in mind. The Corinthians had evidently not left behind "their seditions and immoralities."[1] The Corinthians were guilty of having what might be termed a "prolonged babyhood"—belonging in the Cradle Roll of the church when they should be out witnessing as mature adults to the glorious gospel of the Lord Christ.

● 2   Paul's words concerning milk and meat were frequently used to contrast simple and solid forms of instruction. Evidently the inability on the part of the Corinthians to hear sound teaching was a continuing matter; for in referring to their condition, he used both the imperfect and the present tense. The imperfect refers to the time he was with them (*edunasthe*), while the present tense (*dunasthe*) indicates the worldly life-style of the Corinthians still persisted.

● 3   The emphasis here on the life-style of the Corinthians is not so much on their sensuality and carnal indulgence as on their jealousy and strife. They behaved not like spirit-filled people but like ordinary ones who were untaught and without guidance in the things of the Spirit. It is a literal impossiblity for strife and jealousy to continue to exist among twice-born people. The love of Christ in the lives of his followers could not make room for jealousy and strife to exist for long.

● 4-5   Paul struck a death-dealing blow to factionalism in a church where groups of people line up with their given leaders. In the first place, Christians who pursue this course denigrate their own character as followers of Christ. Such conduct marks them as ordinary people who are unredeemed. All spiritual leaders should be regarded as ministering servants who are merely being used of the Lord as instruments through whom others come to know the Savior. And each is used according to the gifts which the Lord graciously gives. If the spiritual leader realizes that whatever gifts he possesses come from the Lord as free gifts, he is likely to exercise those gifts in a spirit of meekness and with humility. All of us, in a spiritual way, are what we are because of the good and perfect gifts that have come down to us from above.

● 6-7   In verses 6 and 7, Paul came to the heart of fruitful witnessing and the church growth process. As Robertson notes, he "applies his logic relentlessly to the facts"[2] (v. 7). Paul made it clear that the ministering servant of God can only *plant* and *water*. The increase, whatever it may be, is of God. Paul was saying here that, looking at the process, "God is everything, and we are nothing." Certainly God can get along without our help for did he not say, "For every beast of the forest is mine, and the cattle upon a thousand hills. . . . If I were hungry, I would not tell thee: for the world is mine, and the fulness thereof" (Ps. 50:10-12, KJV). Paul's words are certainly enough to give a preacher pause at the Monday morning pastor's conference as he rises to tell about the great day *"I had"* at the services yesterday.

It is interesting to note that the third verb Paul used in verse 6 is in the imperfect tense, signifying a continual process: "He kept on causing the labors of Paul and Apollos to be fruitful," whereas the first and second verbs (aorist tense) merely signify "definite acts."[3]

● 8-9   Paul made it clear that the mission of the Christian is a cooperative undertaking and that there is to be no rivalry or clamor for recognition. God will attend to the recognition. Each one will receive from the Lord his own reward according to his individual labor. Those who plant and those who water are to work together as brothers, and each is to show deference to the other, as though he were more worthy than himself. This spirit, this mood, should be common to all the fellow workers of God when they have the spirit of meekness and humility within their hearts. The Christian is always to regard the Lord as senior partner. We belong to him as his fellow workers. We are his tilled field. We are his building. And both as a tilled field and as a building, we are still on the pilgrimage. We all should say with Paul, "Not that I already attained or have already been perfected, but I keep pressing on if I also may lay hold of that for which also I was laid hold of by Christ Jesus."[4]

Just as the laborers are to be "one," so we are to be one with God both in the labors and in the effort to reach the goal that lies ahead, for *"God is all and in all."*[5] We all belong to him, and as such there can be no place for rivalry and selfishness.

Paul frequently used the words *to build* and *building* "in a moral and spiritual sense."[6] The words *oikodomeō* and *oikodomē* are found many times in the New Testment and all of these uses, with the exception of two cases, are in Paul's writings.

● 10   Paul took no credit either for his call as an ambassador of Christ or for his works. He regarded them as the outcome of God's grace, given to him not because he deserved them, but because of God's love for him and for the lost world. He had met God face-to-face on the Damascus road and had endeavored to respond to his call with all of his physical and spiritual resources. While, like Stephen, Paul was a pathbreaker, he regarded himself as only an instrument in the hands of God—at times almost as a bystander. The Judaizers stirred up trouble for Paul at Corinth, and if his words here appear to be defensive, it is rightly so. After all, the truth must have its spokesman if truth is to be sustained in a given generation.

In calling himself a master builder, Paul seemed to claim "primacy as pastor of the church in Corinth," as Robertson notes.[7] After all, the pastor of a church must have a measure of primacy if he is to succeed as the leader of the people. There are many workers, and all should relate to one another with understanding. But let it be remembered that the pastor is the master builder and that he should be wise in his role, even as was Paul.

● 11   But the foundation of Paul's work was Jesus Christ, and he made it clear that there is no other foundation that mankind can lay beyond the foundation that is already laid, which is Jesus Christ.

● 12   Paul made it clear that it is all important that the superstructure be of the right quality. There is more to this Christian building process than the laying of the worthy foundation. The materials superimposed must have the right character. Some build with rich and durable materials while others use materials that are "paltry and perishing."[8] It would be wonderful if the successive architects of the Christian calling, in building upon the foundation laid by Christ, would be as careful as the subsequent architects have been with reference to Saint Paul's Cathedral. Carefully, it seems, they have endeavored wisely to carry out and sustain the dreams of the master architect of that cathedral, Sir Christopher Wren.

● 13   But whatever the work of the builder, it will one day be "clearly seen" for the day will reveal it—that is, the judgment day of our Lord. Whatever the structure may be, it will be clearly brought to light—every nook and cranny and corner of it. For God is no respecter of persons, and each is to be judged at the last day, according to his own works and not the works of another. It will be brought to light, said Paul, "with fire, and what sort the work of each is, the fire itself will test."

● 14-15   Paul dealt with the matter of rewards at the last day and clearly stated that the rewards will be based upon the character of the work and of its abiding nature. When the superstructure consists of mere stubble (stalks of grain that were used in Paul's day for thatch in buildings, stalks from which the heads of the grain had already been cut), there can be little for the worker to look forward to in the last day by way of reward. A suitable reward, said Paul, will be awaiting those whose work is good.

● 16   Moreover, Paul wanted the Corinthian Christians to know that both separately and collectively they constituted a temple *(naos)* of God and that God's Spirit dwelt within them. In fact, God's Spirit has no dwelling place on earth save in the temples made up of the body of Christ, the church. Paul's words in these verses of 1 Corinthians may well be reviewed against the backdrop of the words of Jesus in Matthew 24:31-46. There simply has to be a final accounting with reference to the fruitfulness or unfruitfulness of the lives of Christ's followers on earth, and that day will be when we all stand before the judgment seat of God (Rom. 14:10-12).

● 17   Paul's reference to the destruction of the temple in verse 17 does not have to do with the defilement of the Temple in the Levitical sense, for the word Paul uses *(phtheirō)* does not have that connotation. It is a word that has to do with injury to the structure and is "to be requited in kind."[9] Certainly the person who wrecks churches incurs the wrath of God and will have his own punishment sooner or later. Paul was not talking about the annihilation of the soul of man, though it is possible for his words to include the idea of "eternal punishment."[10] It is impossible for one to delete the ideas of rewards and punishments as they have to do with the eternal destiny of the saved and the lost without destroying, by so much, the entire premises of the theological structure of the Bible.

• 18   In verses 18-23, Paul repudiated, flatly, the "affectation of philosophy" which, at bottom, is "the wisdom of this world" rather than the wisdom of God. This pseudophilosophy lay at the heart of the problems of the Corinthians. "Those who follow human wisdom exalt human masters at the expense of God's glory, and there are teachers who lend themselves to this error and thus build unworthily on the Christian foundation—some who are even destroying, under a show of building, the temple of God."[11] There is nothing wrong in wisdom, per se, and all of the followers of Christ ought to strive to be learned servants of the Lord, but most learned in the things and ways of God.

• 19-21   There is a sharp and well-marked contrast between the wisdom of God and the wisdom of the world. This seems to be the central thrust of chapters 1—3. This egocentric, worldy-wisdom disposition on the part of the Corinthians becomes the central problem of the church rather than the "surface problems" (divisions, incest, etc.) dealt with by Paul. In the words of Findlay, "the Church's wise are the world's fools, and *vice versa*."[12] In verse 19*a*, Paul told why the philosophy of the worldly point of view is to be rejected by those who aspire to Christian wisdom. "The wisdom of this world is foolishness with God." And Paul supported his premise by quoting from Psalm 94:11. Both the philosophers and "the men of affairs" (the *archōntes*) feel the sting of Paul's biting words. "When the world's schemers think themselves cleverest, Providence catches them in their own toils."[13] It was false wisdom (1:18-20,23; 2:14), along with self-conceit, that helped to bring about the strife in the Corinthian church. "The spirit of glorying in party is a species of self-conceit and inconsistent with glorying in the Lord (1:31)."[14]

• 22-23   In verses 22 and 23 Paul reminded the Corinthians of their great wealth in Christ and how it included "all things, all leaders, past, present, future, Christ, and God."[15] All followers of Christ, therefore, must know that they who have set their lives apart unto him can make no place for strife or wrangling. See Romans 8:12-17.

Notes

1. A. T. Robertson, *Word Pictures in the New Testament* (Nashville, Tennessee: Sunday School Board of the SBC, 1931), p. 92.

2. Ibid., p. 94.

3. Marvin R. Vincent, *Word Studies in the New Testament,* Vol. 3, (Grand Rapids, Michigan: William B. Eerdmans Publishing Co., 1946), p. 200 *ff.*

4. R. Paul Caudill, *Philippians: A Translation with Notes* (Boone, North Carolina: Blue Ridge Press of Boone, Inc., 1980), p. 44.

5. G. G. Findlay, "St. Paul's First Epistle to the Corinthians," *The Expositor's Greek Testament,* Vol. 3, (Grand Rapids, Michigan: William B. Eerdmans Publishing Co., [n.d.]), p. 789.

6. Vincent, p. 201.

7. Robertson, p. 95.

8. Findlay, p. 791.

9. Ibid., p. 793.

10. Robertson, p. 99.

11. Findlay, p. 793.

12. Ibid., p. 794.

13. Ibid.

14. Robertson, p. 100.

15. Ibid., p. 101.

CHAPTER 4

● 1   The apostle Paul emphasized the position of Christ's servants with reference to Christ. They are all subject to and answerable to Christ himself. They are the servants of the church and belong to the church because the church is the body of Christ, the body of which he is the head. They serve the church, and they themselves are not its master. There is one Master, Christ. In Paul's day, the steward (house manager) of the Greek home was usually a slave *(doulos)* who served under his Lord *(kurios)*. But the house manager was also "a master" in that he was placed over the other slaves of the household. He was their overseer *(epitropos)*. Likewise the steward (under rower) of Christ has a responsible role in the administration of the household of God here on earth. Because of that relationship, he is entitled to respect in a measure that the other servants are not entitled to. Better still, his position is to be regarded as one of dignity and presence. "The ministry is more than a mere profession or trade. It is a calling from God for stewardship."[1]

● 2   Paul was speaking here of human relationships as they relate to the office of the servants of Christ and, in a broader sense, to all human interpersonal relationships. "Fidelity is the essential requirement in all such human relationships, in other words, plain honesty in handling money like bank-clerks or in other positions of trust like public office."[2] Lack of integrity and responsible handling of church funds has been the source of downfall for many a religious worker.

● 3   In verse 3, Paul used the ethical dative of personal relation and interest meaning "as I look at my own case."[3] See Philippians 1:21. It did not bother Paul at all that the Corinthians might look upon him with a critical eye, scrutinizing his talents and appraising his motives and his handling of the affairs of his office as an ambassador of Christ. There was nothing in Paul's words to indicate that he disregarded public opinion on the part of the Corinthians; but it did mean that, when his credentials with Christ were called into question, it was not to be done by any human tribunal. Some would say that it may not be to Paul's credit that he was averse to self-examination. What he obviously meant, rather, was that he was unwilling to "set himself up as a judge of himself."[4] There seems to be nothing here to indicate that any formal trial was in prospect for Paul at this point among his Corinthian critics. He merely set the record clear as to his own feelings about such carping criticism.

● 4   Paul did not claim for himself perfection; he was merely saying that he was conscious of nothing against himself that might be brought into question at the moment. But this inability on his part to recall sins that might be against him does not proclaim his innocence. After all, he is to be judged by the Lord, not by himself. It is the Lord who ultimately passes judgment on his fidelity and the fidelity of all of his followers. For Paul, the Lord was the great Examiner. Only his judgment can set one free. Paul's fixed ground of assurance, however, was made possible through the justification that came to him "by faith in Christ, not his innocence, but his Saviour's merit."[5] Vincent puts it this way, "The Lord is the only competent *examiner,* therefore do not *judge* until He comes to judgment."[6]

● 5   In verse 5, Paul dealt sharply with those who had been criticizing and passing judgment. He said, in effect, stop it! The censorious habit is like a fungus, like gangrene, that grows and spreads with each passing day. Human judgments are finite, fallible, incomplete, and are based on the knowledge derived from the wisdom of the world: this is why the critics need to wait for the glorious second coming of the Lord Jesus. That will be early enough for judgment. He himself knows all the hidden things of the darkness, and he will bring them to light in that day. And the praise that comes to people will not be human praise but divine praise, for it will come straight from God. What is more, no one will be left out. For it will come to each (*hekastōi*), according to the judgment of God.

● 6   In verse 6, Paul boldly dealt with the principles involved, applying them to Apollos and to himself for the better instruction of the Corinthians. Since his words fly straight like arrows at the factious spirit that prevailed among the Corinthian church members, the impact was felt by the "puffed up." The warring factions could hardly have missed the point. He wanted to impress the divisive spirits among the Corinthians that they were duty bound by their profession of faith as followers of Christ "to keep their thoughts about men within the lines marked out in Scripture."[7] There was to be no place for glorying "in men" and to act as judges in matters that should be left to the final judgment of God. After all, did not Jesus say, "Judge not, that ye be not judged. For with what judgment ye judge, ye shall be judged: and with what measure ye mete, it shall be measured to you" (Matt. 7:1-2, KJV)?

● 7   In verse 7, Paul exposed the fallacy of the reasoning of the conceited Corinthians. In other words, if you are different, how did it come about? Who made you different? If you have a better mind, more brilliant insight, and a better capacity to perceive, who caused it to be that way? "And what do you have that you did not receive?" "Who gives you the right to exalt one and depress another?"[8]

● 8   In verse 8, Paul continued to confront the self-esteem of the Corinthians. The Corinthians appeared to be "full," that is, sated with the blessings of the messianic kingdom. Already they were "enjoying its banquets, its treasures, and its thrones."[9] And all this was without the help of the apostle. "Already you are become rich; without us you have become kings." Robertson and Plummer suggest that the words "without us" imply "without our company" rather than "without our aid." The Corinthians truly rose in a ludicrous manner, presenting themselves as "perfected saints" while Paul, far from perfection, continued to toil, working with his own hands.

● 9   Verse 9 appears to refer to the custom of "exposing condemned criminals in the amphitheatre to fight with beasts or with one another as gladiators. The gladiators, on entering the arena, saluted the presiding officer with the words *Nos morituri salutamus, We who are to die greet you.*"[10] Paul's use of the words "both to angels and to men" merely seem to imply that the exhibition was complete before the eyes of all who may witness it whether of heaven or of earth.

● 10   Paul's words in verse 10 amount to a withering blow against the conceited self-esteem of the critical Corinthians. "We apostles are fools in the world's eyes *on account of (dia)* Christ, because we know and preach nothing but Christ: You are wise *in* Christ, as Christians, making your Christianity a means to your worldly greatness—union with Christ the basis of worldly wisdom."[11]

● 11   In verses 11 and 12*a*, Paul vividly portrayed the estate of the *atimoi* (that is, the unhonored, dishonored), those "reduced to this position by the world's contempt and with no means of winning its respect—a life at the farthest remove from that of the Gr. [eek] gentleman."[12] The apostle Paul not only felt the lash of this despicable condition but also came to know the pangs of hunger, of thirst, of ill clothing, of the marks of poverty, and of manual toil, harsh treatment, and homelessness. Hardship was his on every side. Moreover, other Christian missionaries came to know these sufferings which extended to physical violence and homelessness.

● 12   Here we have an actual portrayal of Paul's estate while he was writing the first Corinthian Epistle and his response to the indignities and inhumanities of his enemy. See Peter's words about Jesus (1 Pet. 2:23) and how in harmony Paul's response was with the words of Jesus in Matthew 5:44; Luke 6:27. Although persecuted, he retained his Christian composure and was able to hold back and not retaliate.[13]

● 13   Paul's words in verse 13 may refer to a custom at Athens with which he must have been familiar. In times of pestilence, such as famine or plague "or other visitations from heaven," Athenians threw condemned criminals and other individuals who were regarded as worthless and of "the lowest class" into the sea as scapegoats in the hope that such an expiatory offering and sacrifice might "cleanse away" or "wipe off" the nation's guilt.[14] It is interesting to note that in chiding the Corinthians, the apostle referred to them as his children. This seems not only to reflect the affectionate relationship that existed between the Corinthians and Paul but also to indicate the responsibility he felt to set them right on important matters relating to the faith.

● 14-15   G. B. Findlay refers to Paul's admonitions in 4:14-21 as "Paul's fatherly discipline."[15] In turning from his words of concern relative to the divisions at Corinth, the apostle displayed the loving concern of a father's heart "for though you should have many thousands of tutors in Christ, yet . . . in Christ Jesus, through the gospel, I became your *spiritual* father." The pastor who gives his life freely and fully in shepherding the lives of his people, old and young, understands clearly these words of Paul. After all, how can the ties of genuine friendship and interpersonal love be felt so warmly as between the pastor and his people? Such intimate, loving relationships can be surpassed only by the family ties of the home.

The tutor (*paidagōgous*) from boy (*pais*) and leader (Greek *agōgos*) was very much a part of the average well-to-do home in the Rome of Paul's day. "Paedagogus was a slave to whom boys were entrusted on leaving the care of the females, which was somewhere about their sixteenth year. He was often a foreigner, sometimes educated and refined, but often otherwise; for Plutarch complains that seamen, traders, usurers, and farmers are engaged in this capacity. The office was one of general guardianship, not of instruction, though sometimes the paedagogus acted as teacher. He accompanied the boy to school, carrying his books, etc., and attended him to the gymnasium and elsewhere."[16]

● 16-17   Paul must have felt deeply his responsibility as the spiritual leader of the Corinthians. His words of admonition should not be regarded as given in a spirit of overconfidence. "He has received the charge to lead them, and he is bound to set an example for them to follow, but he takes no credit for the pattern (xi.I)."[17] In sending Timothy to the Corinthians, Paul obviously felt that, because of the character of his life and his faithful relationship to the teachings of Paul, Timothy would be able to interpret to the Corinthians, effectively, not only the life-style of the apostle but also his teachings concerning the believer's new life in Christ Jesus.

● 18-19   It appears from Paul's words in verses 18 and 19 that some of the Judaizers had become puffed up in Paul's absence and assumed that, in his sending Timothy to them, Paul would pass them by. "Amongst these, presumably, were mischievous teachers (iii.11-17) who had swelled into importance in Paul's absence, partisans who magnified others to his damage and talked as though the Church could now fairly dispense with him (3,6,8,15)."[18] But Paul made it clear (v. 19) that he would not take cognizance of such conceited individuals but would show regard only for the measure of power that any of them might reflect regarding God's kingdom.

● 20   Paul had no place in his thinking for pretense or other "high-flown" dispositions on the part of the Corinthians or any other people of

God. After all, the kingdom of God lies not "in what is said" but in power, the power that comes from God and belongs to his kingdom. So-called Christians who become little more than "puff bags" and who leave behind them only a trail of windy words have little support to offer in the kingdom of our Lord.

● 21   In verse 21 Paul closed his words of fatherly discipline with a final word of stern reproof. "What do you want? With a rod shall I come to you, or with love and a spirit of meekness?" The word *spirit* here used by Paul hardly refers to the Holy Spirit but rather to the mood and mind of the Christian that stands in direct opposition to that of the conceited, self-appointed spokesmen among the Corinthians.

Notes

1. A. T. Robertson, *Word Pictures in the New Testament* (Nashville, Tennessee: Sunday School Board of the SBC, 1931), p. 102.
2. Ibid., p. 103.
3. Ibid.
4. Ibid.
5. G. G. Findlay, "St. Paul's First Epistle to the Corinthians," *The Expositor's Greek Testament,* Vol. 3 (Grand Rapids, Michigan: William B. Eerdmans Publishing Co., [n.d.]), p. 798.
6. Marvin R. Vincent, "The Epistles of Paul," *Word Studies in the New Testament,* Vol. 3 (Grand Rapids, Michigan: William B. Eerdmans Publishing Co., 1946), p. 205.
7. Findlay, p. 800.
8. Archibald Robertson and Alfred Plummer, "A Critical and Exegetical Commentary on the First Epistle of St. Paul to the Corinthians," *International Critical Commentary* (New York: Charles Scribner's Sons, 1911), p. 82.
9. Ibid., p. 84.
10. Vincent, p. 206.
11. Ibid., p. 207.
12. Findlay, p. 802.
13. Robertson, p. 108.
14. Findlay, p. 803.
15. Ibid.
16. Vincent, p. 209.
17. Robertson and Plummer, p. 90.
18. Findlay, p. 805.

CHAPTER 5

● 1   In chapter 5, the apostle continued his indictment of the Corinthians, dealing with the second stage of it. While he was concerned with particular cases of flagrant immorality, he was more upset by the response of the Christian community to the brazen instances of immorality that had occurred. There appeared to have been no consensus against such. "Their morbid and frivolous self-conceit is untroubled. They have shown no sign of proper feeling: still less have they dealt with the case, as they ought to have done, by prompt expulsion (*vv.* 1-5)."[1] Such immoral behavior stems only from selfish people who are frivolous and unconcerned with the welfare of the larger community. Chapter 5 is linked closely with chapter 4, particularly verse 21.

The code of morals of some of the Corinthian Christians had evidently sunk to a lower level than that of the Gentiles about them. So perverted had they become that it was possible for a man to consort with the wife of his own father without reproof. How the evidence of immorality came to Paul we do not know, but rumor has its way of circulating and eventually being heard. Perhaps the same persons who informed Paul about the strife (1:11), or maybe Stephanas (16:17), brought the word to him. In the background seems to be the basic problem of the dualism between soul and body. In other words, the body, being separate, might sin without affecting the soul or spirit. This view paved the way for incest and other carnal indulgences.

The fornication with which the apostle was concerned was "Illicit sexual intercourse in general."[2] "The woman was clearly not the mother of the offender, and probably (although the use of *porneia* rather than *moicheia* does not prove this) she was not, at the time, the wife of the offender's father. She may have been divorced, for divorce was very common, or her husband may have been dead."[3]

● 2   Paul's words about being "puffed up" do not indicate that the Corinthian Christians were puffed up over this particular immoral matter. They were just puffed up in general for the simple reason that they had become insensitive to the character of their own life-style. In truth, the Corinthians did not even mourn about the tragic state of morals in their midst. Sorrow was the least response they might have shown to the sad story.

● 3-4   Paul's words in verse 3 give bluntly his conclusion of the matter. The conclusion is that of "an imaginary church court where the culprit has been tried and condemned."[4] Whatever one's interpretation may be of Paul's sharp words in verse 3, and however one may regard his apostolic prerogative, he did use such power against Elymas (Acts 13:8 *ff.*). Peter also used it against Ananias and Sapphira (Acts 5:1 *ff.*).

● 5   What Paul obviously had in mind was expulsion from the church. A person who was guilty of such outrageous misconduct could reside only outside the commonwealth of believers, so far as he was concerned. Paul's language, however, does not imply that expulsion amounted to "the damnation of the offender. The wilful offenders have to be expelled and not regarded as enemies, but admonished as brothers (II Thess. 3:14 *f.*)."[5] After all, expulsion is merely a discipline, in its ultimate purpose, to safeguard the influence of the body of Christ on the unbelieving world. The matter of ultimate salvation will be handled by the Lord in the day of Christ, and every Christian should want nothing less than that for all mankind. In the light of the New Testament teaching, the Christians should feel all the more responsible to help restore the brother who has been expelled from the body.

● 6   The Corinthians could hardly have misunderstood the meaning of Paul's words in verse 6. There was nothing beautiful about the condition; rather it was a "plague spot," a "cancer" on the body of the church, and "They needed a surgical operation at once instead of boasting and pride."[6] If anyone has any doubt about the effect of a little leaven on the lump, let him ponder the course of a single germ in disease.

● 7   There seems to be a note of urgency in Paul's words in verse 7. The old and decayed yeast was to be completely removed and a new stock begun. The ideal and normal estate of the followers of Christ is without any leaven whatever. "Paul means that the Lamb was already slain on Calvary and yet you have not gotten rid of the leaven."[7]

● 8   In verse 8, Paul may have had in mind the Jewish Passover, which came just before Pentecost (1 Cor. 16:8). At any rate, Christians are to "keep on celebrating" the feast. It is to be perpetual, and the leaven is to be "kept out." The etymology of the word *eilikrineias* (sincerity, purity) is uncertain. It may have the meaning I judge *(krinō)* "by the light of the sun, holding up to the light."[8] The word *truth (alētheias)* is from an old word *(alēthēs)* meaning true. This with the *a* privative and *lēthō* (meaning to hide or conceal) means "unconcealed, not hidden." With the Greeks, truth was something that was unconcealed, not hidden, out "in the open." See Romans 1:18.

● 9   In verse 9, Paul seemed to refer to an epistle to the Corinthians written earlier than our 1 Corinthians. It was evidently a letter that was not preserved. At any rate, he had already warned them against associating with those whose sexual practices were immoral.

● 10   Verse 10 does not seem to indicate that Christians are to break off all communications with those outside the church whose moral life-styles differ from their own. For to do this, one would have to literally get out of the world. But Christians are not to "keep company" with the licentious and idolaters. They do not walk or stand or sit in the way with them (Ps. 1:1).

● 11   Social contacts with "a brother" who has adopted the life-style of the unbelieving world are to be restricted. Such a person is to be regarded as an outsider. One is "not even [to] eat in company with such a one."

● 12-13   Paul wanted to make it clear that he did not regard it as his business to pass judgment on those outside of the church. To begin with, how could they have a life-style such as his until they had first come to know Jesus as Savior and Lord? As for those outside the church, God will judge them. Let the church members deal with their own evildoers in their own midst.

Notes

1. Archibald Robertson and Alfred Plummer, "A Critical and Exegetical Commentary on the First Epistle of St. Paul to the Corinthians," *International Critical Commentary* (New York: Charles Scribner's Sons, 1911), p. 95.

2. Ibid.

3. Ibid., p. 96.

4. A. T. Robertson, *Word Pictures in the New Testament* (Nashville, Tennessee: Sunday School Board of the SBC, 1931), p. 112.

5. Ibid., p. 113.

6. Ibid.

7. Ibid., p. 114.

8. Ibid., p. 115.

CHAPTER 6

● 1   In verses 1-6 Paul dealt with the matter of Christians going to law in heathen courts. In addition to the problem of fornication, there was the matter of robbery, fraud, and other problems subject to correction and censure. Apparently evil within certain members of the Corinthian church had gotten completely out of hand so that some members of the Christian body had gone to law with the offender in the civil court, "to the scandal of the Church and to Paul's high indignation."[1] Paul's indignation is clearly reflected in the opening sentence in the form of a question. It was not that the apostle was opposed to Roman justice, for he himself had been forced to turn to such; but in no instance had he been known to appear in a civil court except in defense of problems that had to do with his work, never in a case that involved brother with brother. Why would the Corinthians turn from the counsel and judgment of the saints *(tōn hagiōn)*? Truly such a disposition was a denigration of the ability of the Christians to keep their own house in order. A rabbinical inhibition said, " 'It is forbidden to bring a matter of right before idolatrous judges. . . . Whosoever goeth before them with a law-suit is impious, and does the same as though he blasphemed and cursed; and hath lifted his hand against the law of Moses our Teacher,—blessed be he!' "[2] The Jews had the right under the government of Rome to have their own *house of judgment* in matters of internal jurisdiction. They had their Bethdin *(house of judgment)* just as they had their *Beth-keneseth (synagogue).*[3]

● 2-3   Paul's reference to the saints who "will judge the world" was to the coming messianic kingdom (Acts 1:6). The belief was that "the saints were to share God's rule over *the world,* even over fallen *angels* or the angel-guardians of pagan nations."[4] Paul regarded the use of the civil courts by Christians in such trifling matters to be a denigration of the prerogative of the body of Christ. After all, even Plato in his *Republic* showed contempt "for anyone who was so litigious as to frequent law-courts over matters like money and property, issues far too trifling to deserve the notice and interest of a free, good man."[5] Paul's position, however, was purely religious. He wanted the Corinthian Christians to have a life-style that was above that of those who were outside the church.

● 4   It is unreasonable to suppose that there will be times, even among those of the household of faith, when there will not be misunderstandings—perhaps grave misunderstandings. But such matters should be resolved within the body of the saints. That was Paul's premise here.

Two constructions are possible for verse 4. The verb *kathizete* may be regarded as imperative; if so, it would indicate that the Corinthian Christians would have been better off to call upon those within the church who enjoyed the least esteem of their fellow Christians rather than to appeal to the heathen courts.[6] On the other hand, if one regards *kathizete* as indicative, with a sentence interrogative, the words would mean "those who, in the Church, are held of no account," with the same meaning "if the sentence is categorical."[7]

● 5   In 4:14 Paul stated that he was not writing to shame the Corinthians, but he felt different here. He would move them to shame. He would have the Corinthians know that conditions must be bad among them if they found it necessary to go outside their own ranks to find a suitable arbiter to deal with matters between two of their brothers. The sentence is "highly condensed,"[8] but the meaning is clear.

● 6   Paul's words in verse 6 reflect the tragic condition among the Corinthian church members. It is twofold: first, those that were in the dispute were too far removed from the spirit of Christ to be able to settle the thing among themselves. Second, they went into heathen courts about the matter rather than asking one of their own brothers to be the judge.

● 7   "Better undergo wrong yourself than suffer *defeat* in the matter of love and forgiveness of a brother."[9] A lawsuit with a brother is bad enough, but to strive to have the cause vindicated outside the fellowship of believers is defeat to start with. Paul suggested that it is better for one to suffer wrong himself or allow himself to be defrauded than to pursue such a course as the Corinthians had followed in the settlement of their disputes. F. F. Bruce puts it this way: "'There are thus two distinct points:

(a) Christian cases should be tried by Christian courts . . . *(b)* There should be no cases: Christian courts should have perpetual white gloves" (T. W. Manson, *Studies in the Gospels and Epistles* [1962], p. 198)."[10]

● 8 "The very climax of wrong-doings, to stoop to do this with one's brethren in Christ."[11] Surely the Corinthians would have had an opportunity to know something about the substance of the Sermon on the Mount. They needed only to consider Jesus' words in Matthew 5:39-41 to realize there was a better way than the course they had pursued in dealing with their brothers.

● 9-10 These verses fit together. Paul stressed the character of the kind of people who are to be excluded from God's kingdom.[12] He did not deal with the particular sins, per se, but did particularize certain types of wrong-doing that are "incompatible" with God's kingdom. "*Fornicators* is the general term covering all forms of sexual sin" whereas *adulterers* specifically relates to those who "violate the marriage bed."[13] The word translated *sodomites (malakoi)* when used of things like garments means soft garments or soft clothes. When used of persons, the meaning comes to include boys and men "who allow themselves to be misused homosexually (Catamites)."

"The tendency to divorce religion from reality has manifested itself in all ages of the world, and under all forms of religion." Many religions have been "exact in the performance of religious services, and zealous in the assertion and defence of what they regarded as religious truth, while unrestrained in the indulgence of every evil passion."[14]

Paul cautioned the Corinthians about being led astray (*mē planasthe*, present passive imperative with *mē*, negative). "Some Jews held that the belief in one God sufficed without holiness of life. Judaizers may have been teaching in Corinth that faith sufficed."[15] From the Roman satirist Petronius, we know that the common sexual practice rife among the Corinthians "was not seriously or generally regarded as heinous; occasionally it was reprobated and punished, but Christianity first, and from the first, became its uncompromising foe, in line with the best Hebrew and Jewish traditions of morality."[16] Paul made one thing clear. The "wrongdoers" (*adikoi*) were definitely not among the heirs of the kingdom of God. There is no place for them in heaven. Nor is there to be a place for the voluptuous, soft (*malakoi*) who are addicted to sins of the flesh. But

Paul did not limit his biting words merely to the sensual-minded. He also included the covetous, and others (see vv. 8-10).

● 11   In verse 11, Paul stated clearly that not all of the Corinthian Christians were guilty of the sinful life-style that he described. They may have been guilty of many of the things in the past, but then they were "washed . . . consecrated . . . justified." Note that the first verb, washed, is in the middle voice whereas the last two verbs, consecrated and justified, are in the passive voice. Having been delivered from their former sin habit, and having "been declared righteous by God; they had been made his holy people."[17]

● 12   F. F. Bruce suggests that Paul's parallel use of the words "all things for me are lawful" in verse 12 may have been "a slogan of the gnosticizing party in the church which was impatient of the restraints of conventional morality,"[18] but Paul did qualify his double use of the expression by reminding the Corinthians that not all things for him were expedient. The Christian is never to be unmindful of moral issues as they affect others. "There are some things which are not expressly forbidden, but whose results are such as to rule them out for the believer."[19] As Morris adds, "There is a danger that in claiming his Christian freedom a man may bring himself into bondage to the things he does."[20] This Paul refused to do. He considered himself his brother's keeper, and he was willing to change his own life-style to the benefit and lasting advantage of other people.

● 13   In verse 13, we may have a reference to an old proverb concerning the adaptation of the body and food "which had apparently been used by some in Corinth to justify sexual license." Paul met the issue head on and, by "adopting the profound principle of Jesus (Mark vii. 15-23), cuts through these knotty questions at a stroke."[21] It is the old question of two opposing life-styles that have plagued the human race since the Advent of Jesus, namely, his life-style and that of the unbelieving world about him. Among the ancient Greeks of Paul's day, "the two appetites" referred to by Paul were "treated on the same footing" and largely ignored the ethical aspects of sexual passion.[22] Paul dealt boldly with the nobler concept of human sexuality as opposed to the Greek concept of human sexuality in his day.

● 14   The language of the various old manuscripts differ in the rendering of this verse, but the thrust of the verse is the same. God, who raised Jesus from the dead, will also raise up us at the last day. Paul's sudden switch to the matter of the resurrection of the body adds to his premise concerning "the dignity and destiny of the body (*quanta dignitas,* Bengel) which should not be prostituted to sensuality."[23]

● 15   Paul's words are graphic and powerful. The very thought of taking a member or members of Christ's body and making them "members of a harlot" in a union "staggers Paul and should stagger us."[24] The word *God* does not actually occur in the Greek *mē genoito*. But it may well occur there, for it is even repulsive to think of such a union as is posed by the question of Paul, and an appeal to God is certainly in order to the end that it will never take place.

● 16   Paul's words refer to Genesis 2:24, where the sexual act of a man and his wife issues in one flesh. In like manner, Paul said, "Any man who unites with a prostitute by that act becomes one with her. The Corinthians had not realized the implications of their view of sexual laxity. Paul drives home his point with this combination of an appeal to Scripture and to well-known fact."[25]

● 17   The present participle *(kollōmenos)* could be either middle or passive in form, as is true of the same form that appears in verse 16. In the case of the union with a harlot, however, it is a voluntary act which the male by his own initiative accomplishes. Therefore, the word should be treated as middle voice, something the male is doing for himself. In verse 17, however, the participle should be regarded as passive, for the actual uniting is the work of the Spirit, being accomplished by God. It is by the grace of God that one is saved. It is brought about through faith as the gift of God and is neither the result of self nor of works (Eph. 2:8-9).

● 18   Unlawful cohabitation, with which Paul dealt here, "instead of being a purely physical or transient tie, is held to produce a united life in which the two are so closely knit together that they form a single self, as it were. Like a genuine Hebrew, Paul repudiated any notion of the soul being either imprisoned in the body or being able to live its own life irrespective of the body, whether that life was degrading or noble."[26] Paul discovered at Corinth that there were those who endeavored to justify promiscuous sexual indulgence in an indifferent manner, as though it had no effect on the soul. He made it clear that the body is a part of the total self and that the functional natures of both soul and body blend into one perfect whole.

The views of commentators differ greatly concerning Paul's words in verse 18 (*ektos tou sōmatos,* outside the body). "But the general meaning of *vv.* 13b-18 is plain," say Robertson and Plummer. "The body has an eternal destiny, *to sōma tō Kuriō*. Fornication takes the body away from the Lord and robs it of its glorious future, of which the presence of the Spirit is the present guarantee (cf. Rom. viii. 9-11). In *v.* 18 we have the sharply cut practical issue, 'Flee fornication.' Clearly the words that follow are meant to strengthen the *severitas cum fastidio* of the abrupt imperative: they are not an anti-climax. Any exegesis which fails to satisfy this elementary requirement may be set aside."[27]

● 19-20   Paul closed his argument for morality in human sexuality on the highest possible plane. The human body becomes the *naos* (sanctuary) of the Holy Spirit which dwells within the believer. The body is the dwelling place of the Christian and offers the only dwelling place for the Spirit of God which dwells within the person of the believer. There is no room for the sort of dichotomy that prevailed among some of the Corinthians. The body and the spirit cannot be separated from each other into different personalities or things while one is in the flesh. They cannot be regarded as mutually exclusive of each other or in any measure contradictory. It is, indeed, an occasion of lament that even to this day some Christians hold the view that when a person commits an act of sin his spiritual self is not involved, only the body. This viewpoint is particularly reflected by some in their interpretation of the King James Version's rendering of 1 John 3:6-9.

Notes

1. G. G. Findlay, "St Paul's First Epistle to the Corinthians," *The Expositor's Greek Testament,* Vol. 3 (Grand Rapids, Michigan: William B. Eerdmans Publishing Co., [n.d.]), p. 813.

2. Ibid., p. 814.

3. Ibid.

4. James Moffatt, *The First Epistle of Paul to the Corinthians* (New York: Harper and Brothers Pub., [n.d.]), p. 64.

5. Ibid.

6. Archibald Robertson and Alfred Plummer, "A Critical and Exegetical Commentary on the First Epistle of St. Paul to the Corinthians," *International Critical Commentary* (New York: Charles Scribner's Sons, 1911), p. 113.

7. Ibid., p. 114.

8. Ibid., p. 115.

9. A. T. Robertson, *Word Pictures in the New Testament* (Nashville, Tennessee: Sunday School Board of the SBC, 1931), p. 119.

10. F. F. Bruce, "I and II Corinthians," *New Century Bible* (London: Oliphants, 1971), p. 61.

11. Robertson, p. 119.

12. Leon Morris, *Tyndale: New Testament Commentaries, The First Epistle of Paul to the Corinthians* (Grand Rapids, Michigan: William B. Eerdmans Publishing Co., 1958), p. 97.

13. Ibid., p. 97.

14. Charles Hodge, *An Exposition of the First Epistle to the Corinthians* (Grand Rapids, Michigan: William B. Eerdmans Publishing Co., 1956), p. 98.

15. Robertson and Plummer, p. 118.

16. Moffatt, p. 66.

17. Bruce, p. 62.

18. Ibid.

19. Morris, p. 99.

20. Ibid.

21. Findlay, p. 819.

22. Ibid., p. 810.

23. Robertson, p. 121.

24. Ibid., p. 122.

25. Morris, p. 102.

26. Moffatt, p. 72 *ff.*

27. Robertson and Plummer, p. 127.

CHAPTER 7

● 1-2   Paul began his answers to the questions raised by the Corinthians in their letter to him with an elliptical expression, "concerning the things of which you wrote," which is common in the papyri and which would have been readily understood by the Corinthians. Whoever wrote the letter, and whether it was written in the name of the whole church, the letter likely contained questions that the church as a whole wanted answered concerning celibacy and marriage. Apparently the first question had to do with a single life—is it right or wrong? Paul immediately replied that there is nothing wrong about a single life, rather it is good.

For one to understand Paul's position on celibacy and marriage as outlined in this chapter, it is necessary for the reader to keep "a proper perspective."[1] Some of the heretics obviously wanted to forbid marriage (1 Tim. 4:3). But such a position violates the divine purpose of God in the creation of man and woman (Gen. 2:18). Notice in verse 1 that Paul used the word "for a man" rather than "for a husband." There seems to be no disposition in his words to dissuade marriage; he was merely "contending that celibacy may be good" under certain conditions.[2] He apparently leaned toward the single life here at least for himself. And while some orthodox Jews looked upon marriage "as a duty" and opposed celibacy, Rabbi ben Azaï is quoted as saying, " 'Why should I marry? . . . I am in love with the law. Let others see to the prolongation of the human race' (Renan, p. 397)."[3] Certainly in the light of "the variety and extent of profligacy"[4] among the Corinthians (2 Cor. 12:21), marriage was to be desired instead of heathen libertinism and polygamy that had been common practice among the Jews.

● 3-4   Paul maintained "a careful balancing of the terms relating to man and wife, bringing out the equality of the Christian law."[5] Paul made it clear that there are normal conjugal rites, and these should not give way to unnatural abstention from sexual intercourse on the part of both husband and wife. In marriage, each partner "relinquishes the exclusive right to his or her own body and gives the other a claim to it."[6]

● 5-6   If the abstinence is "one-sided," it can amount to disagreement. Hence, Paul's words "do not deprive each other." The important thing is for the husband and wife to have complete understanding, thereby obviating any tension that may exist due to a "one-sided" position on abstinence. The word *concession* reflects the recognition of normal marital relations. Paul's own personal relationship to marriage is unknown. There is no certainty as to whether he had been married. One thing is obvious: his magnificent obsession in life was to know Christ, become Christlike in his life-style, share in Christ's sufferings, and attain unto the resurrection of the dead (Phil. 3:7-14).

● 7   All of Paul's personal references to his present condition, as to marriage, indicate that he was not married. Any final determination, however, must be reckoned with Acts 26:10. At any rate, if he had been married, he was now a widower. If Acts 26:10 indicates that Paul was a member of the Sanhedrin, he would have been married "at that time."[7]

● 8   Paul's reference to "the unmarried" (masculine plural) possibly refers to men only inasmuch as he mentioned virgins and widows later.

● 9-10   Paul drew no firm lines of favor here whether of celibacy or marriage. He did make clear his own preference and said that there is to be no reproach for the non-continent (v. 7) since it is not to be regarded as a virtue to be achieved by imitation.[8] He did make it clear that it is better to marry than to continue to burn with sexual desire. In verse 10 he spoke of divorce in absolute terms that came from the Lord: "the wife is not to be separated from her husband." Paul did not deal with the words of Jesus concerning divorce which by implication make allowance for remarriage of the innocent party (Matt. 19:3-12).

● 11   In Matthew 19:9, it appears that Jesus, by implication, made allowance for remarriage of the innocent party, but Paul did not do so here. Paul flatly left no options for the woman who is separated from her husband other than to be reconciled to him or remain in an unmarried state. He did not deal at all with circumstances that may have been the factors that led to the separation.

● 12   In dealing with the matter of a husband and wife where one had become a Christian while the other remained an unbeliever, Paul first acknowledged that he had no direct command from the Lord on it but declared that there is to be no separation in such a case. According to Roman and Greek law, a wife could divorce her husband.[9] Whether the Corinthians had raised this particular question in their letter to Paul is not known. But it is a grave question, one that has to be faced all too often by youth approaching the marriage altar today. Certainly when a believer is united in marriage to an unbeliever, the two are "unequally" yoked (2 Cor. 6:14).

● 13-14   In verse 14, Paul gave the reason for the course that a husband is to follow when his wife is an unbeliever and likewise the course of the wife who has an unbelieving husband. The "marriage relation is sanctified so that there is no need of a divorce. If either husband or wife is a believer and the other agrees to remain, the marriage is holy and need not be set aside."[10] Paul's words are clear and unmistakable and hardly call for an effort at interpretation. Paul carried the idea of sanctification further and related it to the children born to the believing and unbelieving mate. The children of such a "mixed" marriage are not to be regarded as illegitimate or unclean. This particular passage "has played no small part in Christian jurisprudence, and in the doctrine of Infant Baptism."[11] But there is really nothing in the passage to assume the baptism of a child with a Christian parent. That idea, it appears, did not enter Paul's thoughts. In truth, it would be difficult to find any light thrown on the matter of infant baptism by this particular passage.

● 15-16   The matter of securing a divorce on the part of the pagan partner is no problem. He can have the divorce if he wants it. In that event, is the Christian partner free to remarry? Both Luther and Conzelmann take the affirmative in the matter, but Paul did not make the matter clear. Apparently Paul did not consider the possibility of reconciliation in such a case. (See v. 17.)

● 17-20   The whole point of verses 17-20 is to emphasize the liberation of the individual in Christ, so far as ritualistic practices are concerned. God takes the believer just as he is, whether Jew or Gentile, and requires of him no external ritual to become a child of God. "The Jew has not to alter the 'standing' in which God encounters him, in order to do justice to grace as grace, and the same applies to the Gentile. In the church our natural standing no longer counts; it is abrogated 'in Christ.' It has no further influence on salvation, neither positive nor negative."[12] In Christ there is perfect freedom. Grace makes this possible, for it is by grace the believer comes into sonship. "It is the gift of God: not of works" (Eph. 2:8-9, KJV). "Paul is not advocating a principle of unity in church order. He is indeed attacking precisely the kind of schematization which postulates a specific mode of *klēsis,* 'calling.'"[13]

● 21-24   The dialectic in verses 21-24 which "constitute a self-contained section"[14] may, on first glance, appear incongruous. At the heart of the matter is the fact that, when a person is in Christ, he belongs to the Lord and has lasting freedom not only from the power of sin and death but also in the eschatological sense.[15] This freedom "in Christ" is unaffected by one's civil status, whether that of freedman or slave. "A slave 'called in the Lord' is in relation to Christ a freedman: *apeleutheros,* like *libertus,* is a relative term, used *c. gen.* of the emancipator. Although in his secular condition he remains a slave, in his spiritual condition he has been set free,"[16] free from sin bondage. "The social slave, who has been set free by Christ, and the social freeman, who has become enslaved to Christ, have alike been bought by God, and are now His property. In one sense Christ's death was an act of emancipation, it set free from the thraldom of sin; in another sense it was a change of ownership."[17] Verse 24 merely repeats verses 17 and 20. Conzelmann regards *para* (v. 24) as the equivalent of *enōpion,* "before the face of God." I prefer the reading "with God" since that appears to convey more nearly the root idea of the preposition *para.* Paul made a point of the fact that all who are in Christ are "bought with a price." The same phrase was used in 6:20. (Present middle imperative of *ginomai* with the negative *mē.*) Paul made clear his opposition to the institution of human slavery as he did so forcefully in his Epistle to Philemon. Paul was proud to call himself Christ's slave. He, like the Gentile, was set free from the power of sin by Christ who gave his life on the cross as the ransom *(lutron).* Every Christian was originally a slave to sin and dead in sin (Eph. 2:1*ff.*). But all of the family of God have been set free in Christ and henceforth belong to him.

● 25-26   "This language, so far from being a disclaimer of inspiration, is . . . in no sense a command, but an inspired opinion."[18] Paul's use of the word *enestōsan* (second perfect active of *enistēmi*) means "present" or "at hand." Paul may have had in mind here the second coming of Jesus, for had not Jesus himself referred to the calamities that would precede his coming (Matt. 24:8 *ff.*)? Certainly the eschatological outlook is present in his words. Conzelmann notes the word might be rendered "imminent." In other words, it is impending.

● 27   In verse 27 Paul seemed to "suddenly pass over to the man" to illustrate his point still further. "In this way he can set out from the principle 'each in his own calling,' and now, via the unmarried man, apply this principle to the virgins (v. 28)."[19]

● 28   Paul stated plainly that his words here consist not of a command, but his own advice. Those who would change their life-style, biblically, however, as to marriage, are guilty of no sin (v. 28). But dark days lie ahead in view of the imminent distress. And those who are married are not to seek a separation.

● 29-31   These verses bring "a broad eschatological interpretation of conduct in the world, in which the sequence of thought is plain."[20] Paul did not advise the Corinthians "to withdraw into the safe and unrestricted realms of the inner life, but to maintain freedom in the midst of involvement."[21] The closing words of verse 31 (the present form of this world is passing away) reflect the same eschatological interpretation found in the verses that have gone before. Of course, Paul was speaking figuratively, for the word *schēma* (form or shape) is taken by some to mean "not the form, but the essence"; but we also know that even the "shape" of the earth is changing constantly under the impact of nuclear fission and the ecological blunders of mankind. No one knows what may happen in near and faraway places of the world where the natural oil and gas and coal have been removed, when earthquakes take over in a measure never known before.

● 32-34   These verses provide more than a passing insight into the shepherd heart of the apostle. This type of pastoral concern is readily understood by his "view of the approaching hardships," and his aim "to bring his readers even now to freedom from care."[22] A marriage partner has a twofold responsibility—responsibility to his or her partner and responsibility to God. Paul took the view that things could get out of balance in the marriage relation so that the primal concern of the married one may be that of pleasing the mate rather than in doing that which is pleasing to God. But who is able to demonstrate this principle universally?

What Paul sought for the Corinthians was not complete freedom from all the cares of life, for such could hardly be possible. He was pleading for less anxiety on the part of the relationship of those in marriage concerning the world about them—material things, even the regard for the mate—and more loving concern for the cause of Christ in the world. There can be no place for the split personality with regard to one's relationship to home and to God, no such dichotomy. The two areas of concern do not need to be subjected to a process of dividing where each is mutually exclusive or contradictory to the other. But that is exactly what has happened, all too often, to contemporary people in the increasingly complex culture of which they are a part.

● 36-38   There is a hot dispute over verses 36-38. The traditional view is that the virgin is the father's daughter (his own daughter). (See *gamizōn* in verse 38.) In that case, the matter of propriety is involved and the *patria potestas* (father power). And of course, according to ancient Roman law, the father could do what he wished with regard to any of his children. Linguistically more than one root might be taken by the translator, but more than one root would hardly be "right" in this case. And the idea of applying the interpretation of "spiritual betrothals may present less linguistic difficulties here." There are inherent grounds for rejection of such a view, as Conzelmann notes. "When applied to real betrothals, everything is explained without difficulty as far as the content is concerned. *Gamizein* is then the equivalent of *gamein*, 'to marry.'"[23] To state the problem simply, Paul was obviously merely trying to answer the question which the Corinthians had asked him concerning a father's duty toward his daughter when she became old enough to marry. "Paul has discussed the problem of marriage for virgins on the grounds of expediency. Now he faces the question where the daughter wishes to marry and there is no serious objection to it. The father is advised to consent."[24] "'My marriage is my father's care; it is not for me to decide about that' (Hermione in Euripides' *Andromache*, 987)."[25]

● 39-40   In verses 39-40, Paul dealt with the matter of widows. In verse 39, which comes as "a sort of addendum," Paul dealt with the remarriage of widows. Later Paul discussed the same theme in 1 Timothy

5:9-13. But here the apostle left it up to the widow as to whether she will be married again, but "only in the Lord" (that is, to a Christian and not to an unbeliever) as every marriage ought to be. But Paul boldly declared that the widow will be happier if she does not remarry. The word *happier* (*makariōtera*) is a comparative of *makarios* which is used repeatedly in the Beatitudes (Matt. 5:3 *ff.*). As he concluded his discussion of the "tangled problem of marriage," Paul indicated that his judgment was inspired because he had "the spirit of God." Paul did his duty without wincing but was conscious of the fact that each person, in the end, in the light of the teachings of the Scriptures concerning marriage, must act for himself in his final decision.

Notes

1. A. T. Robertson, *Word Pictures in the New Testament* (Nashville, Tennessee: Sunday School Board of the SBC, 1931), p. 124.
2. Archibald Robertson and Alfred Plummer, "A Critical and Exegetical Commentary on the First Epistle of St. Paul to the Corinthians," *International Critical Commentary* (New York: Charles Scribner's Sons, 1911), p. 132.
3. Ibid.
4. G. G. Findlay, "St. Paul's First Epistle to the Corinthians," *The Expositor's Greek Testament*, Vol. 3 (Grand Rapids, Michigan: William B. Eerdmans Publishing Co., [n.d.]), p. 822.
5. Ibid., p. 823.
6. F. F. Bruce, "I and II Corinthians," *New Century Bible* (London: Oliphants, 1971), p. 67.
7. Robertson, p. 125.
8. Hans Conzelmann, James W. Leitch, trans., *A Commentary on the First Epistle to the Corinthians*, *Hermeneia* Series (Philadelphia: Fortress Press, 1975), p. 120.
9. Bruce, p. 69.
10. Robertson, p. 128.
11. Findlay, p. 827.
12. Conzelmann, p. 126.
13. Ibid.
14. Ibid., p. 127.
15. Ibid.
16. Robertson and Plummer, p. 148.
17. Ibid., p. 149.
18. Robertson, p. 131.
19. Conzelmann, p. 132.
20. Ibid., p. 133.

21. Ibid.
22. Ibid., p. 134.
23. Ibid., p. 136.
24. Robertson, p. 135.
25. Ibid.

CHAPTER 8

● 1   In verses 1-13, Paul dealt with the matter of meat that had been offered as a sacrifice to idols. He began his argument (8:1-6) with a discussion of the function of love in its relation to the knowledge of God. Mere knowledge does not tend, in itself, to *build up* the Christian community. This is the function of love. After all, there are many stages of knowledge—some of the Corinthians were more enlightened than others, but that yet was not all that was required. Only love can build the bridge and provide the substance to stand upon in the Christian community. The problem of meat offered to idols was dealt with in the Jerusalem conference (Acts 15:29; 21:25), but it was a continuing problem. "Knowledge is a good thing in its way, but it needs to be under the guidance of a higher principle,"[1] and that principle is love. Otherwise, mere knowledge might lead one "to despise the poor creature who does *not* know what we know and to use the liberty our knowledge gives us in a way to do him infinite harm. Something else than a knowledge like this is wanted in order to 'build up' the Church."[2]

● 2-3   In verse 2, Paul dealt a devastating blow to mere knowledge. "The really learned man knows his ignorance of what lies beyond. Shallow knowledge is like the depth of the mud hole, not of the crystal spring."[3] Paul here distinguished "between knowledge in the proper sense and the improper. Knowledge is of no value in itself. It is mistaken when it forms a conception of its 'object' and imagines it has thereby acquired the correct attitude towards this object."[4]

"No one is acquainted with God who does not love him (I John 4:8). God sets the seal of his favour on the one who loves him."[5] In the words of G. G. Findlay, "Paul would ascribe nothing to human acquisition; religion is a bestowment, not an achievement; our love or knowledge is the reflex of the divine love and knowledge directed toward us."[6]

● 4   Paul did not mean to dispute the existence of idols—they were literally everywhere. He was saying that the presence of an idol, an image of this so-called God, amounts to nothing in representing God in the world. True, it may have meaning for the person who worships the idol, but in value it is worthless because it brings the worshiper no closer to the living God. Genuine faith consists "in the confession of the true God—a confession whose result is not to deny the 'so-called' gods, but to overthrow them."[7]

● 5   In his concessive clause in which he assumed, for argument's sake, the presence of the so-called gods, Paul did not admit their existence. Rather he "denied the exact actual existence of these so-called gods and held that those who worshipped idols (non-entities) in reality worshipped demons or evil spirits, agents of Satan (I Cor. 10:19-21)."[8] Hence, Paul "indicates *his* criticism, not only of pagan belief in the gods, but of the gods themselves, first of all by using the word *legomenoi,* 'so-called.'"[9] See Ephesians 2:11 where Paul used the same word.

● 6   Paul made clear his concept of creation in its relationship to God the Father and Christ the Son. Herein lies both the source of the universe *(ex)* and the goal of believers, namely, God *(eis auton)*. Even as God is presented as "the intermediate agent in creation" in Colossians 1:15-20, here Paul "makes clear that it is not a question of metaphysical or ontological arguments, but of anthropological judgments which as such include the adopting of an attitude: the gods *become* gods by being believed in, *{by the pagans}* and faith in the *one* God and the *one* Lord creates freedom no longer to recognize these powers."[10]

● 7-8   Verse 7 refers to verse 1 and "corrects the concession made there to the Corinthian thesis. The formal contradiction which thereby arises is not one of content: Paul still grants even now that his opponents have objective knowledge, but not that they have understanding in the proper sense."[11] The point of issue is that of the strong and the weak conscience. Since some people have weak consciences, there is "a situation which neither the strong nor the weak can ignore."[12] "Even if unenlightened, one must act according to his conscience, a sensitive gauge to one's spiritual condition. Knowledge breaks down as a guide with the weak or unenlightened conscience."[13] Conzelmann makes a fine point in saying,

"No work, not even freedom practiced as a work, makes us acceptable before God. The neutrality of food does *not* mean neutrality of *conduct*."[14]

● 9   As Paul said elsewhere, we are all members one of another, and each one is responsible for his conduct in relation to his weaker brother. "The enlightened must consider the welfare of the unenlightened, else he does not have love."[15] In Paul's use of the word *proskomma*, "hindrance," "offense," he brought the issue down to earth in a way that all should understand. Indeed, "the figurative element is hardly felt any more."[16]

● 10-12   In verse 10, Paul pointed out the misuse of the freedom in the way it is exercised by people who are strong in the faith. Not only was it common for persons to participate in meals in idol temples but also it was regarded as "a matter of family and social duty."[17] The emphasis is not on visiting in the temple restaurants but upon the conduct of the strong Christians which may mislead weak Christians for by compliance the idols were honored.[18] Enlightened Christians simply could not afford to eat in an idol's temple for such conduct merely emboldens weak Christians (who are not yet free from superstition) "to go on and do what [they] still [believe] to be wrong, to eat things sacrificed to idols."[19] There is such a thing as "daredevil knowledge."[20] And this is what such conduct amounts to. The selfish pride and vaunted knowledge of the strong one play havoc with the conscience of the weaker brother and may wreck the weak one. Even so, in sinning against the weak Christians, the stronger ones sin against Christ. Such conduct "affects Christ himself."[21] It is just as simple as that. Paul used *smite (tuptontes),* an old word meaning "to smite with fist, staff, whip."[22] The conscience being sensitive, such conduct on the part of the believer is like "a slap in the face" to the weak brother or sister. Paul's words here remind us of Jesus' words to Saul on the Damascus road. In persecuting the disciples of Christ, Saul persecuted Christ himself.

● 13   Paul clenched his argument in the preceding verses by setting forth his own resolve which is clear to all. "Wherefore, if food causes my brother to sin, I will in no wise eat meat forever so that I will not cause my brother to sin." "The strong man's renunciation, too, is an act of freedom, since it recognizes his brother to be one freed by Christ."[23] Paul's use of the word *meat* here means, of course, meat "offered to idols." In laying down his principle of love (v. 2), as it relates to the sacrificial meats of idols, Paul made it clear that he "had rather be a vegetarian than to lead his weak brother to do what he considered sin. There are many questions of casuistry today that can only be handled wisely by Paul's ideal of love."[24]

Notes

1. J. J. Lias, "The First Epistle to the Corinthians," *Cambridge Greek Testament for Schools and Colleges* (Cambridge at the University Press, 1886), p. 95.
2. Ibid.
3. A. T. Robertson, *Word Pictures in the New Testament* (Nashville, Tennessee: Sunday School Board of the SBC, 1931), p. 138.
4. Hans Conzelmann, James W. Leitch, trans., *A Commentary on the First Epistle to the Corinthians, Hermeneia* Series (Philadelphia: Fortress Press, 1975), p. 141.
5. Robertson, p. 138.
6. G. G. Findlay, "St. Paul's First Epistle to the Corinthians," *The Expositor's Greek Testament*, Vol. 3 (Grand Rapids, Michigan: William B. Eerdmans Publishing Co., [n.d.]), p. 840.
7. Conzelmann, p. 142.
8. Robertson, p. 139.
9. Conzelmann, p. 143.
10. Ibid., p. 145.
11. Ibid., p. 146.
12. Ibid., p. 147.
13. Robertson, p. 139.
14. Conzelmann, p. 148.
15. Robertson, p. 140.
16. Conzelmann, p. 148.
17. Ibid.
18. Ibid., p. 149.
19. Robertson, p. 140 *ff.*
20. Ibid.
21. Conzelmann, p. 149.
22. Robertson, p. 141.
23. Conzelmann, p. 149-150.
24. Robertson, p. 141.

CHAPTER 9

● 1-3   In chapter 9, Paul "introduces a new theme," namely, his apostleship.[1] The freedom of which he spoke is not the same kind of freedom that he referred to in chapter 8. It was a freedom that involved the character of his apostleship. Paul had in mind not the freedom of other followers of Christ but his own freedom from his own person.[2] The "wandering Cynic preachers" in Corinth had freedom, but apparently there were those who wanted to deny Paul such freedom. Paul based his claim on his vision of Christ (1 Cor. 15:6 *ff.*; Gal. 1:12 *ff.*). To this basis, however, he added an argument *ad hominem*. Certainly he had the right to claim the Corinthian church as "his work." To deny this would be to deny their own viable character as a body of believers. Paul did not define who the "others" were who would discredit his apostleship, for the Corinthians knew who they were—obviously some of the Judaizers. And by limiting the defense of his apostleship to the work in Corinth, he in no wise renounced "his title for the areas outside the territory of his own mission."[3] Paul's severe "critics" (Greek *anakrinousin*) may have been "outside the Corinthian community," as verse 3 might suggest. But the attacks, whatever the source, were real.

● 4-6   Paul continued to lambaste his opponents with rhetorical questions. The freedom (v. 1) in question "is more precisely defined as a *right*."[4] In verse 3, he harked back to what may appear to be the theme of chapter 8, but not really. In chapter 8 the freedom has to do with "meat sacrificed to idols." But here the question has to do with food in general, and Paul's defense springs from the fact that "his conduct, his renunciation of apostolic rights, had been misinterpreted and used as an argument against him."[5] Hence, Paul went to the root of the matter and dealt with the theological principles that lay back of his action. The basis of Paul's renunciation lay "in the nature of *his* office and is therefore a positive presentation of it, that is to say, an argument *for* Paul."[6] Incidentally, the words *adelphēn gunaika* may well be translated "sister-wife" rather than "a sister *as* a wife." The latter translation may raise a question in the minds of some. The point of issue is the matter of taking a wife along "at the expense of the community." Of course there is no proof that *all* the apostles and brothers of Jesus were *married*. Just why Paul referred to "the brothers of the Lord" and what their relationship to other missionaries was is left unanswered. Likewise, Paul threw no light on the mission of Cephas in regard to the other missionaries. Paul and Barnabas both had a right to work or not to work (v. 6). That is the root of the matter that Paul had in mind. He made it clear that the position that he and Barnabas took with regard to working with their own hands was a subjective matter "freely exercised." "Apparently it has been cast in his teeth that his renunciation shows he has after all a bad conscience in claiming to be an apostle,"[7] as though by supporting himself by gainful employment he might salve that "bad conscience." But this was not the case at all. Paul was free to do as he wished, and he wanted all to get the message clearly.

● 7   The meaning of Paul's words is as clear as the tone of a bell on a frosty morning. In the form of questions, he presented the obvious: "(a) military service at one's own expense; (b) the farmer; (c) the shepherd."[8] See 2 Timothy 2:3-6 for "a similar combination of examples."

● 8-10   Paul went beyond the *ad hominem* approach which some may regard as merely "secular, *human arguments*,"[9] to quote from the Old Testament (Deut. 25:4) in support of his premise, thereby undergirding the purely rational argument with Scripture proof. It is interesting to note that a hieroglyphic inscription at Eileithyas reads, as Robertson points out,

> Thresh ye yourselves, O oxen,
> Measures of grain for yourselves,
> Measures of grain for your masters.[10]

"He that ploughs [v. 10] hardly refers to the ox at the plough as he that threshes does. The point is that all the workers (beast or man) share in the fruit of the toil."[11]

• 11   The copula *estin* is to be supplied as Paul brought his argument to a conclusion in presenting the contrast between "spiritual benefits" *(ta pneumatika)* and material benefits *(ta sarkika*—"things of the flesh," or "earthly goods").[12] People do not live "by bread alone" (Matt. 4:4, KJV), but bread is a part of "the necessities of life" *(biōtika)*.

• 12   Paul set forth "an eloquent example for all modern men"[13] in the matter of "personal rights and liberties." Paul might have insisted on his use of such privileges, but he declined to do so and by his "declaration of free renunciation," set forth "an impressive contrast" to the behavior of some of the Corinthians. His reason for choosing the course he took was simple and clear, namely, that he would not cause a "hindrance to the gospel of Christ."

• 13-14   Paul continued to pile up his arguments by introducing "a rule from the laws of worship." His words "do you not know" indicate that what he was talking about was known already as a rule which held not only among the Jews but was found also in the "basic stock of cultic regulations in general."[14] The word *thusiastērion* is found in the LXX "in the narrower sense to mean the altar of burnt offerings."[15] The whole point of Paul's words here is that the preacher of the gospel of Christ is worthy of his hire, and those who give their lives to proclaiming the gospel should be cared for, adequately, by those to whom they minister. In the words of Robertson, Paul "has made his argument for the minister's salary complete for all time."[16]

• 15   From the standpoint of syntax, this verse is a very tangled affair. Surely "the intensity of Paul's feelings" comes out in this verse.[17] Entitled as he was to "privileges and rights to a salary," he refused to make use of those rights. Neither was he "now hinting for a change on their part towards him in the matter, 'in my case' *(en emoi)*."[18] After his words "it is better for me to die than," Paul abruptly "changes the construction by a violent anacoluthon"[19] (that is, he failed to follow the preceding thought). Vigorously he asserted his spirit of independence and his determination not to rely upon the Corinthians for help. But he wanted nothing to happen that might destroy the grounds of his glorying, his exultation in the Lord. How magnificent! If Paul appeared to be boasting, let him continue to boast, for "his boast lies precisely in his renunciation"[20] of the material advantages that might have come to him had he chosen to use them. Here one comes to the heart of a great aspect of "the theology of the cross."

● 16   Paul made it clear that he deserved no credit for his mission, for he was called by Christ who laid upon him the great necessity to preach the gospel (Acts 9:6,15; Rom. 1:14; Gal. 1:15 *ff*.). Because he was "called," he regarded himself as being forever "under constraint *(anagkē)*." In verse 17, Paul dealt with the "practical consequence" of the "constraint" *(anagkē)* that lay upon him. His real reward lay in the fact that his labor for Christ was voluntary. No other kind of Christian witness deserves reward. Paul's statement "has its obvious auxiliary function in between vv 16 and 18. 'If willingly' is simply a foil for the real case of Paul, for the fact that he 'unwillingly' has a charge of stewardship laid upon him."[21]

● 17   One thing is clear here: Paul had a call from God (not from self), answered it, and performed his service as he was called to do by God. His reward therefore came in the fulfillment of the stewardship with which he was entrusted (see v. 18).[22]

● 18   Paul's great reward came to him in the consciousness that he was able not only to proclaim the good news to all people but also in doing so to set forth the gospel free of charge. What greater reward could any preacher of the gospel want on earth?

● 19   Of this verse Findlay says, "The real aim of this long discussion of ministerial *exousia* comes into view; the Ap. shows himself to the Cor. as *an example of superior privilege held upon trust for the community, of liberty asserted with a view to self-abnegation*."[23] As Conzelmann notes, his action in making himself a slave "is in harmony with the fact that his office is determined by the cross."[24]

● 20   Paul faced a difficult problem, being a Jew from a strictly Jewish background, not being a Gentile. Without compromising his character and mission as an apostle, he had to relate to both groups; perhaps he had the greatest difficulty in relating to the Gentiles. Paul's words concerning his behavior toward the Jews "provides a foil for his observation that in all this he remains free, and at the same time paves the way for the statement on his behavior toward those 'outside the Law.'"[25]

● 21   Notice that Paul merely said, "those without the law." He could have said "to the Greeks." Paul used the genitive case (specifying case) of

Theou and *Christou*. Gould points out that Paul's position may be summarized in these three points: "(1) Freedom from all law as a means of justification. (Rom. 3:20.) (2) Freedom from the Jewish law as a past dispensation, superseded by the gospel. (3) Obligation, in no way annulled, to keep the law of Christ as rule of conduct, which is involved in the idea of being a follower (literally, *imitator*) of Christ."[26]

● 22   Paul reached "the climax in his plea for the principle of love on the part of the enlightened for the benefit of the unenlightened."[27] By exercising the principle of "adaptation," Paul sought to gain a better rapport with all who are without Christ (Acts 16:3). In all this, however, Paul failed to compromise in "matters of principle." See Galatians 2:5.

● 23   Some may sense the sound of "a utilitarian"[28] in this verse, but Paul's words in no way detract from his understanding of and premise concerning salvation. Paul had an obsession to share the gospel with others, and that is where the emphasis lies. He wanted nothing of God's grace for himself that he would not have others to enjoy equally.

● 24-27   These verses fit well into the larger context though the section "is unified in style and content and stands out from its context."[29] Paul's use of sport metaphors should be clear to all. But his analogy may be a bit confusing in that among those who contend in the stadium only one attained the goal, the prize. The followers of Christ, of course, are to strive with all the energy of the runner in the arena, but all of them are to gain the prize bound up in their salvation at the last day. The prize for which the Christian strives "is the future glory of the Messianic kingdom."[30] Everything relating to Paul's body *(sōma)* "is fully and emphatically subordinated to his office."[31] Paul's metaphor of the crowns—the perishable and imperishable—was fitting. The crown of the runners in the arena *(stephanos)* was made of palm branches, and therefore was perishable. Jesus' crown was made of "thorns" (Matt. 27:29; Mark 15:17), but the crown of the Christian is imperishable. For the perishable *(phtharton)* gives way to the imperishable *(aphtharsian)* at the last day (1 Cor. 15:54). Paul did not imply here that he had a fear of final rejection; rather, his confidence was serene (2 Tim. 4:7). On the other hand, his words nowhere in his epistles inspire "smug complacency."

Notes

1. Hans Conzelmann, James W. Leitch, trans., *A Commentary on the First Epistle to the Corinthians, Hermeneia* Series (Philadelphia: Fortress Press, 1975), p. 151.
2. Ibid.
3. Ibid., p. 152.
4. Ibid., p. 153.
5. Ibid.
6. Ibid.
7. Ibid., p. 154.
8. Ibid.
9. James Moffatt, *The First Epistle of Paul to the Corinthians* (New York: Harper and Brothers Pub., [n.d.]), p. 116.
10. A. T. Robertson, *Word Pictures in the New Testament* (Nashville, Tennessee: Sunday School Board of the SBC, 1931), p. 144.
11. Ibid., p. 145.
12. Conzelmann, p. 155.
13. Robertson, p. 145.
14. Conzelmann, p. 157.
15. Ibid.
16. Robertson, p. 146.
17. Ibid.
18. Ibid.
19. Ibid.
20. Conzelmann, p. 157.
21. Ibid., p. 158.
22. Personal correspondence with Dr. John B. Polhill.
23. G. G. Findlay, "St. Paul's First Epistle to the Corinthians," *The Expositor's Greek Testament,* Vol. 3 (Grand Rapids, Michigan: William B. Eerdmans Publishing Co., [n.d.]), p. 853.
24. Conzelmann, p. 160.
25. Ibid., p. 161.
26. E. P. Gould, "Commentary on the Epistles to the Corinthians," *An American Commentary on the New Testament,* Vol. 5 (Philadelphia: American Baptist Publication Society, 1887), p. 81.
27. Robertson, p. 147.
28. Conzelmann, p. 161.
29. Ibid.
30. Gould, p. 82.
31. Gerhard Kittel, *Theological Dictionary of the New Testament,* Vol. 2 (Grand Rapids, Michigan: William B. Eerdmans Publishing Co., 1981), p. 28.

CHAPTER 10

● 1   Verses 1-10 amount to a "self-contained unit" which relates to the biblical narrative of the Exodus of the children of Israel. In rapid succession Paul recalled the various steps of their miraculous deliverance by the providential hands of God and then severely indicted them for their backsliding and sensate desire of evil—they who "sat down to eat and drink, and got up to play like children." Paul's use of the words *our fathers* linked the Corinthian church of the New Testament era with ancient Israel and delivered a withering indictment of Israel by means of the repeated uses of *pantes* (all). "*All* our fathers escaped by miracle from the house of bondage; *all* received the tokens of the Mosaic covenant; *all* participated under its forms in Christ; and yet most of them perished!"[1]

● 2   It is not clear in verse 2 just how far Paul intended to go in his typological interpretation with reference to baptism. Guided by the cloud that hovered over them and delivered by a dry path through the waters of the sea, Israel was baptized "unto Moses." As Robertson notes, "The picture is plain enough. The mystic cloud covered the people while the sea rose in walls on each side of them as they marched across. . . . The immersion was complete for all of them in the sea around them and the cloud over them. Moses was their leader then as Christ is now and so Paul uses *eis* concerning the relation of the Israelites to Moses as he does of our baptism in relation to Christ (Gal. 3:27)."[2]

● 3   Paul's language was highly figurative, and metaphorical, but the point in it all is obvious. The physical food they ate in the wilderness was supplied by God, as was the water they drank.

● 4   "In drinking from the smitten rock the Israelites 'were drinking' at the same time 'of a *spiritual* rock'—and that not supplying them once alone, but 'following' them throughout their history."[3] Paul's use of the imperfect tense *(epinon)* "shows their continual access to the supernatural source of supply."[4] Paul, in identifying the rock with Christ (v. 4), was obviously making a reference to the preexistent state of Christ before his incarnation. There was a rabbinical legend that "water actually followed the Israelites for forty years, in one form a fragment of rock fifteen feet high that followed the people and gushed out water."[5] Paul may have alluded to this legend and "gives it a spiritual turn as a type of Christ in allegorical fashion."[6] Being a scholar, Paul was thoroughly familiar with the rabbinical discourses on the Exodus, and he himself "made use of allegory on occasion (Gal. 4:24)."[7] He endeavored to impress upon the Corinthians that God is "the source" of the water which sustained the Israelites even as he is "the source of supply for us today." Jesus himself typified the manna in the wilderness when he called himself "the bread of life" (John 6:35, RSV).

● 5   Paul put it mildly in saying that the conduct of the Israelites during the wanderings was not well pleasing to God—obviously so when all of those above twenty years of age were "scattered on the ground," save Caleb and Joshua, and never were permitted to see or enter the Promised Land. Even Moses himself, though he saw the land from afar, was not allowed to enter the land.

● 6   The behavior of the Israelites became what Paul called "examples for us so that we should not be desirers of evil as they also desired."

● 7   Obviously some of the Corinthians had already begun to be idolaters, else Paul would not have said "and stop becoming idolaters." The old verb *to play like a child* is found nowhere else in the New Testament, though it is common in the Septuagint. It is quoted here from Exodus 32:6.

● 8   When Moses came down from Mount Sinai, he witnessed the idolatrous festival that was going on with the people dancing and singing around the golden calf (Ex. 32:18 *ff.*). Some Corinthians were already practicing fornication (1 Cor. 6:9; 7:2). It is but a step from idolatry to fornication, as the situation in Corinth proved where as many as a thousand prostitutes were kept at the temple for service as part of the worship of Aphrodite. Fornication, or sexual immorality, bluntly means any and all sex outside marriage. Adultery, in the Bible, refers to sex on the part of a married person with an individual other than husband or wife, as the case may be. Adultery in ancient Israel was regarded as a sin against a husband, that is when the woman was a man's wife. But Jesus rejected this double standard and applied the same standard to both men and women.

● 9   Westcott and Hort, as well as Robertson and others, have *ton Kurion* instead of *ton Christon* which appears to be supported by some of the best manuscripts. But this is a very small point, indeed, for comment since Paul used all three names—Jesus, Christ, Lord—to refer to one and the same person.

● 10   Evidently there were *murmurers* among the Corinthians just as there were among the Israelites (Num. 16:41 *ff.*) who perished by the destroying angel (Ex. 12:23). Paul's frequent references to the Old Testament indicate his thorough knowledge of Jewish history and his own background as a Jew. Mixed and varied as the metaphors employed by Paul are in these opening verses of chapter 10, the meaning of the message is unmistakable: remember the experiences of your ancestors and the wages of their sins and beware; lest by your own backsliding, you suffer a similar fate at the hands of God. After all, as Paul boldly declared in Romans 1:18, "For the wrath of God is revealed from heaven against all ungodliness and unrighteousness of men, who hinder the truth in unrighteousness." (ASV).

● 11   Paul affirmed the "paraenetic sense" of *tupos* in verse 6 and introduces the eschatological aspect.[8] Paul's use of the plural *ta telē (the ends)* merely gathered together the world-age with its limitation.[9] Paul obviously looked for the imminent return of the Lord but went no further with his apocalyptic ideas.

● 12   This verse amounts to a plain and unmistakable warning to all—to both the weak and the strong. The sharp warning falls not upon specific individuals so much as upon "the Corinthian position as a whole."

● 13   Paul did not need to qualify his words concerning temptation, for temptation was "already a reality in Corinth."[10] Paul did not discuss the type of temptation he had in mind but merely said it is "common to man" *(anthrōpinos)*. Whenever and in whatever manner temptation comes, Paul reminded the Corinthians that God is faithful. Notice that Paul used the future tense "will provide" *(poiēsei)*. God will be on hand at the needed moment, and believers know that he does help again and again. Some take

Paul's words to refer to "one eschatological act of salvation," but the sense appears to be otherwise. Conzelmann holds that we have here "a reference to the eschatological manifestation and liberation," and that Paul "does not say that God helps again and again. He is speaking of the one eschatological act of salvation." Nevertheless, the experience of believers would indicate that God does continue to help in the course of the believers' lives as they continue to "work out" their own salvation according to Paul's admonition in Philippians 2:12-13. Paul's words "he will not suffer . . . but will provide," do not reflect "tolerance of temptation on God's part,"[11] but rather the mercy of a loving God who ever responds to the cry of his children in an hour of need. The word *ekbasin* (the way out) means simply a way out "of any situation that arises."

● 14-15   Paul's thoughts at this point evidently refer to verse 7. There is no need for one to ponder the connection between the word *idolatry* here and the *eidōlothuta* (meat sacrificed to idols), for Paul simply dealt with the matter of shunning[12] idolatry whatever its character may be—whether of "meat sacrificed to idols" or otherwise. The appeal, of course, is to the conscience which is based on the ability to discern.

● 16   Here Paul introduced a new subject, the Lord's Supper. Using the word *fellowship (koinōnia),* he presented the supper as a *communion* "centring in Christ, as the Jewish festal rites centred in 'the altar.'"[13] Findlay goes on to say, "Such fellowship involves (1) *the ground of communion,* the sacred object celebrated in common; (2) *the association established amongst the celebrants,* separating them from all others: 'The word *communion* denotes the fellowship of persons with persons in one and the same object.'"[14] Findlay calls *eulogias* attributive genitive (as cup of salvation in Ps. 116:13) whereas Robertson[15] takes the word to be objective genitive. The literal idea of the use of the word, however, implies "a participation in . . . the blood of Christ."[16] The mention of the cup first by Paul, rather than the bread, poses no problem as to sequence. Among the pagan cults, of course, there was a sacral meal which was supposed to establish "communion with the god of the cult."[17] Paul was thoroughly familiar with all of the pagan rites, and in verse 17 provided a further commentary on the subject.

● 17   Paul here continued to develop the fellowship *(koinōnia)* idea of verse 16, "showing how vital to the Church is the fellowship of the Lord's

Table, that was being violated by attendance at idol-feasts."[18] Paul obviously had in mind "the mystical spiritual body of Christ as in 12:12f., the spiritual kingdom or church of which Christ is head (Col. 1:18; Eph. 5:23)."[19] In view of the conditions that prevailed in Corinth, it is easy to see how the observance of the Lord's Supper by the spiritual community should serve as a unifying principle for the body of Christ. "'As one loaf is made up of many grains, and one body is composed of many members, so the Church of Christ is joined together of many faithful ones, united in the bonds of charity,' Augustine."[20]

● 18   Here Paul referred to the practice of Israel in the communal meal at the time of sacrifice and the way it constituted a "fellowship in the sacrifice," while recognizing at the same time "the altar as their common altar and mutually pledging themselves to its service."[21]

● 19-20   In these verses Paul's thoughts "tumble over each other."[22] His preceding words concerning the Lord's Supper were preparatory to his reference to the association of Christians with the idol feasts. After ruling out the reality of both the idol and the meat offered to the idol (v. 19), Paul nevertheless recognized "other terrible presences behind the image," namely, "demons." The pagan worshipers both recognized and worshiped at the idol feast. The word *daimonion,* from Euripides and Plato on, was used (and by the Stoics) in "a depreciatory sense."[23] In Homer it carried the idea of "the *uncanny,* the supernatural as an object of dread." The word was ready at hand for the translators of the Septuagint to render "epithets for heathen gods," while in Judaism the word was used extensively for *evil spirits* as well as to idols. The word offers the root of the word *demoniac* in the New Testament. The "partners" of the idol indicated "a kind of religious guild, brought into mystical union with their god through the sacrificial meal."[24] Paul's argument is a bit tangled here for, while declaring the idols and the meat offered to idols as meaningless, he gave presence to the premise that behind the idol is the demon. In other words, the Corinthian Christian was "not to participate in their cult, since otherwise we make them 'something'; and that is perverse. . . . Sacrifices would make the demons into gods, powers, and bring the participants into bondage to them."[25] Hence the presupposition of 8:5 is found here, namely, that "behind the gods there lurk demons."[26] One thing is clear: the Christian is at no time to share in the rituals of the pagan cult.

Especially is this true with reference to drinking and eating in meals.

• 21   Paul here stated a moral impossibility. One cannot carry water on both shoulders. He cannot be a participant of the Lord's table and at the table of demons. Paul used no definite article here, but the meaning is clear. The Lord's table is simply a reference to the Lord's Supper (1 Cor. 11:20). There are numerous allusions in the Old Testament "to use of the table in heathen idol feasts (Isa. 65:11; Jer. 7:18; Ezek. 16:18 f.; 23:41)."[27] Vincent notes that the altar of burnt-offering in Malachi 1:7 is called "the table of the Lord."[28] Paul was simply saying not to participate whatsoever in pagan cults, and especially so with reference to the idol meals.

• 22   Paul's words here simply intensify the "significance of the *heis theos—heis Kurios* confession, 'one God—one Lord.' It is exclusively valid; God watches jealously over his honor (Deut. 32:21)."[29] Paul's use of the word *stronger (ischuroteroi)* was in no sense an allusion to "the strong"; rather, the rhetorical question was "related to the Corinthian mentality as a whole."[30] See 4:8.

• 23   Verse 6:12 is quoted here without *moi*, "to me," and in shorter form. The meaning of the verse is the same. Paul was saying that though everything is permissible from the standpoint of the believer's freedom, "not everything is for the best."[31] In deciding what is "for the best," one must consider the matter in the light of its effect on others. Will it be the best for them? Paul's words "not everything builds up" (*ou panta oikodomei*) seem to refer to the church.

• 24   Dr. Robertson calls this "Paul's rule for social relations (I Cor. 13:5; Gal. 6:2; Rom 14:7; 15:2; Phil. 21ff.)."[32] In verse 33 Paul carried this idea still further and went on to call upon his followers to imitate him as he imitated Christ.

• 25-26   It was a common practice in Paul's day for one to buy meat in the market place, and much of the meat was from animals which had been sacrificed. After all, since only a small portion of the meat sacrificed to idols was consumed, the rest was sold in the meat market. For the Christians, there were no problems, for they had no need to be "overscrupulous." Paul upheld the liberty of the believer here just as in 8:4. So the Christian, from the standpoint of his own conscience, need ask no questions. Paul justified his position by quoting from Psalm 24:1. Everything belongs to the Lord, for he created the earth and every living thing. Psalm 24:1 was "a common form of grace before meals."[33]

● 27   Paul did not tell us the kind of banquet that he had in mind or the character of the social occasion, but the guidelines are the same. "Paul's ruling can be understood from the same presupposition as that on which Christians do not leave the world."[34] If a Christian is invited to the home of a pagan, "one is to act like a gentleman."[35]

● 28   Here we have a hypothetical case, following the case in verse 27, in which an informer reminds the guests that the meat is "sacrificial meat." What is the Christian to do? Paul answered the question with a blunt, "You are not to eat," for to do so would mean "participation in the cult, and thus an act both of confessing to the gods and also of establishing communion with them in the sense of vv 14-22."[36]

● 29   Paul carried the concept of conscience still further, and here the conscience of the Christian is in relation to the conscience of the pagan, as verse 28 suggests. J. J. Lias cuts the Gordian knot of Paul's involved words here: "But a man's right to think for himself is limited by the effect of his action on others. If his conduct be the means of inducing others less enlightened than himself to act contrary to their conscience, and to do what they believe to be wrong, he is doing harm by the exercise of a liberty which in any other case he undoubtedly enjoys."[37] So Paul's position rests on the same principle as that stated in 8:7-13.

● 30   Here is found further support of the premise of verse 28. In the words of Bengel, "The act of giving thanks sanctifies all the food, denies the authority of idols, asserts that of God."[38] The effect of such a spirit of thanksgiving "associates the act of eating with the worship of God, and so of course leaves no room for the supposition that it is an entanglement with idol-worship."[39]

● 31-32   The meaning of these verses should be clear to all. The criterion is that everything a Christian does is to be "unto the glory of God." In this way, one's Christian freedom operates under the constraint of its effect on both the believer and the unbeliever. In fact, there can be no true liberty without some measure of restraint. A Christian is never to become a stumbling block to others. "The meaning is, Do not by your actions lead others into sin."[40]

● 33   Paul rounded out his discussion by amplifying his position in verse 24. He held himself up as an example not, per se, "to his moral behavior in general, but to his church work."[41] Paul was no opportunist. He was not guilty of seeking his own advantage. His consuming passion was to fulfill, with devoted service, the mission to which he had been called in his apostleship in the unfailing hope "that they may be saved" (v. 33). Paul had no other desire than to spend and be spent in behalf of the salvation of others.

Notes

1. G. G. Findlay, "St. Paul's First Epistle to the Corinthians," *The Expositor's Greek Testament*, Vol. 3 (Grand Rapids, Michigan: William B. Eerdmans Publishing Co., [n.d.], p. 857.
2. A. T. Robertson, *Word Pictures in the New Testament* (Nashville, Tennessee: Sunday School Board of the SBC, 1931), p. 151.
3. Findlay, p. 858.
4. Robertson, p. 151.
5. Ibid.
6. Ibid., p. 152.
7. Ibid.
8. Hans Conzelmann, James W. Leitch, trans., *A Commentary on the First Epistle to the Corinthians*, *Hermeneia* Series (Philadelphia: Fortress Press, 1975), p. 168.
9. Ibid.
10. Ibid., p. 169.
11. Ibid.
12. Ibid., p. 170.
13. Findlay, p. 863.
14. Ibid.
15. Robertson, p. 154.
16. Ibid.
17. Conzelmann, p. 171.
18. Findlay, p. 864.
19. Robertson, p. 155.
20. J. J. Lias, "The First Epistle to the Corinthians," *Cambridge Greek Testament for Schools and Colleges* (Cambridge at the University Press, 1886), p. 116.
21. Findlay, p. 865.
22. Conzelmann, p. 172.
23. Findlay, p. 866.
24. Ibid.
25. Conzelmann, p. 173.
26. Ibid.
27. Robertson, p. 156.

28. Marvin R. Vincent, "The Epistles of Paul," *Word Studies in the New Testament,* Vol. 3 (Grand Rapids, Michigan: William B. Eerdmans Publishing Co., 1946), p. 244.

29. Conzelmann, p. 174.

30. Ibid.

31. Ibid., p. 176.

32. Robertson, p. 156.

33. Ibid., p. 157.

34. Conzelmann, p. 177.

35. Robertson, p. 157.

36. Conzelmann, p. 178.

37. Lias, p. 120.

38. E. P. Gould, "Commentary on the Epistles to the Corinthians," *An American Commentary on the New Testament,* Vol. 5 (Philadelphia: American Baptist Publication Society, 1887), p. 91 *ff.*

39. Ibid., p. 92.

40. Ibid.

41. Conzelmann, p. 179.

CHAPTER 11

In chapters 11—14, Paul turned to deal with internal problems in the Corinthian church, problems that had to do with the relationship and behavior of the members. The three main objects of concern relate to women and their unveiled heads in public worship, the Lord's table, and spiritual gifts.

● 1 Paul's summons for the Corinthians to imitate him is "grounded in his imitation of Christ."[1] Paul did not preach himself, for in his own person he could hardly claim exemplariness—nor can any person. He qualified the summons to imitation with the word *kathōs* (just as, in the manner as). He was an imitator of Christ.

● 2 Following his summons to imitation, Paul immediately plunged into the matter of the conduct of women at the hour of worship as it pertains to "the headgear." Paul apparently intended to lay a foundation for his subsequent discussion of the problem with a brief word of praise for the faithfulness of the Corinthians in holding fast to the instruction "just as" he had delivered them.

● 3 Paul now delved into a sticky subject—the interrelationships of man, woman, Christ, and God. Basically here, Paul had in mind not so much the domestic relationships, for whatever differences there are, they should be "abrogated" in Christ (Gal. 3:28), for Christ is the head of the body, the church.

● 4-6 Apparently Paul had in mind here the custom of the Jews, for it was required that a Jewess have her head covered when in public. Among the ancient Greeks the hairstyle and headgear were more varied. Certainly Paul's words in verse 5, "She is one and the same with her whose head is shaven," call up the matter of custom. Paul did not explain how or why a woman "dishonors her head" when praying or prophesying with the uncovered head. Paul was saying, "A man is not to have any covering on his head at divine worship (and he wears his hair short), while a woman is to have a covering (and she wears her hair long)."[2]

● 7   This verse is apparently a reference to Genesis 1:26, where man was created in God's image. "It is the moral likeness of God, not any bodily resemblance."[3] Man was created in the *image* and glory of God in that he is a sovereign individual with the ability to make choices in life, to know God and have fellowship with him, and to reflect in his words and deeds throughout his life the character and intent of God in all of life's interpersonal relations. In the case of the woman, Paul said that she "is the glory of a man." In reference to Genesis 1:26, however, you wonder if Paul would not have considered it to be generic which would have granted woman by creation similar attributes to those of man. Certainly in Jesus' teachings there is nothing to the contrary.

● 8-9   Here Paul turned back to the biblical narrative of the creation story in Genesis 2:22 in further support of his premise of the preceding verses. The Genesis record "gives the man *(anēr)* as the origin *(ek)* of the woman and the reason for *(dia)* the creation *(ektisthē,* first aorist passive of *ktizō,* old verb to found, to create, to form) of woman."[4] Whatever may have been going through the mind of Paul concerning the relationship of woman to man and to God, one thing is clear: there is neither male nor female in the body of Christ (Gal. 3:28; see 1 Cor. 12:13). However fixed the natural order of the woman-man relationship may be, when one is in Christ there is the "new creation"; and there are utterly no distinctions between male and female with respect to salvation and all of its privileges and all of its rewards.

● 10   Expositors continue to have engaging difficulties with this verse because of the word *authority (exousian)* and because of the angels *(dia tous aggelous).* Robertson takes the woman's veil on her head to be "the symbol of the authority that the man with the uncovered head has over her. It is, as we see it, more a sign of subjection . . . than of authority."[5] In general, the conjectures of the expositors concerning the "startling phrase" *dia tous aggelous* (because of the angels) may be overlooked. Paul was writing in the face of customs that were well known to all of the Corinthians—customs in both the Jewish and Greek aspects of the larger community. The heart of his premise, therefore, calls for conduct on the part of women that would be at all times acceptable to divine scrutiny—even that of angels "present in worship."[6] See 1 Corinthians 4:9; Psalm 138:1.

● 11-12   Here Paul made it clear that there is no distinction "in the Lord" as to sexes—they are equal in him. What might have been regarded as a thesis in cosmology, becomes a new thesis when the participants are brought into the realm of Christ. This transition of thought is marked by the word *plēn* which introduces the adversative clause and brings the preceding words of Paul into clear focus, "Each sex is incomplete without (*chōris,* apart from, with the ablative case) the other."[7] Paul cut the Gordian knot with the words "in the Lord" *(en Kuriōi),* for in him and his sphere of love all problems are solved.

In verse 11, Paul brought out clearly the mutual dependence of the sexes. After all, while the woman was created from the man, man comes into existence "through the woman," and neither is complete without the other. But there is no ground for an air of superiority on the part of either for both owe their origin to God, even as "all things *are* from God" (v. 12).

● 13   Paul laid some of the responsibility for the decision on the shoulders of the Corinthian Christians. After all, they had been rightfully instructed in the concepts of truth and duty according to the Scriptures. Should they not know what is "proper"? Consequently, he said to them, "Judge ye among yourselves," just as he had previously instructed them of their duty to rule in ordinary matters. Rather than take the problems to non-Christian courts for solution, the Corinthians were to assume some responsibility without having to be prompted by Paul.

There is a twofold appeal here: (1) to the Corinthians themselves, and (2) to social custom. "Judge ye among yourselves" means that the Corinthians were to be perceptive enough, in their discernment, to come to their own conclusions in matters like this in the light of their instruction. Paul did not go further into the matter of custom. He merely left the question for the Corinthians to answer in the light of their teaching.

● 14-15   Here again Paul's appeal was much the same as in verse 13 though he referred, in this instance, to nature. In his viewpoint relating to nature, Paul was merely pressing for a harmony that relates both to social custom and to nature. For those who are disposed to wrangle over Paul's words here, the dialogue could go on and on. "Here it means native sense of propriety (cf. Rom. 2:14) in addition to mere custom, but one that rests on the objective difference in the constitution of things."[8]

After all, the Corinthian church had received Christian instruction in such matters, and besides there was the support that should have come to them by the appeal to nature. Paul concluded his instructions concerning the problem by reminding the women (v. 15) that if they wear the hair long "it is a glory" to them, since the long hair was given to them "as a substitute for a covering." It is interesting to note that Homer's warriors wore their hair long, but the youth of Athens "cropped" the head at age eighteen for it was regarded a "mark of foppery or effeminancy" with the exception of the aristocratic knights who did afterwards allow their hair to grow long.[9] Who but the artists tell us about Jesus' custom—was his hair long or short?

Paul's reference to the women's long hair as given by nature does not mean that he implied here that the women's headdress, apart from their hair, was no longer necessary. He was simply saying that the hair, given to women by creation as a covering, is a glory. But men's hair is also given by nature, and Paul left unanswered the problem raised by the discrimination and especially so in the light of Galatians 3:28.

● 16   Obviously it had been customary for a woman in Corinth to wear a head covering, but the custom seemed to be breaking down. In this trend "Paul appears to see the same danger of individualistic disintegration as in the Corinthian practice of the Lord's Supper."[10] Paul obviously did not have in mind here "the custom of contentiousness, but that of woman speaking unveiled. The testimonies of Tertullian and Chrysostom show that these injunctions of Paul prevailed in the churches. In the sculptures of the catacombs the women have a close-fitting head-dress, while the men have the hair short."[11] But the issue in the passage relates to veils as well as to hair.

Paul brought his treatment of the problem to a close by reminding the Corinthians that should there still be "contentions" over the matter, they should remember that "we have no such custom, neither *do* the churches of God." Paul's plea was always for unity in the church, unity without serious compromise, for where there is a lack of unity in a church, there is a lack of peace and of viable witness. There is, as Paul made obvious to all, "neither male nor female" in Christ (Gal. 3:28), and at his feet, all differences can be resolved happily. The matter of individualistic disintegration never ceases to pose a problem for churches in general for the simple reason that church members, by and large, have only a passing knowledge of Christ and apparently put forth little effort to gain an intimate knowledge of him and of his will for the ways of human beings.

● 17   Paul here came to a new theme and a new section. The problem in question was that of a church gathering related to the observance of the supper of our Lord. In a word, he boldly declared that the gatherings "serve not for the better, but for the worse."[12] He outlined the character of the problem in such a way that the meaning is unmistakable.

Paul introduced a new turn in his thought that he expanded in the verses that follow, namely, "the church assembly," and especially here the observance of the Lord's Supper. He had no praise for the Corinthians at this point because of the manner in which the assembly turned out. Paul went on to explain the difficulty.

● 18   First, Paul was disturbed by the divisions in the church which he had heard about. He acknowledged that the word that had come to him was more than a rumor; in fact, he said, "and in part I believe *it*." The presence of these "divisions" *(schismata)* gave him grave concern.

This was a disturbing word, for one of the quickest and surest ways to tear down the viable character of the body of Christ is to stir up "divisions" within the body. When such begins to develop, the real mission of the church begins to suffer neglect.

● 19   Paul indicated that in cases like the Corinthian situation, "there must be also factions" so that "the approved may also become manifest." Certainly truth must have her spokesman and her defense. When heresy rears its head in a church, and there is no obvious voice to contradict the heresy, great and lasting harm may be done. For if the devil himself should arise in person with a cause, he would likely gain some following.

Nevertheless, in this particular case the factions made possible the identification of "the tried and the true," and conditions had come to the point that the line of demarcation between the right and the wrong in things ought to be clearly shown. We get our word *heresy* from the Greek *haireseis,* and heresy is theoretical schism within religious groups. But remember there are times when factions serve a good cause by making "the proved ones" *(hoi dokimoi)* manifest *(phaneroi)*. The bad part about schisms and factions, however, lies in the fact that they invariably serve (as Findlay notes) as "a magnet attracting unsound and unsettled minds."[13]

● 20   In verse 20, Paul's censure comes through clearly. "It is not to eat the Lord's Supper," he said. There were other motives for the gathering, and principal among them was "the *Agapē* or Love-feast (a sort of church supper or club supper held in connection with, before or after, the Lord's Supper)."[14] It was not that the conduct of the Corinthians made it "impossible to eat a Lord's Supper at all." That was not the point; rather, it would be impossible to partake of the supper in a meaningful and proper way, when surrounded with such conduct on their part as Paul had heard about. They had behaved so irresponsibly, in fact, that Paul bluntly told them that their gathering had turned out to be more like Caesar's banquets.

● 21   The reference here appears to be to a sort of private meal in which each one brought his own food and sat down and ate to the full before partaking of the supper of our Lord. This so-called love feast turned out to be an occasion where the more well-to-do gave over to self-indulgence while the have-nots stood around waiting for the Lord's Supper. It is likely that many of those not partaking were slaves who were unable to complete their duties in time to arrive on schedule, and there were the poor who did not actually have their own baskets of food to bring. The feasts which preceded the supper were called *agapē* (love feasts—Jude, v. 12). It was a sort of covered-dish affair, one might say. Each one was supposed to bring his quota. But as Godet observes, "selfishness, vanity, sensuality had prevailed in this usage, and deeply corrupted it. These *agapē* had degenerated at Corinth into something like those feasts of friends in use among the Greeks, where men gave themselves up to drinking excesses, such as we find sketched in the *Symposium* of Plato. And what was still graver, and which had certainly not been witnessed even at heathen banquets, each was careful to reserve for himself and his friends the meats which he had provided."[15] Hence inequality arose among the guests and the poor were humiliated.

From Paul's words, it was more the affair of the individuals than that of the Lord. "Fellowship is canceled when one suffers want and another is drunk; this holds even if the reproach of drunkenness is not taken all too strictly."[16] At any rate, much more went on at these church gatherings than "a sacramental meal." And there is nothing in the New Testament to commend the sort of table fellowship the Corinthians were enjoying prior to the observance of the Lord's Supper.

● 22   The question here has to do with the haves and the have-nots (Findlay). Paul appeared to be drawing a line between the mere satisfaction of hunger and the supper. It was difficult for the supper to reflect its true meaning and purpose when preceded by that type of fellowship meal. But more than that, the issue rises sharply between the haves and the have-nots. The issue was not on houses, or those who have houses and those who do not have them. Paul was talking about the property owners who came well supplied for their slaves, while the less affluent were apparently left standing on the sidelines. In such a situation, it would be difficult for one to observe much of the spirit of *agapē*.

● 23   Here Paul stood on solid ground in his claim to have received directly from the Lord that which he was passing on to the Corinthians. He thereby "classifies himself as a link in a chain of tradition, as in 15:3ff, yet breaks this chain by declaring that he has received the tradition *apo tou Kuriou,* 'from the Lord.'"[17] Paul, therefore, spoke not on the basis of "human authority" but on the basis of revelation that came straight as an arrow to him from the Lord. Without attempting to deal with the historical aspects of the Lord's Supper as commentators often do, Paul went directly into his discussion of the acts of "the historical Jesus" as "the exalted Lord."

● 24   Some of the old translations read, "This is my body which is *broken* for you"; but the oldest and better Greek manuscripts do not use the word *klōmenon.* Jesus broke the bread, but the account of the crucifixion in the Scriptures does not indicate that the body of Jesus was broken. The primal significance of the Lord's Supper is set forth in the phrase *eis tēn emēn anamnēsin,* "in remembrance of me." The purpose of the supper, then, is not that God may remember the participant, but that those partaking of the supper may remember Jesus.

● 25   Conzelmann notes that the corresponding formula as presented here "is not bread and wine, but bread and cup."[18] And Paul referred to the cup as the "cup of the blessing," in 10:16. The words "after the supper" (*meta to deipnēsai*) indicate that the institution of the Last Supper was preceded by a meal. Conzelmann takes it to mean that "the agape was originally enclosed by the two sacramental acts of administering the bread and the cup."[19] Jesus commanded the disciples to continue the observance of the supper, but he gave no explicit directions concerning the frequency of the observance.

● 26   Paul's own words begin with verse 26. One's interpretation of the verb *kataggellete* (you proclaim), as to whether it is considered to be indicative or imperative, will determine whether proclamation is merely the observance of the supper or whether there are to be explicit words of proclamation in connection with the supper. However one may look at it, "The Lord's Supper is the great preacher (*kataggellete*) of the death of Christ till his second coming (Matt. 26:29)."[20] The eschatological outlook of the supper therefore should be obvious to all. It is simply "an institution for the age of the church from the resurrection of Christ to his parousia."[21] Jesus' own words concerning the institution of the supper (vv. 23-26) should give pause to sacramentalists who would attempt to add meanings to the observance of the supper not intended by the Savior himself who instituted it.

● 27   The question here is not upon who is worthy or unworthy to partake of the Lord's Supper. For that matter, who of us, as followers of Jesus, would ever feel the true sense of worthiness in partaking of the supper? The point here has to do with the "manner" of the observance. In verses 29 *ff.*, Paul clarified the meaning of verse 27. It is simply this: the person who partakes of the supper in an unworthy manner is "guilty of a crime committed against the body and blood of the Lord by such sacrilege (cf. Heb. 6:6; 10:29)."[22]

In his conclusion of the issue, Paul pulled no punches. The principle has to do with the worthy or unworthy manner of the supper's observance on the part of those who profess to be followers of Christ. He said bluntly, "If you partake of the supper in an *unworthy manner,* you are *guilty,* for in so doing the guilty one nullifies Christ's command concerning the proclamation of the supper, the proclamation of 'the death of the Lord, until he come.'"

● 28   Paul then commended to the Corinthian church members the principle of "individual, self examination." Again the issue rests not on the worthiness or the unworthiness of the participant. Instead it has to do with the propriety of the observance. In other words, does the participant really understand what he is doing as he partakes of the bread and the cup? Is his motive right? And has he prepared himself and been prepared so that his individual participation in the observance will be meaningful both to himself and to others?

● 29-30   Paul was saying plainly that guilt has its punishment here as elsewhere. In this instance, Paul said the consequence was manifested in mental and spiritual stupor on the part of great numbers of the Corinthians. Did Paul have knowledge of specific instances of those who had experienced the consequences of such sin? Possibly so.

● 31   Paul here harked back to verse 28 where he admonished the participants in the Lord's Supper to "test" themselves and so to eat of the bread and drink of the cup. If after a careful testing of self, a right verdict is reached, there will be no condemnation, no divine punishment. And the judgment which Paul had in mind was not the judgment at the last day, but the operative wrath of God which is continually revealed upon every impiety and wickedness of humans (Rom. 1:18).

● 32   All believers, of course, are under constant judgment of the Lord, but Paul's words here were a plea for a discipline to the end that the believer will not eventually "be condemned with the world."

● 33-34   Paul's conclusion was brief and to the point. The verses refer to verse 22, and Paul intensified his words there with the flat command of verse 34, "If anyone is hungry, he is to eat at home, lest you come together unto condemnation."

Notes

1. Hans Conzelmann, James W. Leitch,. trans., *A Commentary on the First Epistle to the Corinthians, Hermeneia* Series (Philadelphia: Fortress Press, 1975), p. 179.

2. Ibid., p. 184.

3. A. T. Robertson, *Word Pictures in the New Testament* (Nashville, Tennessee: Sunday School Board of the SBC, 1931), p. 160.

4. Ibid., p. 161.

5. Ibid.

6. Ibid.

7. Ibid.

8. Ibid., p. 162.

9. G. G. Findlay, "St. Paul's First Epistle to the Corinthians," *The Expositor's Greek Testament*, Vol. 3 (Grand Rapids, Michigan: William B. Eerdmans Publishing Co., [n.d.]), p. 875.

10. Conzelmann, p. 191.

11. Marvin R. Vincent, "The Epistles of Paul," *Word Studies in the New Testament*, Vol. 3 (Grand Rapids, Michigan: William B. Eerdmans Publishing Co., 1946), p. 248.

12. Conzelmann, p. 193.

13. Findlay, p. 877.

14. Robertson, p. 163.

15. Frederic Louis Godet, *Commentary on I Corinthians* (Grand Rapids, Michigan: Kregel Publications, 1977), p. 570.

16. Conzelmann, p. 194 *ff.*

17. Ibid., p. 196.

18. Ibid., p. 199.

19. Ibid.

20. Robertson, p. 165.

21. Conzelmann, p. 202.

22. Robertson, p. 165.

CHAPTER 12

● 1   In moving on to a new topic, Paul still dealt with questions (*peri*, concerning) raised in the letter to him, and he continued to deal with the problem throughout chapters 12, 13, and 14. Of course, we have no record of the exact content of the questions raised by the previous Corinthian letter, for the letter itself is not available. The core of the issue seems to be "the theological existence of believers, their concrete determination by the Spirit."[1] There seemed to have been no issue here concerning the character of the Spirit. And the matters he turned to are intended for the edification of the Corinthians. He did not want them to be "ignorant" concerning the basic concepts of truth as they relate to salvation and to the "Spirit of the Lord."

● 2   Opinions differ with reference to the precise allusion in verse 2. Paul certainly addressed the Corinthians as "Gentile Christians," for that was the nature of the community. Most likely Paul had in mind "the ecstatic character of pagan cults"[2] and the association of some of the Corinthian Christians with those cults in the past. How or in what manner they were "led away" to the voiceless idols, we are not told. Were the demons the chief actors in draining away some of the weak Christians from their original position? Or did they relate to experiences that took place before the Gentiles came to know Christ? Paul was merely concerned here with an analogy that would enable the Corinthians, whatever their past may have been, to reason now and to make decisions concerning the true Christian posture in a pagan world.

● 3   G. G. Findlay calls the words *Anathema Iēsous* (Jesus is anathema) and *Kurios Iēsous* (Jesus is Lord) both the "battle-cries of the spirits of error and of truth contending at Cor."[3] At this point, Paul did not deal critically with the ecstatic experience of the Corinthians, nor did he allude to his own experience in this area of spiritual gifts. He did make clear that "ecstasy alone is no criterion for the working of the Spirit, but itself requires such a criterion."[4] Spirits, per se, are not all from God (1 John 4:1). Later on in his letter to the Corinthians, Paul dealt more specifically with the criteria of ecstasy as it relates to tongues. Caesar wanted his followers to call him *Kurios* (Lord). In the ancient inscriptions (*ostraca* and *papyri*), there are allusions to Roman emperors who were called *Kurios,* for example, "Nero *Kurios.*" Polycarp was called upon to say *Kurios* Caesar, but each time he replied *Kurios Iēsous.* For his refusal to obey Caesar's command, in his loyalty to Christ, he was put to death.

● 4-6   In these verses, closely linked together as a unit, the essential unity finds expression in "multiform fruit" (Findlay). These fruits are fruits of assignment and all are acts of the undeserved, freely given grace of God. The variety of the designation of the spiritual gifts (*pneumatika*) is really not the point, but rather the "*trinity* of blessing associating its possessors in turn with *the Spirit, the Lord,* and *God* the fountain of all."[5] There is really an overlapping of the terminology, per se, for the *diakonia* includes every type of work of ministration (Eph. 4:12). The narrowing of the sense of the word "to the duties of the *diakonos*" was a later development.[6] Paul's words amount to a leveling off of the concept of the different word concepts of the spiritual gifts (*pneumatika*). There are no three-star ratings given to one over another. "The essential point is precisely that everyday acts of service are now set on a par with the recognized, supernatural phenomena of the Spirit."[7] Every believer, according to Paul, no matter the character of his gift, who does his own thing under the guidance of the Spirit, is on a par with the Christian whose experience has abounded in the ecstatic mood. In other words, the grace of God makes all believers of one kind in relation to the *pneumatika* (spiritual gifts). This means that there can be no believers of high and low degree in relation to the gifts of the Spirit and to the service performed. Special gifts, areas of service, and special activity are ideally allotments (assignments) of God in behalf of the furtherance of his eternal kingdom.

● 7   "To each one is given the manifestation of the Spirit that is appropriate"—appropriate for the eternal purpose that God projected in Jesus Christ his Son. The emphasis here is not so much on the variety of the manifestation of the *pneumatika* (gifts of the Spirit) but upon the fact that "the Spirit is again the sole Giver of all the gifts."[8] And while there is wide differentiation in the manifestations of the *pneumatika,* there is at the same time differential unity, for each allotment is made with a view to what is for the best, that is, for the strengthening and upbuilding of God's redemptive mission in world history. The genitive *(tou pneumatos)* may be regarded as either subjective or as objective (Robertson and Plummer), but the end is much the same.

● 8-10 Here all the gifts stand side by side, being distinguished one from another in character, but not in divine preference, unless there be a preference in the placing of the tongues last. Altogether, there appears to be little if any suggestion that there should be a distinction felt among any of the gifts as over against the others, while at the same time the Holy Spirit is regarded as the cause or intermediate agent *(dia tou pneumatos)* and at the same time the "norm *(kata to auto pneuma,* 'according to the same spirit'), without it being possible to take the distinction strictly."[9]

● 11 Here Paul did away completely with any supposed occasion "for conceit, pride, or faction."[10] All the gifts are the result of the unmerited grace of God who makes the assignments (the allocations) "as he desires." The mood of one Spirit so obvious throughout this section lays the foundation for the same unity (one body) in the section that follows.

● 12 In this section the *body* (the church) comes to the forefront as did the *Spirit* in the preceding passage. Here the same unity of the body (the church), though composed of many members, is ideally the same as the unity that is in Christ. The thought jumps here in the passage from the *figure* of the one *body* to that of the *body of Christ.* But it appears that "the real thought of the section is that of the church as the body of Christ."[11]

● 13 Paul spoke here, as the verb indicates (first aorist passive indicative of *baptizō),* of a definite event in the past when people of different ethnic groups, different nations and stations "each of them put on the outward badge of service to Christ, the symbol of the inward changes already wrought in them by the Holy Spirit (Gal. 3:27; Rom. 6:2ff.)."[12] Paul's words "and we all drank of one Spirit" apparently refer to the inward salvation experience attested to and symbolized by the act of baptism. The emphasis here lies on a unity made possible by the salvation experience marked by "the abrogation of the (physical and social) differences between believers."[13] Certainly as the believer becomes a part of the body of Christ, the church, human differences are never the same again.

● 14 Here again the focal point of the dominant idea is the body (the church) of which Christ is the head. Even Socrates recognized the absurdity of the disposition on the part of people to fail to cooperate with one another, to work against one another, and God decreed otherwise.[14]

● 15-16   Some have felt that Paul had in mind here the "all too humble self-assessment of inferior ones," but we are disposed to think that his attack is not against these, but rather against those, perhaps, more fortunate individuals who had a tendency to draw apart from their fellow Christians and dwell with a sense of false security in the pursuit of their "enthusiastic individualism."[15]

● 17   Verse 17 merely projects the idea of verse 16, emphasizing how undesirable and how grotesque the body would be should it consist of only one organ.

● 18   Here Paul abruptly ended the train of thought from the preceding verses in which he has stressed "the appropriateness of the structure of the body and to the necessity of cooperation"[16] and emphasized the fact that the body in totality—structure and all—is the handiwork of God. It was he who "arranged" each of the members in the order that was pleasing to his will.

● 19-20   In these two verses, Paul's logic shifted from that of "differentiation" (v. 29) to that of "unity" in verse 20. But the meaning is clear any way one looks at it. The application is obvious for it applies to the church members. "It is particularly pertinent in the case of a 'church boss.' "[17]

● 21   Paul continued his dialogue of absurdity with reference to the superiority of one member over another or one member standing in the place of the whole. Apparently there is no intended emphasis in placing the eye before the head, and vice versa. For that matter, the relation in the dialogue of any of the organs would seem to have no viable significance.

● 22   Paul's reference to the members of the body that are regarded as "weaker" (*asthenestera*—comparative of the adjective *asthenēs*) actually relates to members of the church who were thought to be less important, whether of their abilities or of their influence. The idea here seems not to be so much the physical as the sociological and psychological. Actually those members are a part of the whole and are necessary just as the more influential, stronger ones are. Here is a passage that every pastor and church leader might well ponder.

● 23   In verse 23, Paul projected still further the thoughts of verse 22 in "a kind of apologia for the weaker parts by means of reference to the 'natural' attitude toward them, namely, the compensation provided by custom." The thrust of Paul's words here appears to be still further emphasis on the *real* significance of the insignificant. All the members of the body have their places and their gifts. No one is to be looked down upon or disregarded because of rank or station. In truth, all the children of God are "charismatics." All have experienced the grace of God, for it is by grace we all have been saved (Eph. 2:8-9). The gifts of some may be insignificant or greatly inferior in the eyes of others, but all gifts are of God; all believers are the recipients of the divine charisma.

● 24-25   The later Gnostics held to the dualistic concept of things. To them all matter was evil, and they tended to denigrate the physical structure of the body. To the contrary, Paul presented the human body as wonderful, beautiful, and worthy, a structure made of God as a fitting temple for his Spirit (6:19).

In verse 25 Paul emphasized again the necessity for having no divisions in the body, as he did in 11:18. If there exists dissensions or schisms, it is impossible for the body, which is composed of all of the parts, to be in working order.

● 26   Here Paul stressed the interrelationship of all members of the body. When one member (a hand, a foot, the eye) suffers, the whole body picks up the load of suffering and helps the member to bear it. Like middle C on the piano, all of the parts are members one of the other, and no part is an island apart unto itself. If church members could only realize the necessity for such an interpersonal relationship among the members of the church body, how wonderful the days could become for all.

● 27   Here then Paul left the figure of an organism or the "body of Christ" and completed the analogy. The same idea of unity avails here, and Paul brought it into clearer perspective by use of the "idea of an organism" as an illustration.[18]

● 28   Paul listed some of the leading types of service in the church in order (apparently) to emphasize not only the necessity for cooperation but also the meaningful character of the types of service rendered. Paul mentioned three of the significant forms of service and set them apart by the use of ordinal numbers. Paul apparently did not have in mind, in mentioning them, that they are any more charismatic in character than others who are called to special tasks in the church. Paul did not indicate that he was naming all of the kinds of service that are performed or should be performed in a church. But he did mention some that might be regarded as the more significant types of service to be rendered by the members of the body of Christ.

• 29-30   "In this list the technical forms of service, which Paul was the first to exalt to the rank of *charismata,* are omitted."[19] See 12:4-6. Notice that Paul placed prophecy and other aspects of the *charismata* ahead of "tongues" "from the standpoint of *oikodomē,* 'upbuilding.'"[20]

• 31   Paul issued a stirring summons for the Corinthians to be up and striving "earnestly" for the "greater gifts" and then went on to point out the higher way of love (agapē). The "higher gifts" to which Paul called the Corinthians "allow of no self-development and no self-contemplation on the pneumatic's part."[21] To these words every preacher of the gospel and every church-related servant of the Lord should give a ready and constant ear.

Notes

1. Hans Conzelmann, James W. Leitch, trans., *A Commentary on the First Epistle to the Corinthians, Hermeneia* Series (Philadelphia: Fortress Press, 1975), p. 204.
2. Ibid., p. 205.
3. G. G. Findlay, "St. Paul's First Epistle to the Corinthians," *The Expositor's Greek Testament,* Vol. 3 (Grand Rapids, Michigan: William B. Eerdmans Publishing Co., [n.d.]), p. 886.
4. Conzelmann, p. 206.
5. Findlay, p. 887.
6. Ibid.
7. Conzelmann, p. 208.
8. Ibid.
9. Ibid., p. 209.
10. A. T. Robertson, *Word Pictures in the New Testament* (Nashville, Tennessee: Sunday School Board of the SBC, 1931), p. 170.
11. Conzelmann, p. 212.
12. Robertson, p. 171.
13. Conzelmann, p. 212.
14. Xen., *Mem.* II. iii. 18.
15. Conzelmann, p. 212 *ff.*
16. Ibid., p. 213.
17. Robertson, p. 172.
18. Conzelmann, p. 214.
19. Ibid., p. 215.
20. Ibid.
21. Ibid.

CHAPTER 13

Chapter 13 is in itself a complete unity and depends not upon the context for its meaning. Conzelmann calls it "an aretalogy of *alētheia,* 'truth.'"[1] The chapter falls logically into three clear-cut divisions: (1) the necessity for the love (vv. 1-3); (2) the character of the love (vv. 4-7); (3) the permanency of the love (vv. 8-12). Leaving the critics to answer the questions concerning the stylistic form and other matters relating to biblical criticism, let us turn to the chapter and consider it on its own merit.

● 1   All in all, the thrust of chapter 13 seems to indicate "the superiority of love to all the special charismata, and thus proves the pursuit of it to be a more excellent way than to desire even the best of those gifts."[2]

Paul first discussed the necessity for this "superlative" way by the use of a series of hypotheses "respecting *tongues, prophecy, knowledge,* and *devotion of goods or of person.*"[3] Paul began with the last of the charismata mentioned in the preceding chapter (tongues) and says that this charisma in its highest form without love amounts to no more than "a noisy gong or a clanging cymbal." Though "tongues" be raised to its highest station, that "of angels," the result is the same. The "noisy gong" and "clanging cymbal" figures doubtless refer to the use of these instruments by the pagan religions. There was no spiritual heart to the sound, no soul message. Paul's message rings clear concerning "the surpassing beauty of love." As Robertson and Plummer note, Paul "may be pointing out the worthlessness of extravagant manifestations of emotion, which proceed, not from the heart, but from hollowness."[4] Certainly the hollow nature of the cymbal which makes the sound adds to the gripping analogy. At bottom, Paul was saying that, apart from love, the loftiest utterances of which human beings or angels are capable of making amount to nothing more than noise.

● 2   Paul placed love on a higher level than the gift of prophecy, knowledge of the mysteries, all knowledge, and all faith. In doing so, he was "not condemning these great gifts. He simply places love above them and essential to them."[5] Even wonder-working faith takes second place to love, the originating cause of our salvation (John 3:16). It is interesting to note here that Paul in following "the Corinthian order of merit in the spiritual gifts . . . emphasizes prophecy more strongly than speaking with tongues." But all the gifts he mentioned fall below love without which, said Paul, "I am nothing" *(outhen eimi)*. Paul could hardly have spoken more bluntly.

● 3   Paul used a striking figure in his ascending scale of symbolism. The picture is that of doling away one's possessions bit by bit. It is like the procedure of a mother bird in breaking up the food for her tiny baby, or a mother placing tiny portions of solid food in the mouth of her infant. "The verb implies *personal* distribution to *many,* and that the act is done once for all: he could not habitually give away *all* his goods."[6] The better manuscripts have here *kauchēsōmai* (that I may boast, or glory, or take pride in myself) instead of *kauthēsomai* (future passive indicative of *kaiō,* to burn). There were those of course who "courted martyrdom in later years (time of Diocletian)."[7] Of course martyrdom by fire was frequent in the years of Diocletian, and at times it was totally *voluntary.* Such heroic attitudes in the face of death were common to Greco-Roman thought. But in either translation, the result is the same, for the person who gives up his body whether to be burned or whether for the purpose of boasting or glorying is "helped in no way."

● 4   Here Paul began another independent section where the subject is love *(agapē)* "in personifying style. The content and style are not hymnic, but didactic."[8] In these words Paul set forth ways of love, and in doing so defined, in a limited way, the character of love. Love has patience *(makrothumei).* Love is kind *(chrēsteuetai)* with a kindness that is of a useful nature. The word *jealousy (zēloi)* is found widely in both the good and the bad sense. One can be zealous without being jealous. Love is not a braggart in the sense of vaunting oneself. Paul's other words here hardly need comment.

● 5-6   Love does not "behave disgracefully, strives not for its own advantage, is not habitually irritable, does not place evil to its account," that is, love does not set down an evil matter in the credit side of the ledger.

● 7   The words "bear all things" *(stegei)* come from a word meaning roof and therefore a covering or shield. It could mean to "draw a veil of silence over."[9] The sense of *bear* seems to be preferable here in the light of *hypomenei,* endure which follows. Paul's word "continues to have faith in spite of all things, continues to hope in the face of all things" go together perfectly. Hope "sees the bright side of things. Does not despair." Even so love "keeps on enduring all things." Love "perseveres. Carries on like a stout-hearted soldier."[10] Paul was now ready to round out his profile of Christian love by stressing the eternal character of the love of which he had been speaking.

● 8   Paul used strong language here with reference to the gifts of prophecy, tongues, and knowledge. These will go. They will be "set aside," rendered ineffective; but love, he says later, will remain. This amounts to setting love and the charismata "in antithesis to each other," and in view of the eschatological "the latter will cease."[11] These special manifestations of the charisma serve us in "a provisional way," but love abides forever. Paul's reference to "knowledge" called to mind the *gnōsis* slogan of the Corinthians.

● 9-10   In these verses, we have an explanation as to why the charismata mentioned in verse 8 "pass away." Though they are part of the charismata as a whole (12:31) and are "rich in edification (xiv.6), these charisms are partial in scope, and therefore temporary."[12] The full knowledge will come at the last day when we are with the Lord in our "house not made with hands, eternal in the heavens" (2 Cor. 5:1).

● 11-12   Here again Paul emphasized through the verbs "the aspect of discontinuity."[13] The contrast between youth and adulthood further supports the premise. Paul fortunately made a clean break with the age of immaturity and passed on to maturity—the mature person no longer talks, thinks, and reasons as a child. How wonderful it would be if every follower of Jesus could make this transition effectively. So many of us do not know Jesus well. We have only a passing acquaintance. That is why we do not turn to him in the crisis moments of life saying, What would you do, Lord, in this case? What would you have me to do? Here again we have the antithesis "of now . . . but then." "The full *vision* of God is attained only on the 'royal way,' when the human *nous* is expelled by the divine *pneuma,* 'Spirit.'"[14] Knowledge in the present is fragmentary, *(ek merous).* But the perfect knowledge will come in the end. Throughout these verses Paul reflected his eschatological longings, as all true believers in the second Advent would do.

● 13   In the triad of faith, hope, and love, Paul scaled the topmost heights of spiritual understanding. Faith, hope, and love all have their validity. It is necessary at this point to understand the type of contrast Paul had in mind in the triad. He was not saying that faith and hope pass away. Rather, it seems he meant that the three remain valid in contrast to the transitory nature of other spiritual gifts. But one is greater than the others. Other gifts may pass away but faith, hope, and love remain forever. And the greatest of these is love, for love is necessary for both faith and hope and keeps on growing in proportion to the believer's knowledge of and fellowship with Jesus.

Notes

1. Hans Conzelmann, James W. Leitch, trans., *A Commentary on the First Epistle to the Corinthians,* *Hermeneia* Series (Philadelphia: Fortress Press, 1975), p. 218.

2. E. P. Gould, "Commentary on the Epistles to the Corinthians," *An American Commentary on the New Testament,* Vol. 5 (Philadelphia: American Baptist Publication Society, 1887), p. 111.

3. G. G. Findlay, "St. Paul's First Epistle to the Corinthians," *The Expositor's Greek Testament,* Vol. 3 (Grand Rapids, Michigan: William B. Eerdmans Publishing Co., [n.d.]), p. 896.

4. Archibald Robertson and Alfred Plummer, "A Critical and Exegetical Commentary on the First Epistle of St. Paul to the Corinthians," *International Critical Commentary* (New York: Charles Scribner's Sons, 1911), p. 289.

5. A. T. Robertson, *Word Pictures in the New Testament* (Nashville, Tennessee: Sunday School Board of the SBC, 1931), p. 177.

6. Robertson and Plummer, p. 290.

7. Robertson, p. 177.

8. Conzelmann, p. 223.

9. Ibid., p. 224.

10. Robertson, p. 179.

11. Conzelmann, p. 225.

12. Findlay, p. 900.

13. Conzelmann, p. 226.

14. Ibid., p. 228.

CHAPTER 14

● 1   Here Paul referred to 12:31 with a sort of summary of what has immediately gone before (chs. 12—13). Paul departed abruptly from the emphasis on love *(agapē)* to that of "edification, upbuilding." It is obvious that prophecies did not have the proper regard of the Corinthians "but ranks after speaking with tongues. Thus the gifts are evaluated in Corinth according to the intensity of the ecstatic outburst; in fact, even according to the degree of unintelligibility. The latter is considered to be an indication of the working of supernatural power."[1] However much the gift of tongues may be desired, as any of the other gifts mentioned in chapter 12, tongues do not edify and build up listeners for the simple reason they are not understood. Tongues may benefit the individual, for they become for him an instrument of communion with God, but the communion is unintelligible to others. Others hear the sound (as in Acts 9:7) but they do not understand the sounds; hence they are meaningless.

● 2   It should be clearly understood that Paul did not here condemn the use of tongues, per se, but rather held that the tongues have value for others only through mediation. There has to be an interpreter, either the one who speaks in tongues or another. Paul did not say that tongues are unintelligible to the speaker, but only to others when there is no mediation. However much the speaker may be inspired and uplifted, the inspiration and the uplifting do not pass on to others who do not comprehend what is going on between the speaker and God. By speaking the mystery, namely, "truth about God, once hidden, but now revealed," the mystery remains a mystery still. The speaker may receive personal improvement but is actually made morally no better by the gift, for the character is improved through personal effort as the gift is used to further the kingdom of God.[2]

● 3   In prophecy the results are just the opposite, for "the one prophesying to men speaks edification and exhortation and encouragement." Here "the accent is plain: *theō—anthrōpois* 'for God—for men.'"[3] Paul's use of prophecy here does not refer to "foretelling of the future." See verse 24. Paul marked the difference between tongues and prophecy boldly and, in doing so, delineated the character of prophecy. Prophesying is "the power of seeing and making known the nature and will of God, a gift of insight into truth and of power in imparting it, and hence a capacity for building up men's characters, quickening their wills, and encouraging their spirits."[4] "Edification, cheer, incentive in these words."[5]

● 4   There is no article with the word "church" (*ekklēsian*), but the meaning is clear. Paul likely had in mind the Corinthian church, whereas the principle with which he was dealing applies to all churches. The meaning in verse 4 is merely an extension of the meaning in verse 3. It is again the case of the individual instead of the assembly—one person instead of many persons is benefited.

● 5   Paul boldly expressed his preference when it came to tongues as against prophecy. The criterion is inescapable. He would do nothing to disallow the use of tongues in a church, but he gave his own evaluation clearly stated in the preceding verses. The criterion is not based upon the phenomenon itself, but rather upon the edification, the value of each with reference to the body of believers. But even the value standard changes when there is an interpreter, for with the right interpretation the message of the tongues may acquire "the same function as prophecy."[6] But whatever the gift, whatever the function, those proclaiming—whether through tongues or prophecy—are to have in mind the edification of others. This is always to be primal in places of public worship. Otherwise, a few are benefited and others go without help.

● 6   Paul's words "but now" are not to be taken in a "temporal" sense, but rather as a point in logic. "The use of the first person is rhetorical; it serves, in diatribe style, by way of illustration. Yet it may also contain a hint that Paul actually could appear on the scene as one who speaks with tongues."[7] Here again the meaning is obvious. What would be the point of Paul's speaking in tongues to the Corinthians if, in doing so, he failed to edify them, to make known God's erstwhile hidden truth to them, to inspire them by adding to their knowledge and understanding of

Christian doctrine? Paul's logic in dialogue was clear, and he apparently struggled hard to make himself understood by the Corinthians. There is no disposition manifested to denigrate the use of the tongues on the part of any of the Corinthian fellowship, except what is implied in his words concerning the necessity for edification at all times. The larger body deserves to be in on any and everything that is spoken if it has to do with the kingdom of the Lord.

● 7-11   The word "lifeless" (v. 7) could be translated soulless for the word *apsuchos* means literally without a soul. Paul's words in verse 9 are a bit confusing, for if one speaks in tongues intelligibly that would in itself be a contradiction in the light of all that has gone before. There is hardly any way to misunderstand Paul's meaning here with the words that follow. Conzelmann thinks that Paul chose the word *phōnē* (v. 10) "to designate language, because *glōssa* has already another meaning in the context."[8] Conzelmann also notes that Paul's words in verse 11 have found "an excellent piece of evidence for the basic meaning of *barbaros*, 'foreigner,' lit. 'gibberish talker.'"[9]

● 12   Paul's language here seems to indicate that the Corinthians were to employ their zeal, their striving, in behalf of "the edification of the church" rather than "self-edification." In the larger context, the thrust of Paul's idea seems to be "edification" (*oikodomē*) as it relates to the community of believers, the body of Christ, the church.

● 13   Paul clearly stated that the one speaking in tongues has the responsibility; he is "to pray that he may interpret." The long view again is that of edification of the church. The tongue speaker is not to drift off into his own garden of spiritual satisfaction to the exclusion of the understanding of others. He is to pray that he may be able to interpret what he is saying. Interpretation is a charisma, just as is tongues. The prayer that Paul had in mind is "not ecstatic, but conscious prayer."[10]

● 14   Paul set a state of ecstasy in tongues in contrast with the "mind" (*nous*). The mind is to have its proper place, even in tongues.

● 15   The singing of psalms, as well as prayer, is a part of the worship in the synagogue for the Christian era and was in Paul's time a part of the service of worship in Christian churches. Paul, it appears, endeavored to present both the mind (*nous*) and the spirit (*pneuma*) in the proper perspective. Both are to be recognized, but there is a balance to be maintained, and the balance is to make for the edification of the church. Ecstatic prayer and ecstatic tongue speaking leave the mind barren said Paul. And this type of unfruitfulness does not make for the building up of the church.

"There was ecstatic singing like the rhapsody of some prayers without intelligent words. But Paul prefers singing that reaches the intellect as well as stirs the emotions. Solos that people do not understand lose more than half their value in church worship."[11] The original meaning of *psallō* was to play on strings. Later it came to mean to accompany the stringed instrument with song (Eph. 5:19). There was no reference here to the type of instrument (if any) that Paul had in mind.

● 16   This reference is to the situation that prevails when a person in the congregation is praying "in the Spirit." The lay person who is in his appointed place during the worship does not understand the prayer and, therefore, is at a loss as to when to utter his own expression of approval, his own amen. The other person here presumably has neither the gift of speaking with tongues nor the ability to interpret tongues, hence the problem.

● 17   Paul recognized the validity of prayers that are spoken in the spirit (v. 16). But the same criticism revealed in verse 15 is stated here. The person praying in a tongue fails to build the other person up.

● 18   In this verse, we have "one of the few allusions to the psyche of Paul."[12] Paul told the Corinthians, clearly, that he himself did speak in tongues "more than" they all, and he was thankful to God for the ability to do so.

● 19   But Paul went on to explain his own position concerning the speaking in tongues in the assembly (the church). He would have rather spoken "five words" that "instruct" than "ten thousand in a tongue."

● 20   Paul resorted again to the use of the antithesis, and in this case the "child" as opposed to the "mature" person. The word *phresin* (understanding) is found only here in the New Testament. Some see Paul's words here as paradoxical, but only because many of the translations have "be babes in evil." *Alla* may be a "misrendering of an Aramaic word meaning *and not*" (Souter). This, if taken as the proper translation in this instance would relieve the paradox. The kind of "perfection" Paul called for is "a practically attainable state."[13] It is a type of spiritual maturity that all believers may achieve with proper faith and works.

● 21   The essence of Paul's thought does not follow altogether either the Hebrew text or the Septuagint,[14] but this is the train of his thought: "Scripture predicts speaking with tongues as a God-given sign, but this sign has no attention paid to it. . . . Thus the quotation is made use of only for the *one* thought, that speaking with tongues is a 'sign' (namely, for unbelievers, see v 23)."[15]

● 22   Paul took a new turn in his argument. He held up "tongues" as a "sign" for unbelievers. But it is a bit difficult to follow his reasoning in view of all of his statements concerning speaking in tongues in the preceding chapters. Here it indicates that signs may have a missionary effect upon the hearers—even unbelievers. At any rate, it is all a working of the Spirit, even though the process may be unintelligible to them. The sign is there even though they do not understand the content. Concerning prophecy, however, Paul made it clear that it makes an impact on unbelievers as well as on believers.

● 23   Paul gave us in these verses and others an intimate glimpse of what went on in the early Christian gatherings for worship. Where tongues were in great evidence, Paul indicated that the speakers could easily give the impression of madness. The uninformed, and the new-comer, would simply not know what to make of the phenomenon. "These unbelievers unacquainted *(idiōtai)* with Christianity will say that the Christians are raving mad (see Acts 12:15; 26:24). They will seem like a congregation of lunatics."[16]

● 24   The persons referred to in this verse are similar to those in verse 23. We have here also added insight into Paul's "understanding of prophecy: it is not prediction of the future, but unmasking of man."[17]

● 25   Here we have a gripping picture of the work of the Spirit in relation to conversion. In this instance, the experience is "manifest in adoration,"[18] an aspect frequently witnessed by those who are privileged to share in the conversion experience of another.

● 26   The opening words in verse 26 *ti oun estin* are a bit difficult to translate. Conzelmann suggests, "What does this imply?"[19] Findlay has, "How then stands the case, brothers?"[20] The *oun* is resumptive and casts a look back over all of the events that have taken place at the Corinthian church. By his words "each one has" *(hekastos . . . echei)*, he probably did not mean to imply that every Corinthian Christian "has one of the gifts mentioned, but means: one has this—another has that."[21] Every believer has some gift, but not necessarily the gift of tongues or of prophecy or one of the other gifts mentioned by Paul. But each has a gift to exercise under God. The thing Paul was striving for was edification; whatever gift a person has should be used to building up the body. The criteria continues, therefore, to be for "edification" (oikodomē).

● 27   This verse lays down clearly ground rules which the speakers in tongues are to observe. They are to speak "in turn," and there must be an interpreter present to explain what is being said. Otherwise, the speaking in tongues would be fruitless for others who are present. Paul was merely bringing to a head what was implied in verses 13 ff.

● 28   Paul did not tell us clearly what he had in mind concerning the interpreter in verse 28. As Conzelmann notes, the translation might be rendered "but if no interpreter is present" or "but if he is .not an interpreter." Either way the sense is clear, and the language allows the interpretation. If there is no one to interpret, then the tongue speaking should be done at home.

● 29-30   Here the ground rules for those prophesying called for the same orderliness that is required for those who speak in tongues. Perhaps the matter of injunction for those who listen to the prophecy to "examine" the word spoken may have been occasioned by evidence of the false prophets who are always present in every community. Certainly prophecy should not require an interpreter in the same sense that speaking in tongues does. Paul did not tell us who "the others" were that he had in mind. They may have been "members of the community, or the rest of the prophets."[22] At least the necessity for a close look at the prophecy will always be in order in the light of 12:1-3. Verse 30 seems to indicate that customarily the speakers stood in addressing the congregation.

● 31   Here again the emphasis is on orderliness, for the prophets are to speak singly, one by one. The purpose of this, of course, is so that those listening can understand what is being said. It appears that Paul's word "the others" (hoi alloi, v. 29) refers to the other prophets.

● 32-33   Paul was saying that the prophets should be always in control. They should be "the master of . . . spirit."[23] The Spirit of God inspires, but the prophet is responsible for the administration of the gift in an orderly and upright way for the building up of the congregation. After all, the object of prophecy is that all may "learn" and all may "become encouraged." For God is not "a God of disorder but of peace."

Here again the emphasis is on orderliness, and the object seems to be to keep the prophet who is speaking from colliding with the one who is rising to speak. They are not to speak at the same time, and the one who has had the floor and had his turn in speaking should give way to the one who is rising to his feet to speak. The "disorder" *(akatastasias)* to which Paul referred apparently means "the disturbance that would arise if the Spirit were at variance with himself." The prophet is to remain in charge of his own spirit and not allow it to run riot in collision with the spirits of others.

• 34-35   In verse 34, the flow of thought is interrupted by a new train of thought relating to the participation of women in the worship services. In 11:2 *ff.,* Paul referred to their participation but only with reference to their decorum, namely, whether they have the proper headdress. But here he plainly said that it was "not permitted" for the women to speak in the churches. Some hold that Paul's words "as in all the churches of the saints" belong with verse 33, rather than with what follows in verse 34. Be that as it may, Paul's words are clear. Certainly in view of the role of woman in the secular world of Paul's day and especially womanhood as it was represented by the temple prostitutes at Corinth and their decorum as they went about the streets of the city, it is easy to understand why women of the church at Corinth would need to dissociate themselves, in every needed measure, from the ways of the women of the secular community about them. These words can be understood clearly only in the context of pagan life of the Corinthians in general. Whatever Paul's meaning may have been here as to the future of women's relationship to the churches, we know that, in our day, there would be a great void in the work of the churches were it not for the gifted, faithful, devout service of our women. As teachers of Sunday School classes, as committee members throughout the full range of the church service, as members of the church choirs, as clerks of the assemblies, now as special ministers of God in the various chaplaincies of our service institutions, and in some instances even as pastors set apart to proclaim the gospel, they serve. We know that the daughters of Philip were prophetesses and that Lydia led the prayer meeting by the riverside attended by Paul. Surely it is clear today "that we need to be patient with each other as we try to understand Paul's real meaning here."[24]

● 36   There are those who regard this verse as an interpolation and find its meaning difficult to perceive. The passage is not difficult at all if one will let the Greek speak. Verse 36 amounts to nothing short of a rebuke as with irony Paul made inquiry concerning the origin of the word of God and its destiny. Inordinate pride of the Corinthians must have led them to feel that they had superior knowledge as if "the word of God took its earthly origin from the Corinthians," and "it was to them only that it came." Paul's withering words must have been to them an embarrassment that cut to the bone.

● 37-38   Paul continued to pull down the lofty and the mighty among the Corinthians. Those who regarded themselves as *pneumatics* needed to understand fully one thing, namely, that Paul's words to them were nothing short of a command of the Lord. "They must not think that they alone know what is Christian."[25] Paul was speaking for God, as his prophet, and his words were commanded by the Lord.

● 39-40   In these concluding statements, Paul affectionately turned to his "brothers" in Christ with a final exhortation concerning prophecy, an exhortation begun in verse 1 and at the same time a parting recognition of the gift of tongues in commanding his brothers not "to forbid" the speaking of tongues while they, in the meantime, earnestly continue to seek the gift of prophecy. Paul closed his remarks with the final admonition to the Corinthian Christians, namely, that "everything is to be done respectably and in an orderly way."

Notes

1. Hans Conzelmann, James W. Leitch, trans., *A Commentary on the First Epistle to the Corinthians, Hermeneia* Series (Philadelphia: Fortress Press, 1975), p. 233 *ff.*

2. Archibald Robertson and Alfred Plummer, "A Critical and Exegetical Commentary on the First Epistle of St. Paul to the Corinthians," *International Critical Commentary* (New York: Charles Scribner's Sons, 1911), p. 305.

3. Conzelmann, p. 234.

4. Robertson and Plummer, p. 306.

5. A. T. Robertson, *Word Pictures in the New Testament* (Nashville, Tennessee: Sunday School Board of the SBC, 1931), p. 181.

6. Conzelmann, p. 235.

7. Ibid.

8. Ibid., p. 236.

9. Ibid.

10. Ibid., p. 237.

11. Robertson, p. 183.

12. Conzelmann, p. 239.

13. Ibid., p. 241.

14. Ibid., p. 242.

15. Ibid.

16. Robertson, p. 184.

17. Conzelmann, p. 243.

18. Ibid.

19. Ibid., p. 244.

20. G. G. Findlay, "St. Paul's First Epistle to the Corinthians," *The Expositor's Greek Testament*, Vol. 3 (Grand Rapids, Michigan: William B. Eerdmans Publishing Co., [n.d.]), p. 911.

21. Conzelmann, p. 244.

22. Ibid., p. 245.

23. Ibid.

24. Robertson, p. 185.

25. Leon Morris, *Tyndale: New Testament Commentaries, The First Epistle of Paul to the Corinthians* (Grand Rapids, Michigan: William B. Eerdmans Publishing Co., 1958), p. 202.

CHAPTER 15

● 1   Chapter 15 falls logically into three sections, each of which can be logically subdivided. *Section 1* deals with the resurrection of Christ as "an Essential Article of the Gospel, 1-11."[1] *Section 2* proclaims the resurrection of the Christian on the basis of his relationship to Christ, verses 12-34. *Section 3* has to do with the character of the resurrected body of the believer and with objections raised concerning the resurrection of the dead. Paul's premise is that "Christianity stands or falls with the fact of the Resurrection."[2] The certainty of Christ's resurrection becomes the certitude of the believer's hope of life after death.

Paul introduced the theme of the resurrection abruptly, maybe because of rumors that reached him concerning the Corinthian's views on the resurrection. Paul's discussion of the resurrection, therefore, came like an arrow to the heart of his theology and to the theological basis of the believer's hope in Christ and in the resurrection of the dead. In truth, Christ *had* to rise from the grave, for he had clearly taught that he would die and rise again. Over the space of forty days he appeared some eleven times to his followers, always under the premise that he had been dead and that now he is alive again. Had Christ not risen from the grave, he would have been the world's greatest mountebank, a quack of the first order. "Christ is not merely the first to be raised, but is constituitive for our being raised: the dead will be made alive 'in him.' "[3] Paul dealt here only with the resurrection of believers, "Resurrection is for him not a question of the world picture, but of faith in Christ."[4] Paul did not discuss the character of the views of the Corinthians concerning death and the future of the dead, but their views must have been disturbing. In verse 1 Paul laid the foundation for what he was to say in the verses that follow. The foundation is "the gospel" as he proclaimed it to the Corinthian church.

That which he had proclaimed to them was the good news, the staple of his message, and the foundation which is the structure of the entire system of Christian thought.

● 2   It is through the gospel that the Corinthians were being saved. The verb *sōizesthe,* present indicative passive, emphasizes a present, continuous salvation. The process is going on all the time as others come to know Christ as Savior and Lord, that is, said Paul, "unless you believed to no purpose." The words "to no purpose" *(mē eikēi)* seem to indicate that, as in our own day, there were those who proclaimed their faith in Christ in genuine conversion, but failed to exercise the kind of *faith* that the gospel experience calls for. Genuine faith is the leaning of the entire person upon God in Christ not only for salvation but also for wisdom, for guidance, and for strength in behalf of the new life-style that is in Christ. Evidently some of the Corinthians had merely become joiners of the church and had done so thoughtlessly, haphazardly, and to no thoughtful purpose. Paul's words not only commended the Corinthians but also warned them of the shallow, superficial approach to the Christian faith in conversion. He presented, therefore, the resurrection of Christ not "as an isolated fact, but from the very start as saving event, that is, in its soteriological reference— which means, however, in its conjunction with death/cross."[5]

● 3-4   Paul laid the foundational surface for the entire structure of the thought that follows. That foundation consists of the fact that "Christ died for our sins according to the Scriptures, and that he was buried, and that he has been raised up on the third day according to the Scriptures." Paul used the perfect passive indicative of the verb *egeiro (egēgertai)* to indicate that the resurrection was a *past event* and that the event is *still a reality* —Christ was raised up, and he is still raised up and living in our midst. And all this took place "according to the Scriptures." Paul's reference to the death and burial of Christ is affirmed in the use of the aorist tense, since it was a historical event. To emphasize the continuing character of the resurrection, however, he used the perfect tense, showing that the action took place in the past but still holds.

Ten appearances of Jesus, following the resurrection, are recorded in the New Testament in addition to his appearance to Paul. Nine of the appearances are as follows: to Mary Magdalene, the two women (in Matt.), the two disciples en route to Emmaus, Simon Peter, the ten apostles and others, the eleven and others, the five hundred, the apostles in Jerusalem, and James. Paul mentioned but five of the ten appearances, but one of them (to James) is not listed elsewhere.

● 5   Paul did not tell us why Christ appeared to Peter (Cephas) first before appearing to the twelve. This appearance is not recorded in the Gospels, but Luke alludes to it in 24:34. Some relate this initial appearance to Peter's position in the early church and to a special relationship that he was to have with the twelve, subsequently, but this is all mere supposition. There is nothing in the Scriptures to support this premise. The order of the appearances, as given by Paul, apparently reflects no special significance. Paul was merely recording the historical facts as they relate to the living Lord.

● 6   A bit of the mood of apologetics is reflected in verse 6 as Paul alluded to the fact that the majority of those who witnessed the resurrection of Jesus "remain until now." He also mentioned those who had fallen asleep in Christ, thereby linking them with the future resurrection of all believers, whether living or dead. Findlay notes that since Paul was writing at least a quarter of a century after the resurrection event, the majority of the followers alluded to, and their witness to the resurrection, must have been "mostly young in age."[6]

● 7   James was our Lord's brother (Gal. 1:19). All of the apostles saw Jesus after his resurrection.

● 8   Jesus appeared last of all to Paul *as unto one born out of due time.*[7] Paul used the word *ektrōmati* which means miscarriage or premature birth (abortion). What Paul meant by these words is not clear. At any rate, Paul was no less an apostle, and he became a living testimony to the resurrection of Jesus. For he had seen Jesus face-to-face, whether after the ascension of Jesus or before—that is of no consequence.

● 9   There was no boasting on Paul's part concerning his apostleship. He was aware of his unworthiness, not due to "his personality in general, but on his concrete past as a persecutor of the 'church of God.'"[8]

● 10   Paul took no credit for his position as an apostle. It was up to him, however, to see that the grace of God did not come his way "without result, without profit, without effect, without reaching its goal." After all, God's grace put him to work, and he labored "more abundantly than they all." Paul "relativizes the *human* differences in favor of the essential thing, proclamation and faith,"[9] and his words refer to verses 1-3. After all, it was unnecessary to go on with the comparison between the other apostles and himself.

● 11   No matter who did the preaching, Paul or the twelve, Cephas, James, or any other of the disciples, all proclaimed the same truth and received, in return, the same result—people believing in the message. All those who deliver the message are in perfect accord and preach "with one mind and one mouth, that the crucified Jesus rose from the dead."[10] After this, Paul "closes the case on the ground of testimony."[11]

● 12-13   Here Paul spoke specifically of the resurrection of the dead in Christ. He did not have in mind, at this moment, the dead in general, rather the hope of believers and their existence after death. Paul's whole argument, of course, rested upon the resurrection of Christ. His resurrection is an established fact that is based on the testimony of the witnesses to whom Christ presented himself alive during the forty days prior to the ascension. His resurrection is a historical fact that "lies in the past and is distinct from our own, yet it is directed as such to us."[12]

● 14   Upon the resurrection of Christ, Paul went on to say, rests the credibility of our witness as Christians and our faith. Apart from his resurrection, any testimony becomes as mere empty words without any basis and wholly without any truth and power. His resurrection and ours, though separate, are bound together by an indissoluble bond of faith.

● 15-16   Again, Paul said that the validity of our witness rests completely upon the resurrection of Christ. Otherwise we are false witnesses of God and thereby false witnesses concerning the raising up of the Christ. In a word, "if the fact is untrue, *the testimony is untrue*."[13] If "the message is empty," so is "the faith, . . . building on the thing that is not; preaching and faith have no genuine content; the Gospel is evacuated of all reality."[14] Paul presented the dilemma from which there is no escape. Christ either arose from the grave or he didn't; but the facts say he did, and to dispute the facts is to render testimony empty and void of meaning.

● 17   The word *vain (mataia)* used by Paul here is substituted for the word *empty (kenos)* in verse 14. Both words have a similar meaning which at bottom indicates that we have not been delivered from our sins—that is, if Christ has not been raised from the dead. Notice the plural of the word *hamartia* (sin) as in verse 3.

● 18   Paul's conclusion was final concerning the dead, apart from the resurrection of Christ. They would not be delivered from the consequences of their sins and hence would remain forever "a prey to death. . . . at the mercy of the *power* of death."[15] Then "the last enemy" (v. 26), which is death, would still have dominion over the dead—that is, apart from the resurrection of Christ.

● 19   Paul merely called attention to the "infinite bitterness of such a deception"[16] of believers who had put their every hope in Christ on the basis of his resurrection from the dead, should such resurrection not have taken place. Hope that pertains only to this life would only leave people to be pitied. Such would amount to "letting earth go and grasping at a fancied heaven."[17]

● 20   But such is not the case. Believers are not to be pitied. They have more than a false hope that pertains only to this life. For Christ now "has been raised from the dead ones, [and become] the firstfruits of them that sleep." Truly, in the resurrection of Christ the resurrection of the dead has already begun. The word *aparchē* (firstfruits) was sometimes used by Paul of "the first converts of a community." The term was also used by him in an eschatological sense of the Spirit. (See Rom. 8:23.) Hence, the resurrection of Jesus is the constitutive force behind the resurrection of the dead who will follow in his train at the last day.

● 21-22   The antithesis in verses 21 and 22, the antitypes Christ and Adam, are clearly seen. Adam is the intermediate agent of death, and Christ is the intermediate agent of life. Just as man became "the channel conveying death to his kind" (Rom. 5:12), in the same manner Christ became the channel for the "counter current" of life to flow.[18] Both events are historical. While man was the instrument of his calamity, Christ is the instrument of his salvation. "A firm and broad basis is now shown to exist for the solidarity between Christ and the holy dead."[19]

● 23   But each in his own turn, Christ the firstfruits, thereafter those who are Christ's at his coming. Here Paul brought the apocalyptic order clearly into view as he argued for the resurrection. He did not go into detail concerning the progressive development of the apocalyptic plan concerning the Lord's order of last events, for he dealt here only with Christ and believers. The word *order (tagmati)* is a military term, a metaphor for troop, rank, band, company. Here the figure is that of each group assuming its proper order. In this case, it is Christ "who has already reached the goal of Resurrection; and Christ's Own, who will reach it when He comes again."[20] Unbelievers, as is obvious, are not dealt with here, only Christ and those who are in Christ (v. 22). This fact may have occasioned the use of *parousiai* rather than *krisis* or *hēmera* and *kriseōs*.[21]

● 24   When will the end come? "Whenever he shall deliver the kingdom to the God and Father, whenever he shall abolish [annihilate] all rule and all authority and power." Christ has already accomplished his own resurrection, and the resurrection of believers will be accomplished at the last day, when "the end" comes. The second resurrection takes place after the first (Christ's) and is, therefore, subordinate to it. At the exaltation of Christ, God delivered to him his kingship, the sovereignty which Christ will deliver back to him when the end comes. One finds here the typical Jewish designations of demons: namely, *archai, exousiai, dunameis,* "authorities, powers, forces," which in themselves may mean "either good or evil spirits."[22] There is nothing of mythology reflected here. But Paul's concept has to do with both existence and power.[23] The word *whenever* simply marks the uncertainty of the time element. Jesus himself said that not even the angels in heaven know the time of his return. In Paul's concepts, "we need not think of Christ as losing anything or as ceasing to rule, but as bringing to a triumphant conclusion a special dispensation. It is His work to put an end to all that opposes the sovereignty of God."[24] Only when this comes to pass, "the reign of God, which is the reign of love, will no more have let or hindrance."[25]

● 25   Here the apocalyptic order is clearly in view again. The language affirms that "the whole messianic prophecy and the whole fulfillment agree with each other. The purpose is not the temporal limitation of the sovereignty of Christ, but the fact that it is guaranteed by God and attains its goal."[26] Christ himself reigns and subjects the enemies to himself and finally annihilates them.

● 26   The last of all enemies is death, which is treated here as a person. See the apocalyptic reference in Revelation 6:8. It is interesting to note that Paul designated "not the devil, but death" as the last enemy.[27] As an enemy, therefore, death is represented as "a *historical* power" that has to do with the whole existence of man, and that death is the adversary not only of man but also of God.[28] The reign of death, therefore, continues until the resurrection. But from that day on, death's power will be at an end, and death will then be "swallowed up in victory"[29] (2 Tim. 1:10; Rev. 20:14).

● 27   Paul advanced his argument further with scriptural proof by quoting from Psalm 8. There is a difference of thought, among expositors, as to the subject of *hupetaxen* (he has put in subjection), whether Christ or God. In the light of verse 24, it seems that Christ is the subject. Gould makes God the subject of "he saith" *(eipēi)*. "In putting all things under the Son, the Father plainly leaves himself out. The nature of the act, and the proper position of the Father, both imply this."[30]

● 28   Paul's play on the word *hupotassō* (to subject) is understood clearly if one keeps in mind the fact that during the messianic age, Christ "accordingly exercises the sovereignty of God in a specific area," and that when he has fulfilled his mission there, "God once more rules alone and directly; for then there is no more struggle, but only pure sovereignty."[31]

● 29   Conzelmann calls this "one of the most hotly disputed passages in the epistle."[32] In truth, there have been more than thirty different interpretations offered concerning the passage. Possibly there was a custom in Corinth which allowed vicarious baptism—live people being baptized in behalf of dead people.

Over and above all of these so-called interpretations, some essential truths come from the act of baptism in itself. Why not allow these truths to emerge?

In the first place, is not the act of baptism merely a symbol of vital truth but without any saving efficacy? If so, then what does the act of baptism symbolize? Basically, is not baptism the symbol of a burial and resurrection? If so, did it not symbolize, in the first place, the burial and resurrection of the believer's old self, the self to which Paul referred in Ephesians 2:1, "And you being dead in your trespasses and sins in which you formerly lived according to the contemporary life-style of this world"?[33] And was it not this same old self who was transformed and raised up with him and made to "sit with him in the heavenly places in Christ Jesus"? And does not the act of baptism symbolize also the burial and resurrection of Christ, and consequently the burial and resurrection of our own dead bodies when we are raised from the dead at the last day? Aside from possible Corinthian practice of vicarious baptism, the interpretation

I have just offered may cut the vexing tangle of interpretation and offer a reasonable explanation of Paul's words. Remember that the thrust of Paul's argument throughout chapter 15 is on behalf of the validity of the resurrection. So here it seems he was saying that if there is no such thing as the resurrection of the dead, why are you going to all the trouble you are to memorialize something that is never to take place?

● 30 In other words, if there is nothing to life beyond the grave, if there is no hope of immortality, if there is to be no resurrection, what are we doing in pursuing the kind of life-style that is now ours? "I am constantly in peril," as he wrote in 2 Corinthians 11:24-33. "If there is nothing to our hope, our faith, why should I go on—why should you go on?"

● 31 Paul used his own experience to refer to the "external" perils that surrounded him from day to day. What is the advantage of continuing to face these perils if there is no resurrection of the dead? At any rate, he "once again shows that 'his' glory is a glory that is 'not his own.'"[34]

● 32 Paul's expression "If according to man I fought with beasts in Ephesus" is likely a figurative expression. As a Roman citizen, if such a thing had happened, he would have lost his citizenship which he still possessed at Caesarea. The expression somewhat parallels Paul's words *ti baptizontai* (why do they have themselves baptized?) and *ti kinduneuomen* (why do we stand in jeopardy?). Dangers were his daily, and the figure of fighting with beasts would be a natural one for him to employ in his argument. Here again Paul was saying that, if there is no after life, what is the purpose of it all? There is a quotation from Menander (*Thais* fr. 218 kock) that has such a warning as Paul gave here.

● 33 The word translated "bad company" is *homiliai* from *homilia* and means association, company, something like our words *crowd, gang, bunch.*"[35] Whether Paul's words were intended as a warning to those who deny the resurrection or against the tendency on the part of the Corinthians to conform to the world (Rom. 12:2), the admonition is equally relevant.

● 34 Paul's opening words here refer to verse 33. The use is figurative, of course, but relative to the case in hand. "The enjoying of our earthly life is intoxication, and intoxication is *agnōsia*, 'ignorance.'"[36] *Agnōsia* is a strong word and literally means without knowledge or lacking in knowledge. Paul was trying to rouse to their senses the Corinthians who had been misled and had been caught up in the life-style of the pagans of Corinth. Christianity calls for a line of demarcation that is bold and clear between the believer and the unbeliever, and this is what Paul was pleading for.

• 35   The question Paul raised here may be in response to the diatribe of some of the Corinthians. Nevertheless, he answered it in a "fourfold reply": "(1) vv 36-38; (2) vv 39-44; (3) vv 45-49 (or 50, see below); (4) vv 50(51)-57."[37]

• 36-38   It is not hard to see "needs to be quickened," as some of the translations put it, for it is already a viable seed and needs to sprout, germinate, come up. This is the thought Paul had in mind here. Conzelmann notes here an obvious fact, "the necessity of death as the condition of life,"[38] and also speaks of "the discontinuity between the present and the future life" of which Paul spoke. Rather, I regard Paul's words as just the reverse. There is a very definite continuity, for the physical gives way to the spiritual, and God bestows the gift of new life in accord with his own will. The fact that this physical body gives way to the spiritual body which God wills—unto each of the seed its own particular body—only accents the continuity. In truth, if there were not some sort of continuity, where would the meaning in the afterlife come?

• 39-41   In verses 39-41 Paul answered the questions raised in verse 35. In these verses the words *sarx* (flesh) and *sōma* (body) are used but not synonymously. He is not dealing with bodily substance, per se, but merely endeavoring to point out that humans are to be given different bodies. This new body, as Paul subsequently explained in this chapter, is a spiritual body and perfectly adapted to the order of its new existence. Paul did not use the word *sarx* (flesh) with reference to the heavenly existence. Instead he used the word *doxa* (glory). The analogy is that of the seed in nature, though a rather crass analogy and one that need not be pressed minutely; for life that springs from the seed that dies is still a physical matter conforming to, and perfectly adapted to, the physical.

• 42-44   These three verses contain four antitheses and a conclusion. Conzelmann holds that "the emphasis is again on the contrasts, that is, the discontinuity, the miraculous character of the future life."[39] Perhaps the use of the word "discontinuity" here is loose; then we face the fact of a future life as it relates to the earthbound life. The contrast, by necessity, is between the physical and the spiritual; and if there is an interrelation between the two, as Paul said, there has to be a continuity as it relates to the soul. The "diff. is not a matter of condition merely, but of *constitution*."[40] A "frame suited to man's earthly life argues a frame suited to his heavenly life."[41] Some render *sōma psuchikon* psychic body and others natural body, but neither seems to be quite adequate. Perhaps the words *physical body* will do as well for the whole. One encounters the same problem in dealing with the *sōma pneumatikon* for the simple reason that "the resurrection body is not wholly *pneuma*."[42] Though the physical body is sown "in weakness," it is raised in "power" over which death has no power because it is "conformed to the body of his glory" (Phil. 3:21, ASV).

● 45   Here we have the contrast between "the first man Adam" and "the last Adam." The first represented humanity in the beginning, whereas the second Adam became "a life-giving spirit." "Christ is the crown of humanity and has power to give us the new body."[43] In Romans (5:12-19) Paul referred to Christ as the second Adam. Paul had nothing to say about when the last Adam became a "life-giving spirit"—whether at his creation "before all time, or at his resurrection? The context points to the resurrection."[44]

● 46   Findlay sees an emphasis in Paul on "the historical relation of the two Adams in the development of mankind, Christ succeeding and displacing our first father."[45] At any rate, this is what Robertson called "the law of growth."

● 47   Here the antithesis continues. The first "man" described as made "out of dust" and second "out of heaven." "Christ had a human (*psuchikon*) body, of course, but Paul makes the contrast between the first man in his natural body and the Second Man in his risen body."[46] See Romans 5:12 *ff.*

● 48   The antithesis continues in the two types of humanity, the first coming *ek gēs* out of the earth, and the second *ex ouranou* out of heaven—a reference to the preexistent state of Christ before his incarnation. All people "correspond" to the first Adam in that all are of dust (*choïkos* from *chous*—dust). See Genesis 2:7 for "dust of the ground."

● 49   Some old manuscripts have *phoresōmen kai* (volitive aorist active subjunctive, "let us bear," and Westcott and Hort follow this reading).

Perhaps the emphasis here is not so much on the volitional aspect of the experience as upon the factual. The believer who has been born of the Spirit will come to bear a form or likeness of the heavenly in the last day. As verses 46-48 indicate, Paul contrasted the spiritual and the physical and in both instances whether in the physical stage (earthy) or the spiritual stage (heavenly) the Christian's likeness conforms to earthly or heavenly existence.

● 50   Here Paul dealt with an impossibility. The perishable nature of humanity (flesh and blood) is not fit to have possession of the kingdom of God which is imperishable. In this case, the perishable would be dealing with the imperishable. This is why there has to be a transformation, "a change by death from the natural body to the spiritual body."[47] Paul did not deal with the change that took place in the body of Jesus during the transition stage between the resurrection and ascension. His argument did not rest on that. He merely emphasized the fact that there has to be a change, a transformation, and this is accomplished through death and the resurrection.

● 51   Paul followed the proclamation in verse 50 by the revelation of the change that is to be effective on the part of all believers whether living or dead at the last day. They will all *(pantes)* be changed. Not all are to pass away, for there will be believers living at the time of Jesus' coming. But all will be changed believers—both the living and the dead. The change, therefore, will be universal on the part of believers, and in accord with "the necessary development" that is to be effected at the time of the resurrection.[48]

● 52   Note that Paul said, "The dead ones will be raised up imperishable," and then added "and we shall be changed." Did Paul imply here that those that have been "asleep" in Jesus will have an opportunity to greet the living before the transformation takes place? At least the order of Paul's words here is interesting and suggestive.

● 53   The word *athanasian* (immortality) comes from an old word *athanatos* which in turn comes from "*a* privative and *thnēskō,* to die."[49]

Paul gave the basis for his words in verse 50. The transformation is an absolute necessity, for "flesh and blood cannot inherit the kingdom of God." Note the parallelism in the passage: *to phtharton—to thnēton, aphtharsian—athanasian.* The word *athanasian* (immortality) is used only here and in 1 Timothy 6:16 in the New Testament.

● **54-55** In verses 54-55, Paul said that this victory over death which is accomplished by the resurrection of Christ, and in which we as believers share, is the fulfillment of prophecy for "then shall come to pass the word that has been written." Paul quoted in Isaiah 25:8, using the word *katepothē* (first aorist passive indicative of *katapinō*) which means to drink, swallow down, drink down. Death is literally swallowed up, devoured, made totally extinct. Victory over death accomplished by the resurrection was a total victory; it plucked the sting out of death and wrested from death its own victory. The word *to kentron* (sting) was used of the sting of an animal, or the goad, or "pointed stick that served the same purpose as a whip" (Bauer). Paul's use of the words *eis* and *nikos* (in victory) means literally *unto* victory "so that victory is to be established."[50] The image held up by the prophet's word *kentron* (sting) is "that of a beast with a sting; not death with *a goad*, driving men."[51]

● **56** The "sting" of death is "the power of death to destroy."[52] By "the power of the sin is the law," Paul meant that "since responsibility depends on knowledge, the condemnation and curse of sin come through the law and, further and deeper, that it is through the law that the dormant power of sin in the soul is awakened, so that, with the knowledge of the law, comes the quickening of sin and the death of the man."[53] Death itself, therefore, had to be overthrown, for only in this way could sin lose its dominion.

● **57** "Who is giving" *(tōi didonti)* is a present participle and indicates continual action. Victory is a process, coming to believers constantly as they turn to Christ by faith. And the victory comes about "through our Lord Jesus Christ." He is the intermediate agent "through" whom the victory comes. It is "through" this victory that Christ's redemptive work is fulfilled, a work "which includes the renovation of both soul and body. The sting of death is sin; and Christ, in removing sin, removes the death which it causes."[54]

● **58** Paul brought his discussion to a triumphant close with the admonition to loyalty and faithful performance. Corinthian believers were to be steadfast and immovable in response to God who gives to all the glorious victory through Jesus Christ. The participial clause, with which verse 58 closes, assured the Corinthian believers, and all who are servants of the Lord, that their labor in the Lord would not be fruitless, empty, and void of meaningful effect. This knowledge is to be a continual realization, and the glad consciousness of it is to spur us on. And all should know that, as Robertson says, "The best answer to doubt is work"[55] in the Lord. And all should remember that every believer is to "keep on becoming steadfast, immovable, always abounding in the work of the Lord." There is to be no letup.

Notes

1. Archibald Robertson and Alfred Plummer, "A Critical and Exegetical Commentary on the First Epistle of St. Paul to the Corinthians," *International Critical Commentary* (New York: Charles Scribner's Sons, 1911), p. 329.
2. Ibid., p. 330.
3. Hans Conzelmann, James W. Leitch, trans., *A Commentary on the First Epistle to the Corinthians,* *Hermeneia* Series (Philadelphia: Fortress Press, 1975), p. 249.
4. Ibid.
5. Ibid., p. 251.
6. G. G. Findlay, "St. Paul's First Epistle to the Corinthians," *The Expositor's Greek Testament,* Vol. 3 (Grand Rapids, Michigan: William B. Eerdmans Publishing Co., [n.d.]), p. 920.
7. A. T. Robertson, *Word Pictures in the New Testament* (Nashville, Tennessee: Sunday School Board of the SBC, 1931), p. 188.
8. Conzelmann, p. 260.
9. Ibid.
10. Findlay, p. 922.
11. Ibid.
12. Conzelmann, p. 265.
13. Findlay, p. 923.
14. Ibid., p. 924.
15. Conzelmann, p. 266.
16. Findlay, p. 925.
17. Ibid.
18. Ibid., p. 926.
19. Ibid.
20. Robertson and Plummer, p. 354.
21. Ibid.
22. Conzelmann, p. 272.
23. Ibid.
24. Robertson and Plummer, p. 355.
25. Ibid.
26. Conzelmann, p. 272 *ff.*

27. Ibid., p. 273.

28. Ibid., p. 273 *ff.*

29. Charles Hodge, *An Exposition of the First Epistle to the Corinthians* (Grand Rapids, Michigan: William B. Eerdmans Publishing Co., 1956), p. 331.

30. E. P. Gould, "Commentary on the Epistles to the Corinthians," *An American Commentary on the New Testament,* Vol. 5 (Philadelphia: American Baptist Publication Society, 1887), p. 132.

31. Conzelmann, p. 274 *ff.*

32. Ibid., p. 275.

33. R. Paul Caudill, *Ephesians: A Translation with Notes* (Nashville, Tennessee: Broadman Press, 1979), p. 28.

34. Conzelmann, p. 277.

35. Robertson, p. 194.

36. Conzelmann, p. 279.

37. Ibid., p. 280.

38. Ibid., p. 281.

39. Ibid., p. 282 *ff.*

40. Findlay, p. 937.

41. Ibid.

42. Robertson, p. 196.

43. Ibid., p. 197.

44. Conzelmann, p. 287.

45. Findlay, p. 939.

46. Robertson, p. 197.

47. Ibid., p. 198.

48. Findlay, p. 941.

49. Robertson, p. 198.

50. Marvin R. Vincent, "The Epistles of Paul," *Word Studies in the New Testament,* Vol. 3 (Grand Rapids, Michigan: William B. Eerdmans Publishing Co., 1946), p. 286.

51. Ibid.

52. Gould, p. 142.

53. Ibid.

54. Ibid.

55. Robertson, p. 199.

CHAPTER 16

● 1   Findlay titled this last chapter (division 6) "Business, News, and Greetings."[1] Some see in the chapter a lack of literary unity, but Paul's message to the Corinthians is easily understood; and all of the emphases are relevant to the material of chapters 1—15. Leaving behind "the Cor. atmosphere of jealousy and debate, of sensuality and social corruption, infecting their Church,"[2] Paul came directly to some matters of personal interest and dealt with them briefly. While on his third missionary journey, Paul initiated an offering in behalf of the poor saints in Jerusalem. Apparently the offering had not moved along too well, for Paul devoted two chapters in 2 Corinthians to the matter. The offering already had been initiated among the churches of Galatia. Paul gave the same order to the Corinthian churches in behalf of the offering. The offering was especially needed in Jerusalem because of the chronic conditions of poverty that afflicted the Christian community there. The employment situation was bad and added to this was severe persecution.

Paul did not say how much time had elapsed since the collection for the saints in Jerusalem had been initiated in the churches of Galatia. He merely desired that the churches of Corinth follow the same pattern in the effort and to respond as the churches of Galatia had done. The reference to the offering among the Galatian churches indicates that other churches through the territory touched by Paul's missionary endeavors were likely involved. This was certainly in accord with the consensus of the apostolic council referred to in Galatians 2:9-10. The offering was a *freewill* offering and is in no sense to be thought of as any sort of tax collected for the support of the Jerusalem church in general. There is nothing judicial about it, as Paul's devotional expressions such as "gift" (*charis,* v. 3; and 2 Cor. 8:14 *ff.*) and "fellowship" (*koinōnia,* Rom. 15:26) point out. Rather, this voluntary effort on the part of the churches symbolizes "the unity of the church."[3]

● 2   Paul's businesslike approach to the offering among the churches of Galatia had evidently proved satisfactory, or he would not have suggested the same procedure to the Corinthians. Obviously, up to this time there existed no prearranged type of organization to deal with such matters. From Paul's words one assumes that already Christians of the various communities gathered for their meetings on the first day of the week (our Sunday) rather than on the Jewish sabbath.

● 3-4   Paul took steps to ensure that the offering was properly dispatched to the Jerusalem church. He would not go alone with the offering but would send it by messengers approved by the congregation and the apostles. Paul was careful in handling the offering to see that his own action was above reproach. He wanted no one to be able to accuse him of using any part of the offering for his own benefit. Of course he might decide to (v. 4) accompany those appointed to bear the gift to the Jerusalem church. He could hardly have acted more wisely.

● 5-9   As the passage indicates, Paul was in Ephesus as he made plans for his journey through Macedonia to Corinth. His intimation that he might spend the winter in Corinth may have been occasioned by difficulties in ocean travel in those days. Paul knew from experience that journeys by sea could prove hazardous. See the account of his journey to Rome (Acts 27:9-12). The use of the word *door* is a metaphor for *opportunity* "*great* as to its extent; *effectual* as to the result."[4] What Paul meant of course, was that a great opportunity awaited him for fruitful service. His words in verse 8 suggest that he was either at Ephesus or near Ephesus at the time of the writing. Notwithstanding the presence of those who opposed him, "Paul rather finds in the fact a new motive for prolonging his stay. As he is under obligation to those who are disposed to listen to him, he also feels it a duty to confront those who oppose him."[5]

● 10-11   Timothy had already left with the letter (4:17), and he would likely arrive in Corinth before Paul, whose journey through Macedonia would delay his own arrival in Corinth. The mission of Timothy was a sensitive one because of conditions in the Corinthian church. Paul wanted the church to treat Timothy with respect rather than with contempt and to give him no cause to be afraid. Moreover, he wanted to be sure that

Timothy's departure was "in peace." "The brothers" (v. 11) seem to be the same brothers as those in verse 12.

● 12   Paul earnestly desired that Apollos go on the mission with Timothy and the brothers, but Apollos did not feel disposed to do so. Apollos was, in a sense, Paul's rival in Corinth because of the strife there which involved both him and Paul (1 Cor. 1—4). But Apollos wanted nothing to do with "partisan strife over preachers" and, consequently, had left Corinth "in disgust" at the time of the strife.[6]

● 13-14   In staccatolike fashion, Paul brought to a close his admonitions. The commands are terse, bright, clear, and all to the point: (1) "Stay on the alert"—that is, be watchful, stay fully awake. Be conscious of what is going on around you. Keep a perceptive eye always open for observation and evaluation of the daily counter currents. (2) "Stand fast in the faith." Hold your ground. Do not waver. Be not ambivalent in facing up to life's choices. Let every decision be marked by loyalty to the faith—the faith set forth in the gospel and made manifest in the incarnation of our Lord. (3) "Act like men." Behave like mature persons in the face of life's tensions. Be not as children tossed to and fro by the waves of circumstance. (4) Be loving in all your ways. Let love prevail in the home or out of the home, among your friends or among your enemies. "All your doings are to be in love." Paul could hardly have laid down guidelines more effective in the quest for unity in a church and in the larger community.

● 15   Stephanas and his household were baptized by Paul (1:16). As the firstfruits of Achaia, they were held in special esteem (see 1 Cor. 16:15). Achaia, then a Roman province, comprised what was then central and southern Greece, "a senatorial province since A.D. 44."[7] Corinth was the capital of Achaia. It should be noted, as Conzelmann points out, that here one finds "the roots [*diakonian,* service] of the office of the *diakonoi,* 'deacons.'"[8] See Philippians 1:1 and Romans 16:1. Of course at this time, there was no organization in the churches and no formal offices such as that of our diaconate.

● 16   Paul appealed to the Corinthians not only to show due respect to Stephanas and his leadership but also to submit themselves in a similar way "to everyone who is hard working and striving together with us *in the work.*"

● 17   The coming of these three messengers was a boon to Paul's spirit.

As Conzelmann has it, "'because they have made up for your failings, that is to say: 'they have given me what you failed to give.'"[9] Did these words contain a mild hint of rebuke for the type of support that Paul had received for his ministry from the Corinthians? If so, the words were delicately phrased. Of course Paul's greatest support came from the Philippians. How could he have helped from loving them as he did! They were so poor, yet genuine in their regard for him, and unselfish.

• 18   The coming of the messengers brought a spirit of refreshment both to Paul and to the Corinthians.

• 19   Such greetings as Paul used were customary in the conclusions of his epistles. Paul may have been a path breaker in this respect since "Before him, greetings are found in letters only exceptionally."[10] Asia, a Roman province in which Ephesus was headquarters of the procurator, lay in the western part of Asia Minor and became a great center of missionary activity. Apparently Paul met Aquila and Prisca (Priscilla in Acts) in Corinth. Acts 18 also records a relationship with Apollos. In Paul's day, many assemblies (church meetings) were held in homes. If a synagogue were not available for use, Christians met wherever they could—in safety.

• 20-21   Here Paul reflected his closeness to the believers. The brothers sent their greetings through him to the Corinthians. It seems that the letter was read to the community of believers, but whether at the "community meal" we do not know. If the "holy kiss" were a customary part of the ritual at a time of gathering, we do not know. Some light is thrown on the matter at the close of 2 Corinthians.

• 22   Paul's use of the word *philei* for "love" is a bit surprising. One might have expected him to use the word *agapē* (the lofty word for love— the word that characterizes God's love for people, people's love for God, and people's love for others as motivated by God's love). But Peter's word to Jesus when he asked Peter *"agapais me?" was "thou knowest that I love thee (philō se)"* (John 21:15 *ff.*).

Anathema, the curse formula, in verse 22 implies a "negative relation to the Lord" on the part of the one accursed. The word *marana tha* (which Conzelmann calls "an element in the liturgy" of the early churches) may be rendered "Our Lord, come!" or "Our Lord has come."[11] The rendering "Our Lord, come" seems preferable, in that it was likely a petition in behalf of his *parousia* or second coming.

● 23-24   Paul could hardly have chosen two words other than *grace* and *love* (*charis* and *agapē*) that would have conveyed more fully the affectionate regard of his heart for all believers. For Paul, indeed, wore the garments of grace and love at all times after his conversion, according to the Scriptures. None before him, and none after him, has so surely impressed the Christian communities of the world as one who sought to know and to do God's will in all things at all times—no matter the price. The consuming passion of Paul's heart, yea, his magnificent obsession was (1) to know Christ fully, (2) to achieve the righteous life that is in Christ, (3) to share in the fellowship of Christ's sufferings, (4) and to attain unto the resurrection of the dead. Underneath all this was the motivating desire to lay hold on that for which he was laid hold on by Jesus Christ (Phil. 3:7-14).

Notes

1. G. G. Findlay, "St. Paul's First Epistle to the Corinthians, *The Expositor's Greek Testament*, Vol. 3 (Grand Rapids, Michigan: William B. Eerdmans Publishing Co., [n.d.]), p. 944.
2. Ibid.
3. Hans Conzelmann, James W. Leitch, trans., *A Commentary on the First Epistle to the Corinthians, Hermeneia* Series (Philadelphia: Fortress Press, 1975), p. 296.
4. Marvin R. Vincent, "The Epistles of Paul," *Word Studies in the New Testament,* Vol. 3 (Grand Rapids, Michigan: William B. Eerdmans Publishing Co., 1946), p. 289.
5. Frederic Louis Godet, *Commentary on I Corinthians* (Grand Rapids, Michigan: Kregel Publications, 1977), p. 88 *ff.*
6. A. T. Robertson, *Word Pictures in the New Testament* (Nashville, Tennessee: Sunday School Board of the SBC, 1931), p. 202.
7. Conzelmann, p. 298.
8. Ibid.
9. Ibid., p. 299.
10. Ibid.
11. Ibid., p. 300.